ALMOST RAPIST

PUBLISHER'S FORWARD

The Enthusiast Press is a publisher of handmade books and zines focused on affordable and unique bindings that draw on a punk and camp aesthetic. And while our about statement has been criticized on rather specious grounds—and compared to a Dr. Bronner's soap label—we really are a socialist political project that advocates for the creation of literary space outside the restrictions of traditional institutional control. We are run out a small alcove built into the wall of a boarding house in Queens and are committed to no less a cause than the welfare of animals, plants and people, as well as the continuation of democracy itself. In queer fashion, we will leave the specifics of our hydra-headed opposition to the stultifying conformity of the ideological state open to our authors — not wanting to impose our vision on their work. We stand as a statement of alterity in what has been called the "extreme conservatism" in the history of the book, and we see ourselves as a populist venture vested in an anti-capitalist and anti-imperialist agenda, aiming at the cultivation of art outside the stranglehold of an increasingly isolated, ludicrous, but hopelessly self-satisfied cultural elite.

ALMOST RAPIST

BY JÖYCE

PUBLISHED BY
THE ENTHUSIAST
QUEENS, NY
2025

EDITED BY GEOFFREY BRIDGMAN. PUBLISHED
BY THE ENTHUSIAST PRESS.

COVER ART BY JOYCE MILLER. COVER
DESIGN AND INTERIOR DESIGN BY GEOFFREY
BRIDGMAN.

ISBN 978-1-968141-02-8 (hbk)
ISBN 978-1-968141-00-4 (pbk)
ISBN 978-1-968141-04-2 (ebook)

ENTHUSIASTPRESS.COM

TO LEMON

"It is not enough to win a war; it is more important to organize the peace."

–Aristotle

CHAPTER 1

GRAVEYARD GIRL

Jooks teetered at the edge of his grave. Like the Ghost of Christmas Yet to Come, my finger, overgrown with cuticles, pointed across the path of Lyme Meadows Cemetery. He never did make good on his promise of a weekly manicure.

"Can you put your goddamn arm down? Jesus Christ." He was in good spirits.

"See, Jooks?" I kept pointing. "Joseph Heller's gravestone looks like a Party City one that people might stick in their yard for Halloween. It's understated."

Heller's grave was why Jooks was getting buried here, across from the author of *Catch 22*. It was a slim marble outfit with the epitaph: There was only one catch.

Jooks had wanted me, not Mimsy, to go to the Hamptons. I dodged hints all week like I couldn't bear the thought of him passing. I didn't want to work on a Saturday. Mimsy was offended. She got the paltry $5,000 Rolex his call girl left behind, but I was trusted in matters of eternity, where my lack of punctuality had no bearing. Mimsy was his show pony. I was his graveyard girl.

The low ceiling of clouds drowned our shadows. Sound congealed in the fog. I was trying to convince Jooks that engraving his Oscar, Emmy, Grammy, and People's Choice trophies on $600,000 Italian marble was impractical, given his legal expenses.

Jooks' claim to fame, a chart-topping love ballad, had garnered every award. In recent months, celebrity had found him again for the alleged rape and assault of a dozen women. The DA had granted special permission to leave Manhattan on condition he return by nightfall.

Jooks owned a family plot for himself, the three children he chose to acknowledge, and their plus ones. Depending on who got on his bad side, he wrote them in and out of his will. At the moment, he'd bequeathed all eight graves to himself.

"What if nobody can find me?" he said.

GRAVEYARD GIRL

"Go minimalist," I said. "Name. Date. Epitaph. People will figure out who you are and say, 'Wow! What a cool guy! He was famous, but his grave is humble!'"

His eye gleamed. False modesty was a novel tactic compared to his characteristic aggression.

Jooks was the biggest tyrant I knew. Neither rejection nor law could dissuade him. He sussed out weakness to calculate how far he could push. The narcissistic tendencies that let him rise in the world also overwhelmed him. Obscured in an ether of self-absorption and physical afflictions from the stroke, his mind was not always his own. This didn't make it easier to sympathize with him. His predatory ways remained intact, if more transparent.

I rationalized our association by serving his wholesome needs, subverting his pathological ones with artful incompetence.

Discouraging this half-million-dollar monument to his resume would be my greatest feat besides his switch from Diet Coke to caffeine-free Diet Coke, and eating more fruit with breakfast. I had my paycheck to consider.

"I want the quote by O-O-Oscar Wilde." Jooks spoke in his controlled stutter.

"'We are all in the gutter, but some of us are looking at the stars,'" I confirmed. "I'll fax it."

Compared to my usual shifts, the mood was light. I took pictures of comedically perfect headstone names and texted them to Hazel. Hogarth... Bogfaith...Digby...Bacon. No first name, just Bacon, like the meat.

Hazel lived with our friend Ryan in Astoria. I'd known them since I was eleven. After college, they moved to New York, where I did theater and talked about my job, making them listen to my unending catalog of Jooks' insufferable misconduct.

"Did he set aside one of the graves for you?" she asked.

I was conditioned never to show blood in the water and told no one about my financial panic, why I was actually terrified to leave Jooks. So I played along.

GRAVEYARD GIRL

"To be buried at the foot of his coffin. Like Mr. Burns and Smithers."

"You realize," Hazel wrote back, "this makes you the Assistant Rapist."

"No," I said, "I'm Assistant to The Rapist. There's a difference."

Hazel worked nine-to-five jobs and internships, had been accepted to Stanford, and spoke Mandarin. Even though I was the actress, she was taller and lankier like a model. She dyed her hair and dressed fashionably. She had been studying the makeup section of MAC and Sephora since the seventh grade, whereas I didn't wear makeup unless I was explicitly required to for photos or film, and barely knew how to use foundation.

Our mutual friend Ryan had the appearance of a curly haired doll who had one day become very serious. With minimal effort but maximum results, she progressed quietly into analyst jobs and boyfriends, a normal person and a good friend, patiently accepting the strange and unnecessary antics of my and Hazel's various cultural experiments.

JÖYCE

Even as a student, she had always given the impression that she had finished all of her homework in an hour and was bored waiting for the rest of us so that she could have company.

I hadn't fully bonded with anyone in college. Hazel and Ryan were so much fun, I forgave them for sending me the black PR about people dying because of Scientology after I did an eighth-grade social-studies presentation on why it is the world's fastest-growing religion, and all the parents became jealous over the math grades and scholarship for classical piano lessons I got thanks to Scientology Study Technology.

Someone once told me that becoming roommates always ruins the friendship anyway, so I chose to live with strangers, where my art could escape the influence of familiarity.

On the morning I was supposed to walk at graduation, I woke up on the student couches of the twenty-four-hour common area inside the Kimmel Center with several Failed and Incomplete academic credits. It didn't make sense to rent a gown when I didn't have enough money for food or books.

Then I visited my parents in Philadelphia to find our house up for a forced Sheriff's sale. Back home, my father had sat in a La-Z-Boy chair gazing at the empty space where the television had been, in a maze of furniture marked "keep" and "sell," and my mom had cried out that she couldn't argue because of the pain in her stomach. They'd been going hungry.

In my last two years of college, my father's strawberry blond hair had started to go white and his walk had become a stiff, teetering, painful shuffle that left him wincing. My mother's hair was grey. It had gone grey before I was born. I was helpless when it came to Mother's self-improvement. She was so irrational that she never embraced Scientology in the first place. Having signed me up for the Communications course at age ten, I tried to get my father to admit that she was a Suppressive Person, but he wasn't strong enough, and eventually, he gave up Scientology as well.

"Stop suppressing me," my mother would say, "You're a Suppressive." This was not how you were supposed to apply the technology. Still, I was weak too, I suppose, and I could not leave my parents to die, even though they had succumbed to my mother's urge towards destruction.

Before Jooks, I'd got a full-time job at Starbucks and traveled to Philadelphia to bring my parents groceries on weekends. They gathered what they could and retreated to an extended-stay motel in Lansdowne for six months. The artifacts of our foreclosed home lined the walls of their tiny room. After years of taking the lead, my father propped himself up in the bed disoriented. I offered to drop out of college, but they begged me to finish.

I went to the financial aid office in my black barista Dickies and no-slip shoes, spattered with steamed milk, holding a stack of predatory loan approvals. As I was about to indenture myself, the administrator Sandy Bowie maneuvered me into the four seminars I needed with $10,000 in government loans. My teachers often said that every student was on their own individual journey. Sometimes, the journey meant having a lot of money, or a teacher who liked you, making sure that you got an agent right out of school. My journey was as sacred and beautiful as any, bestowed upon me by the Universe itself, and it was one that I had chosen. I was responsible for everything that happened to me—I had even chosen the family and the body I was born in—and so was sure to prevail.

"If you knew how many artists she's saved in this situation..." the receptionist nodded, "a lot of people owe her some free Broadway tickets." I silently vowed to send her free Broadway tickets but could only envision a fancy gift basket. Broadway was one more sacred place I couldn't afford. I re-took my failed credits.

At least my parents wouldn't suffer for nothing.

JÖYCE

That Christmas Eve was the best ever. Only the kosher pizzeria was open, with one whole pie left: pineapple and ham. I cheerfully paid for it, and we drove home to eat on the unfurnished carpet of the apartment they finally managed to secure in Lansdowne, PA. I'd spent the previous months staving off images of my parents living out of a shopping cart. There was no sentiment left for our evacuated house. The sheriff's sale had leveled my father's debt, with enough money left over for a few months of a bare-bones existence. We had never been at a net profit as a family unit, and it was our first time together without holding our breath for a phone call from the debt collector.

Three months later, "recession" was the buzzword of the decade. The economy couldn't keep up appearances and the office temping that let me quit Starbucks had dried up. Dad's HVAC business and health had collapsed, Mom hadn't been on the job market, outside working for him, since I was born, and social security eligibility was a year away. My dreams of interpretive dancing into a TV and Film career as a debt-free child of Bohemia were dead. By the time Jooks interviewed me, I was getting thirty-five dollars a day to stick business cards in doors for a locksmith on the Upper East Side. The sales demands of this job were easy compared to my experience selling copies of *Dianetics: The Modern Science of Mental Health* in Times Square, but every day, I lived with the guilt of abandoning the very Church that had given me the tools to succeed. I would return, as soon as I handled my family dynamic and got my finances in order, so that I could contribute as a staff member or at least get back into the course room and start having Big Wins again in life.

Everyone said I was lucky for any job in this economy, especially right out of college, especially a glamorous novelty job like "Personal Assistant." Fifteen dollars an hour under the table, free meals, and long hours, thanks to Jooks' chronic insomnia and friendlessness.

Friends living off their parents,

unemployment, or savings were envious. I envied them. I didn't have those options. But I couldn't afford to see what would happen if I dropped the illusion of prosperity, so I let people wonder how I got lucky. In Scientology, a being is either expanding or contracting and never static, so I made it a point: Always Be Expanding.

Jooks was driven straight to his grave. Irma took us in her teal minivan. Her eyes were wide open and alert, her complexion healthy from the fresh air. She wore her salt and pepper hair in a smart, pageboy cut. She was the cemetery coordinator. Irma was so dedicated to her job that a jumble of budget zombie films on VHS tapes rested in a brown paper bag under her seat. Professionally dealing with all those bodies who just got dropped by their Thetans would probably leave anyone somewhat aberrated.

We passed row after gap-toothed row of headstones until Jooks rapped on the window at a cluster of graves attired in handsome alabaster.

GRAVEYARD GIRL

"W-w-w-whose graves are those?"

"That's the Tobin family," said Irma.

"I want a stone exactly like that. What's it cost?"

"About six hundred grand."

"You h-h-have gotta be k-k-kidding me."

"It's heavy Italian marble. It has to be shipped by boat."

"So ship it. I need to see it before I buy it."

"Well, we can't ship it unless it's paid for. Six hundred grand is the cost of the raw marble and shipping alone, even before the engraving and polishing."

"Irma, th-that's ridiculous. What if I don't like it?"

"That's why we plan it carefully."

"Also, I'd like to add a tree. Plus a bench where someone can sit."

I pictured Jooks' girlfriend, Corinne, keening in a shroud of black lace against a relief of his Oscar. Corinne was fifty years his junior and one of three call girls he'd proposed to over the course of my employment. He never quite found that balance of commerce and romance needed to date his call girls.

Still, he wanted a bench by his grave in case somebody wanted to sit down. He could be generous like that.

CHAPTER 2:
THE KEY TO THE CITY

It was ninety degrees in the shade, not long before I met Jooks. I was putting up business cards for Schlomo. I stopped at The Donut Plant on East Houston for a lavender donut and raspberry lemonade. It cost me an hour's pay.

Schlomo had started to cheat me. He was making my locations bigger without adjusting compensation. He paid thirty-five dollars per "location," which took roughly six hours at a speedy pace. I could be only so meticulous without decimating my pay grade. I wondered if Schlomo was testing me, grooming me for management. A position with a respectable locksmith was nothing to scoff at.

On workdays, I lined up with a dozen men who spoke in Spanish and two Ukrainian students—lovers—in front of the shop by 86th. The job did not require citizenship. When it was my turn, I walked down the long, narrow shop to the end of the pegboard wall displaying locks and mechanical parts where Schlomo sat, wearily, in jeans, sneakers, and a T-shirt hovering his pencil over a stack of photocopied maps of the city, behind a tiny fold-top counter in an unending waltz of canvassers, phone calls, dispatching, and twenty-four seven service.

"How are you ?" I asked.

"I feel tired. Went out partying, last night. Don't tell my uncles." He nodded to a man dressed in religious garb milling round with some others in v-neck sweaters and tailored pants.

"I won't tell them," I said.

"You like to party too?" he asked.

"I can't drink or stay out late," I said. "I'm an actress."

He gave us each a bag of business cards and a photocopied map of Manhattan with our thirty square blocks outlined in pencil. We were to stick a card in every door. Schlomo insinuated that our work was monitored by an unmarked white van that drove around town on jobs, not that I would have cut corners.

THE KEY TO THE CITY

Schlomo didn't set a schedule. You had to call on the day you worked, choose the morning or afternoon shift, pick up your bag of cards, and return it full of competitor cards at the end. Major locksmiths have a team of people out for twelve hours a day, taking down their competitors' cards and putting up their own. Sometimes I'd see a competitor several doors down, turning one of my fresh placements into confetti. Lockouts are the biggest moneymaker. The point is for your locksmith's card to be the last one standing at 2:00 a.m. when some young stockbroker whose cab sped off with the keys will pay $400 to change the lock so they can sleep before the trading floor opens.

A sizable percentage of my wage was reinvested into cold beverages once the two water bottles in my backpack ran out.

When I worked for the Church two summers before that, I would pass out postcards for Scientology's free, mandatory introduction film to every single person who walked past me in Times Square without hesitation, but there were sometimes a few left over, and it was considered suppressive to throw them away. That same summer, I was also working for the University Fundraising Phonathon and as an immersive actor playing Lucrezia Borgia at the Renaissance Faire in Tuxedo, New York, where an older man dressed as William Shakespeare would always appear in the woods and distract me from showing off my improv chops to the fairegoers. He was probably a Church spy, or a CIA agent attempting to blackball my acting career because I hadn't defected from the Church yet. My friend Matt, who invited me to split his sublet of DeWanda Wise's Henry Street room while she was on tour that summer, was also probably CIA, knowing I'd be forced to hoard my excess Scientology postcards in the room for everyone to see.

I now realize that whatever division of the CIA Mimsy's Aunt Dill was a part of made sure that the Williamstown

THE KEY TO THE CITY

Theatre Festival rejected me that summer—so that they could wait to get me there the next summer, when Floyd Lumber, who had written a musical that mocked Scientology, would be there along with Mimsy.

I never did make it go right with those leftover postcards, which is probably where the downward spiral began. After betraying the human race, not much else seemed to phase me.

I was meticulous with the locksmith cards also and didn't miss a single door if it was legally accessible from the street. A major perk of the job was solitude. I was left to my thoughts without the nattering of coworkers or supervisors. I had found other jobs spiritually intolerable. The flattery of restaurant work and the cordiality of offices were suffocating to me. It was vulgar to pretend that I, an artist, yoked to an economy I neither chose nor understood, was there for any reason but room and board.

With Schlomo, it was constant walking up and down sidewalks and stairwells, my legs in ideal form. Life was an adventure, just like L. Ron Hubbard taught, and because I had seized that adventure, I didn't need a gym membership and could stay in shape for my acting career. I sun-proofed myself in a baseball cap, shades, long sleeves, tights, and a navy blue paisley kerchief around my neck. Supers chased me from their property for soliciting. Overdressed, unpaid interns smelled the college on me as they passed with trays full of espresso.

Still, even if Schlomo was straight, my days on the locksmith scene were numbered. Winter was coming. My parents had little margin for error, and I was worried my exploited laborer status could shift from tourism into something permanent. I needed income.

I'd walked away from the Church's recruitment efforts, for now. They said you can create more time and money as you go up The Bridge, so I wrote out a chart of how many hours there are in a day, how many days there are in a week, and all the hours I'd need to spend on sleep, survival jobs, rehearsal, and auditions. To my surprise, there were no hours left to join staff at the Church of Scientology. I showed my findings to the recruiter, and they seemed to accept my explanation, if only to indicate how much of a loser I was for not taking planetary responsibility.

I forked over seven dollars to the cashier at the Donut Plant and noticed a voicemail from a blocked number.

"Hello, my name is Vel. I'm calling regarding the Personal Assistant position you responded to on Craigslist for an Academy Award-winning composer. We'd like you to interview tomorrow. Please call back at (xxx) xxx-xxxx."

The youthful, feminine voice suggested safety. My laptop was broken, so I'd been using my soon-to-expire NYU ID to apply for jobs online in the school computer lab. The Craigslist ad had read:

Oscar and Grammy-winning recording artist seeks female personal assistant. Position Includes: Accompanying the artist to appointments and meetings, household errands, light office work.

Ideal for aspiring actress, model, or student types.

GREAT pay.

Send picture AND phone number to be considered.

Applicants without both will not receive a response.

I wondered why an Oscar winner was shilling for employees on Craigslist rather than through friends or a staffing agency. Maybe it was some creep. Maybe it was someone famous, like Chaka Khan, downsizing because of the stock market dip. I'd collaborated with Chaka while a barista at Starbucks, suggesting she try the orange cream coffee cake. At a time when most people dismissed the orange cream as too out-there, she got my aesthetic and bought a piece. I'd had no idea who she was until my co-worker said, "That was Chaka Khan." Great spirits always seem to find one another. I had no illusions about personal assistant work. I'd heard enough anecdotes to be certain it would take over my life. I called and booked my interview for the following day.

CHAPTER 3

DOORMAN BATES

Unable to afford a MetroCard, I walked seventeen blocks to my interview from the posh yoga studio on 86th where I work-studied. My cellphone was dead and I didn't know the time. I sweatily stated my purpose to a doorman wearing a black tailored suit with red trim, a matching visor cap, and white gloves, standing before a black marble facade, and I was invited to sit in the vestibule.

A cluster of women pierced through, their features honed past nature. Their joy was an infantile mesmerism that survives only in unbroken leisure, as exponentially beyond reach as interest income to the wage earner. Delicate shoulder bones bore the chains of buttery leather purses. Pulpy shopping bags were embossed with crests of elite designers.

With porcelain teeth and fingernails like freshly painted cars, they transported from one regulated environment to the next, in summer furs and skins. Flattened to the wall, I stopped breathing—they even claimed the air.

The elevator ejected a girl more like myself, dressed in the factory couture of the hourly class. Mistaking my indifference for confidence, she cast a look of rivalry. The doorman sent me up to 16B.

A manicured thing my age greeted me in a tiny pleated skirt, polo shirt, Tiffany heart tag bracelet, and leather flip-flops.

"Hi, I'm Vel." Vel had the air of a personal assistant, like in the movies. I thought, *what a well-paying job this must be.* Behind her, a powdery old man smiled shyly and struggled to keep his balance. He had dark gray hair splayed long and unevenly over his scalp with a long, emaciated frame almost swimming in a crisp, grid-patterned, red-and-white button-down shirt. "This is Jooks. Come on in."

I dared not look at a piano, across the living room, boasting the Oscar Craigslist had promised. "Hello, nice to meet you! Thank you so much for taking the time to see me." Financial duress brought out my people skills.

Jooks looked me up and down. "Huh, cute!" he said, as if commenting on a hat, or an umbrella.

"You can sit down," said Vel, crossing her legs and sinking into the armchair with a single motion. I took the chair opposite and Jooks took the sofa, draping one thigh over the other, accentuating their scrawniness through his khakis.

"Do you kn-know who I am?" he asked, like I was in for a real treat.

"I'm really bad with recognizing famous people," I said. He flickered his eyes at Vel. Behind him hung framed record covers of Johnny Mathis, Debbie Boone, Whitney Houston.

"See those?" he gestured towards his awards.

"I'm trying not to. It's intimidating!" I said.

"I won the Grammy, the Golden Globe, the Oscar, the People's Choice, and on...and on...in a single y-y-y-year."

"It's very nice to meet you," I

squeaked.

"'Nice to meet you,' she says!" He chuckled.

"That's amazing. One year."

"Honey. That's a small portion of my whole career."

"I'd love to hear about all of it."

"D-do you have a b-boyfriend?"

"No," I knew the answer would be yes pretty soon, once Japetto returned my text messages. "What makes you ask if I have a boyfriend?" I asked, careful to remain pleasant. The eBook *Well Behaved Women Seldom Make History... but Never Die Alone* said to do stuff like smile and laugh gently, which makes men protective, and avoid using words and logic, which make men defensive.

"This job can be very long hours. I've had girls whose boyfriends got upset."

"Weird. I thought lots of girls have jobs and boyfriends at the same time."

"That's odd," he said.

"Maybe they were jealous that their girlfriends were spending so much time with you, specifically."

"Maybe," he chuckled and shrugged.

Then, a serious look came over him. He sat up and bore his eyes into mine. I didn't blink for fear of insulting him. "Now this," he spoke softly. "Is a very. Important. Job. I am very. Very. Busy." He grasped his chest and threw his head back. "So busy! Vel has been wonderful." He cast her a fond glance. "I've had her all summer, every day, twelve-hour days. Once her school resumes in September, she can only work part-time. I need someone to fill in."

"Oh! What's your major?" I asked.

"Nursing and home care. I'm getting my master's," she said.

"H-h-h-hold on," interrupted Jooks, "you really don't know who I am?"

"I—I don't, I'm ashamed to say. I don't know who anyone is," I shrugged.

"Vel, go ahead and give her that thing."

"What thing, Jooks?" she said.

"The piece of paper."

"Oh, I forgot to print it," said Vel.

"What? I told you to print it!"

"I forgot. I'll go and print it." She went quickly out of the room.

DOORMAN BATES

"You are so stupid!" he shouted, with the forced joviality of an abusive dad being visited by social workers. I took Vel's dethroning to indicate that he liked me. If I played my cards right, I'd be taking the same abuse.

"Hurry!" he called.

Vel re-entered with a manilla envelope containing two pages of densely printed text. At the top, it read, "Jooks: Brief Overview of Biography, Career, and Achievements."

"Should I read this now?" I asked, delighted.

"Later. When you get a ch-ch-ch-ch... chance. I'm sorry, I talk like this because I had a stroke."

"I'm so sorry." My face dilated in sympathy.

"Last April, I was in bed with a beautiful twenty-two-year-old. She was in love with me. The week prior, I had heart surgery. I have a pacemaker. When we made love, I would joke and pretend to get a heart attack. Thank god she had the smarts to call an ambulance when I got a real one, or I'd be dead!"

"Thank god, how terrifying. I'm so sorry. My father had a series of mini-strokes and started having neurological issues this year." Although I knew better, I spoke in the accepted language of Western medicine. As an outsider, Jooks would be unlikely to understand that the underlying causes of my father's ailments were based in things that could only be addressed by the Church. Jooks became immediately bored with the focus removed from him. "I mention this only because," I added quickly, "given my father's condition, I might have some familiarity with what you've been through."

"Ahhh, sweetheart," he clasped my arm and sighed, "you can never know what I've been through. My children were on the floor of the hospital room, sobbing. I was as good as dead. The head surgeon recognized me from my movies and said, 'I cannot let this man die.' They had me on the operating table for five hours. Usually, they give up after three. I woke up—I couldn't talk...couldn't move. Ugh!" He clutched his heart and threw his head back. "Finally, I began to figure out where I was, what had happened. My children knew I was back to my old self when I started bossing everyone around. Those nurses were terrible. Terrible! I refused to talk to anyone except the head surgeon. I'd say, 'Get me the surgeon.' He was wonderful. Wonderful! He saved my life. Saved my life...

"Now, though, you see, this whole left side of my body can barely move. I am in excruciating pain. My whole body aches. I have physical therapy two times a week. Occupational therapy once a week. Speech therapy twice a week. Doctors every day. I take so many pills. I have to go for walks. I'm the same up here," he tapped his skull, "but in my body, I'm not the same. The worst part is, I can't play my music. My fingers can't move the way I want. I tried playing the piano—no good. No good. It's so difficult. Oh honey, you can't imagine. That poor girl who was fucking me when I had my stroke. She begged me to let her visit. I had to tell her, 'Honey, there's nothing for you here.' I was too sick. She was in love...so

(37)

young...she saved my life. I told her to come to me if she ever needed anything. Isn't that true, Vel? But what I miss most: being able to play my music."

Vel nodded sadly.

My eyes moistened. "It must be so difficult, having to relearn what you've mastered," I sighed.

"Honey. You have no idea. I'm going to get back to where I was, though."

"Oh, I have no doubt that you will!"

"You don't understand. I won an Oscar! I made millions! One day soon, I know I'll be back. Every day, I'm getting stronger, better, bit by bit. It just needs time. But I'll get there. So, you see, I need somebody good for an assistant, and I mean good."

"Of course," I nodded with purpose.

Vel interjected, "Jöyce, we noticed on your resume that you studied piano. Jooks, did you want her to play something?"

"C-c-c-can you play?" he asked.

I got up and played the one composition I still had memorized from twelve years of study. It was a dark and stormy concert étude by Soviet composer and Stalin Prize winner Nicolai Petrovich Rakov. It consists of a warped arpeggio progressing with obsessive rapidity through incremental keys and variations. It bursts at the climax into renegade chromatic scales, until, exhausted by escape into the less complicated, equally rigid structure, contentedly resuming its initial imprint, and retreating to a finish.

"Huh, sounds pissed off," Jooks muttered to the air. I could not tell if he meant me or the composer. "Follow me," he beckoned. We went through a short corridor. The wall boasted a large photograph of himself, fifteen years younger, on a boat at sea. Beside him stood a grinning boy holding up a freshly caught fish.

"That's my youngest, Will, when he was six or seven. I took him on my boat and he caught that fish. Later that day, I caught the bigger fish!"

"That's so sweet! How old is he now?" I asked.

"He's in college. He was terrible in school. I got him tutors every day. Now he gets A's and B's."

"That's fantastic. Plenty of really smart people don't do well in school," I said.

I followed him into the den. The west wall was covered by a media bookshelf ornamented with photographs of girls my age.

"Those are some of my girlfriends!"

"Oh, how nice."

"Sweetheart, it's not nice, it's GREAT!" He stuck a proud thumb into his puffed-up chest. "I'm a seventy-year-old man, and I only date girls in their early twenties! T-t-t-twenty-five...thirty... that's too old for me! So I wouldn't call it nice, I'd call it GREAT!"

"It's great! Wow! You're seventy? I don't believe it! You could be in your fifties!"

"Ah, shut up, ya jerk."

"Are those your family?" I pointed to some middle-aged people and small children on less prominent shelves.

"Them? Oh. Yeah. I guess. Hey, c'mere, I wanna show you my songs!" He shuffled to the desktop computer.

DOORMAN BATES

There were hundreds of MP3 files. "This is all the music I wrote for advertising before I won my Oscar." He fumbled with the mouse. A chorus swelled in praise of Dr. Pepper. "This was my first big hit! I knew before it aired, so I bought the stock, and it tripled! Then, every major company was hiring me. Rival companies hired me. There simply wasn't anyone better at it than me! Get this—I'd write the music, the lyrics, and sometimes I'd hire myself to play one of the instruments or sing harmony. That way, I'd get the biggest paycheck."

"Wow. You were, like, the Mozart of jingles."

"I was. I wouldn't call them jingles though."

"Of course not."

"I used full orchestration. I gave jobs to a lot of musicians. Nobody did full orchestration in commercials in the sixties. Once I did it, everybody did it!"

"Wow."

A love ballad came on.

"This song is my big hit, from my first movie. It got the Oscar, the Grammy, the People's Choice...it was top of the chart longer than any song during the seventies. It broke the record."

"Oh, yeah, I know that song. You wrote it? Amazing."

"You think that's amazing? I've done much, much more than just some songs."

"I'm sure of it."

"Movies...Broadway...poetry... acting...I do it all. I conducted the New York Philharmonic twice."

"Wow."

I hired the Philharmonic for a movie. I played the character who conducts them—we did two takes. That means I conducted the New York Philharmonic twice," he chuckled. "Listen to this." An ode to coffee came blaring through the speakers.

"Gahhh, what a great song," he said, tilting back in his leather office chair. "Boy, this song is great." He gazed at the ceiling in ecstasy.

"Oh yes, it's great," I said.

The music stopped.

"Vel!" he shouted, jabbing at the mouse.

"Yeah? What is it, Jooks?"

"Where's that Pepsi one? I can't... get...the fuckin'...clicker..."

"Here, I'll do it." She leaned over him.

"Uggghhh. God! Fix it! You're so slow." He turned to me, straining to appear gentle. "You see, I get frustrated with the simplest things. Because of the s-s-s-s-stroke."

Then came his Pepsi number. It changed keys upward, again and again. When it seemed like there were no more keys, it went up one more in a triumphant swell, until the pay-off, "Yooooooou've got a lot to live...and Pepsi's got a lot to giiiiiiiii-iiiiiiiiiive!"

"Yes, that's it!" He waved Vel out of the room. "I wrote this song when I was brand new to advertising. I wrote hundreds. I won the CLIO Award twenty-one times. The second-most CLIO Awards any single person has won is four."

"I'm so sorry to ask, but what is a Cleo?"

He smacked his open palm onto his forehead and threw his head back.

"Ahahahahahahah! You're so fuckin' dumb! A CLIO Award? It's the Oscar of advertising!"

"Oh, wow. I'm so sorry. Ha ha. I am dumb. I know so little about pop culture. I'd love for you to teach me all about it though." If my survival didn't depend on this man's ego, I'd have locked him into a cold, dead stare and told him, "I'm not dumb. I'm not dumb at all."

Jooks hummed along to a MetLife theme, one languid hand conducting in the air.

"Jooks, we're late for your psychiatrist," Vel said.

So here it is, I thought: *the Great Artist, just as Scientology describes.* Ailing, medicated with psych drugs, whittled down into a materialistic shell of himself by societal suppression—just like the Church says.

We reconvened to the living room.

"I take it you, ah, come from money," he asked, giving me the once-over.

"Oh, not at all!" I took the opportunity to showcase my rags-to-riches tale. "I'm completely self-supported. My parents lost their house, their health, and their business, all in one year. I had to get through my last year of college on my own."

He cast a sly look over to Vel, impressed, I thought, by my self-sufficiency. "And, eh. What do you like to do when you're not working?"

"Well, I'm an actor. I'm doing a play in October." As if choreographed, Vel and Jooks winced simultaneously.

"Oh," I grinned, "I thought your Craigslist posting said that you preferred actors?"

"Honey, I n-n-need to know if you can do the job."

"Of course," I said.

He sighed, deeply burdened. "Here's what we'll do. Come back Friday. I'll try you out then. Just to see what it's like. Come at three o'clock."

"I'm performing in a play Friday. It doesn't end until three. It's our last show. I can come right after."

"Why can't you j-j-just quit the show?" He looked perplexed.

"I really wish that I could quit the show, so I could get here by the time you prefer—unfortunately, I already agreed to perform. I play a very minor role, but I'm in a lot of scenes, and if I don't go, it would mess everything up for the other twenty cast members who are also performing in the show, this Friday. I'm so, so sorry. I had no idea when I accepted the role three months ago that it would conflict with you asking me to come in this Friday at three. Had I known, I would have done everything differently. I always honor my commitments, but I would love to come by as soon as the show is finished. Would four o'clock be all right?"

"I see," he thought, unable to locate anything distasteful in my response. "Come this Friday at four and don't be late. Here," he held out a twenty-dollar bill, "take a cab."

"I'll leave right after the show." I breathed an audible sigh of gratitude.

"Oh," I held up his artist's bio as Vel escorted me out, "I'll make sure to read this tonight! I want to know all about your amazing career."

"Honey," he shook his head, "that's just the beginning."

CHAPTER 4

SUNSET TOOLIVARD

After the final performance of *Don't Deny Delancey!* I stepped out of my costume and into a taxi. Jooks had yet to mention pay, and I did not want to offend him by holding to contemporary labor practices.

Japetto was a non-speaking wino opposite my singing dancing prostitute. He was secretly dating a producer on the show the whole time we'd been flirting, turning all of her friends against me in a cruel smear campaign that I did not yet know a thing about.

Vel was going to train me for the first hour. She microwaved leftover Indian food while Jooks watched TV in the den.

"This is for Jooks, not me." She placed it steaming on the polished stone two-person breakfast bar attached to the kitchen wall.

Jooks scuffed in to join us. He tipped himself into place, looked at the plate, and groaned, "No. I don't want it."

Stone-faced, Vel slopped his supper

into the garbage. I could see that he enjoyed saying the word "no."

"And h-h-h-how are you?" he asked me.

"I'm great, thanks, how are you?"

I stood at attention with a warm but neutral facial expression.

"Get me my milkshake," he croaked. Vel handed him a plastic tumbler from Häagen-Dazs. "A-A-A-Advil," he said. Vel rifled through a basket of prescription bottles on the counter and pried open the cap. Blue gel capsules bounced across the marble counter.

"You idiot!" he cried.

"It was an accident! Whaddaya want me to do, Jooks!" she yelled right back at him.

My instinct would have been to shrink in apology, fearing that to shout back would provoke him, but to my surprise, Jooks retreated. In an instant, I absorbed the lesson that would return to me in reflexive self-defense many times over: Jooks' aggression was only aroused further by meek propriety, but would promptly recede from attack if matched with an equally robust offensive. She stooped and gathered the painkillers.

"Give me my m-m-m-medicine," he said.

Vel brought a plastic bowl containing a dollop of applesauce flecked with crushed tablets. "I-I-I'll just have the Japanese for dinner. You can go." He flicked his wrist at Vel without looking at her. Twenty minutes had passed since my arrival.

"That's it, you want me to go?" she stammered.

"Yeah," he said.

"Goodnight, Jooks." She got a black cardboard take-out box from the refrigerator, placed it between his utensils, and stalked out of the kitchen. The apartment door slammed.

We were alone now.

"Sit, sit," he motioned.

I sat straight as an arrow as he wrested a shrimp tail from his lips.

"What's the pill you take?" I asked, trying to breathe evenly.

"I can't sleep. So I gotta take T-T-T-T-Trazodone. And Klonopin. And I take

Lipitor, Warfarin. You don't need to know all that."

But now I did know, and I wondered if any of those were mind-altering drugs distributed by psychiatry—the industry of death—to irrevocably change the brain chemistry and make it impossible for a person to go clear in this lifetime. If I ever gave him his medicine, I wondered, would that make me a Suppressive Person who would then be blacklisted from the Church?

I decided that it wouldn't count, because he'd already taken the medicine on his own. And I would be doing nothing to exacerbate his situation. I was only trying to earn money to continue my own religious journey. I would never do anything to interfere with his medicine either, because the Church taught us it was dangerous to interfere with psychotropic drugs unless a doctor was supervising, and the Creed of the Church of Scientology stated that we were to always comply with the laws of the land.

SUNSET TOOLIVARD

"Would you like me to get you another Diet Coke?" I asked. "Is there anything else you might need."

"No, no, no," he said. "W-w-w-would you like some?" He offered me the gem-pink strip of sashimi on the end of his chopsticks.

"Oh, no, thank you!" I smiled, implying that I was too professional to show up hungry for work. If I managed to keep this job, I figured I would possess the resources to obtain however much sushi I want. Jooks chuckled, not unkindly. He was no stranger to the pretense of down-at-heel girls who refused hospitality. He saw through my pauper's grandeur.

"I can't finish it. It'll only go in the garbage."

"Oh, I'm fine, fine. Thanks."

"Look, I haven't touched it!"

"Thank you so much for the offer. I ate beforehand."

"Suit yourself," he shrugged. I tightened my abdomen around an audible growl. Jooks raised a yellowtail sashimi to his lips. A lump of soy-

drenched rice tumbled down the front
of his sweater. "Ahhh...damn it."

I didn't know how to react, but I shed
my timidity when I saw that he wasn't
embarrassed.

"Here, I'll grab a paper towel," I said,
seizing the opportunity to convey my
efficiency.

"Don't worry about it."

"I'm happy to do it. I'm eager to work."

"There won't be much for you to
do. Th-th-this is just so you can get a
feel for what it'll be like." He dropped
his food into the garbage. "Here," he
handed me a bottle of Fiji water, "that's
for me. N-now, l-l-l-let's go for a walk."

The elevator rose toward us in the hall.

"C'mahhhhhn!" Jooks banged on the
door when he heard it stop at a lower
floor. "Fuckin' asshole."

Inside, we joined a striking woman
about Jooks' age who looked as if she'd
stepped out of a Barney's shop window.
She examined my face and said, "I just
now remember how beautiful young
people are." I beamed right back at her,
like an infant to its grandmother. It was

the first nice thing anyone had said to me in some time.

Jooks stared ahead like we were being harassed by a panhandler.

"Don't talk to the people here," Jooks said when she got off on the tenth floor. "I'm serious. They're all jerks."

Two doormen in white gloves and visor caps greeted us.

"H-h-hi there, Donny!" Jooks said. "Donny is the oldest. He's the only one who doesn't h-h-have too good of English. He's gonna retire soon. They're giving him a pension," he whispered. Donny seemed euphoric with anticipation.

"Why, HELLO there, Mr. Jooks, and how are YOU today?" crooned Crawley.

"Hello C-C-Crawley."

Crawley's eyes were pried open over a newly installed smile. He had either snapped or was ironically acting like a Metro-Goldwyn-Mayer doorman, to see who thought it was funny and who thought it was how doormen ought to behave. Maybe if I had been clever enough to think of that, I could have excelled at a normal job.

JÖYCE

"What are those holes in the doors?" I asked as we left the building.

"The super had to lower the handles. They were leaning on the job."

Jooks muttered at his own faltering feet.

His leather driving shoes scuffled in quick little steps along the pavement as we moved forward, inches at a time. I had infinite patience, because we have infinite lifetimes.

Other than the psych drugs, Jooks could be fully rehabilitated. There was no point in doing anything imperfectly, because we would all have to deal with the consequences together on the same planet for all of eternity.

I crept alongside him, down Madison, across 62nd, and up Lexington, ready to prop him back up. A girl my age came towards us. Jooks stopped walking, dragged his eyes up the length of her and fixed a stare to her face. He rotated his body to watch her pass and recede from view. I had never seen anyone violate another person so hard, using only his eyes.

SUNSET TOOLIVARD

"God. I gotta get better. You have no idea. I had so many women. Now, look at me. Even taking a walk is incredibly painful. My doctor says I gotta go for a short walk every day. Just a couple times around the block."

"Well, only do what you're comfortable with."

"I'm not comfortable with anything. It hurts."

"I'm so sorry, Jooks."

"My body is in so much pain...you can't imagine."

"Do you need to stop?"

"Not yet. Even if I do, I'm still in pain. God. The whole left side of my body."

"I'm so sorry, Jooks."

"Why are you sorry?"

"That you're in pain, I guess."

"I just have to go around the block a few times."

"Well, even little things can be helpful."

"Gosh, thanks," he said, sarcastically. "Ugghhhhhhhh. This is torture. You don't understand! I rode horses. I used to sail. I went to the gym every day. Now I'm limping around the block with an idiot like you." He scraped along, left foot pigeoned inward. After two more determined laps, we returned to the apartment with Jooks a few shades pinker. "Well, I feel much better." He looked up, suddenly remembering I was a separate being from himself. "W-w-w-would you like to come back tomorrow?"

"I'd love to."

"Come tomorrow at f-four."

I left the building, Crawley hustled to the door with his eyes bugged out and smile hanging crooked. "Have a good night, Miss. We'll be seeing you again, I hope?"

"Tomorrow, apparently," I grinned, slipping out the door and rushing toward the F train. Japetto had invited me to The Four Faced Liar after the cast party I'd just missed, so I chased him to the East Village.

CHAPTER 5

ALMOST RAPIST

Recall when there was no word for 'fuckboy.'

I arrived to Jooks' apartment the next afternoon in total serenity. Japetto and I had conversed that morning over bagels and coffee, following our night at The Four Faced Liar. I'd said it seemed like he wanted me to like him, but it also seemed he had a girlfriend with long blond hair from LA who wore sunglasses and maxi dresses, much more than he'd initially let on. What fortune of all fortunes when he replied, "Oh, she's gone now. She flew away," making a bird motion with his hands, "to Los Angeles."

He had the touch of a poet and the sensibilities of a true genius with a greying T-shirt, pensive cigarette, electric, wild eyes, and the ability to charm his way into people giving him things and opportunities. He aspired to a wolf-like appearance and state of being. I was never interested in men who fit the moral definition of "good character" and only wanted to spend my time with men who fit the actor's definition of "a good character."

A James Dean from two summers ago, when my parents still had a house, passed by our cafe table on the sidewalk, almost as a sign. Back then I'd had the strength to deflect my attraction to his charisma in favor of my professional relationships and artistic goals. I threw my drained paper coffee cup into his path in joyous greeting. Two conquests forced to encounter one another's scent in my presence.

Finally, with all lost, I could rest my hope on Japetto. Infatuation would make the effortless leap into reality.

For lunch, Jooks wanted delivery.

"What would you like?" he asked.

"Jooks, I brought my own."

"Nonsense!" he waved his hand. "Me eat a nice lunch while you just sit and watch? That w-w-wouldn't be right. The question is: what should we order?" He crouched in his chair like Rodin's Thinker, cellphone caged in a loose fist.

ALMOST RAPIST

"I just remembered!"

"What is it, Jooks?" I sat up, eager to take part in his rehabilitation.

"P-P-P-P-Petaluma!" He seized the name like forgotten pocket money.

"Petaluma?"

"Call them."

"Uh. Do you have the number?"

"Here," he handed me a sleek, plastic slab whose density contained a glowing roster of places and names that only his memory could unlock. I opened the unfamiliar Samsung 4G flip phone, the newest model on the market. "C'mon, c'mon, hurry, I'm hungry!" He bounced in his chair. I hated being rushed. "Order something for yourself," he insisted.

Jooks ordered a prosciutto pizza. Following a display of reluctance, I ordered a plain.

"Now, let's go to the roof."

Jooks loved to collect energy from the sun. Summer was closing out.

"Would you like me to bring the newspaper and bottled water?"

"Sure," he said, "a-a-and a Coke."

JOYCE

"And sunscreen? Do you have sunscreen?"

"Nah."

"I wear sunscreen every day. Even in the winter. You really should. My mother does too."

"Wh-wh-what kind do you wear?"

"It's this organic stuff from Whole Foods."

"Nah, forget it. We're just gonna be up there a minute."

"Okay! I'll go grab everything." I scurried about the apartment, gathering beverages and the New York Times.

"C'monnn," Jooks moaned. "Now!"

We heard the elevator stop on a floor below us. Jooks rolled his eyes and banged on the door. "C'maaahhhhhhn!" he shouted to the unseen passengers. "Fuckin' assholes." Forty-five seconds later, we were one floor up at the Penthouse. Jooks limped with purpose. "Ah, shit." The narrow cement stairwell shot up into darkness. In his time since visiting the roof, he'd forgotten the climb.

"Jooks, is this gonna be okay for you? Maybe we should go back."

ALMOST RAPIST

"Shit," he sighed, "I'll do it." He braced himself on the banister, anchored one foot to the step, and hoisted his body. He took a rest, then proceeded this way up the remaining stairs. "Go and get the door," he growled. I scurried ahead and turned the handle, but it didn't budge. A panic came over me and I gave it another firm pull. The door was locked.

"Uhhh, Jooks..."

"What is it?" he huffed, levering his body up one more step.

"The—the door won't open."

"Ah. SHIT!" With his last bit of strength, he lurched to the door and rattled it himself. I willed his breath to slow and heart rate to return to normal.

"There's a code to unlock the door," he huffed.

"Want me to run down and ask for it?"

"No! Call the lobby," he thrust the phone in my direction.

"There's no contact here that says 'Lobby.' Is it under something else?"

"FIGURE IT OUT!"

I called "Doorman." Ten minutes later, Areef, the building handyman, came and entered the code.

Out on the roof, Jooks lay on a wooden lounge chair, and I dragged over a little table for his reading and beverages. It was cloudy and muggy.

"G-g-g-get a chair for yourself!" I obediently dragged one beside his and lay rigidly on my back. I disliked that I was aging myself in the sun's rays for him.

"Aren't you going to get yourself a cushion?" The cushions were stored in a large Rubbermaid trunk in case it rained. I didn't want to go to the extra trouble of getting another.

"Oh no, I'm fine. Hard wood is supposed to be good for your back!"

"Get a cushion!" he cried.

"No, really, Jooks, I'm okay."

"You're crazy." He closed his eyes.

When the pizza came, we returned to the kitchen.

"You eat too fast," Jooks rasped. I looked at my greasy square of wax paper.

"I have a strong survival urge, I guess."

"If you go out to dinner with someone,

you're going to make them feel bad! My pizza has three-quarters left!"

"I've always had a very healthy appetite."

"Much too fast." He shook his head. "I-i-i-i-is there a boy you're seeing?"

"Well, one I like."

"W-w-who is he?" Jooks perked up with interest.

"This guy I went to acting school with."

"H-h-h-have you fucked yet?"

"Um—"

"I said, did you fuck 'em?!"

"No."

"Why not?!"

I had ended the stigma of my virginity the year prior with an ex-ballerino who had dropped out of the American Ballet Theater following a motorcycle crash. Only much later did I realize that his pronounced limp, and our perfectly timed meeting at a background actor gig after I texted Hazel that I was going to end my virginity, was not a message from the Universe that I would receive everything I asked for, or portent of one day pulling in the job with Jooks because I had been nice enough to sleep with a down-and-out dancer who had a limp, just like him. It was all planned by people and not god.

"It's not like that."

"It's all like that. Did you fuck him?"

"Anyway."

"What's he l-like?" he asked, alive with fascination.

"Well," I sighed, "he's an amazing actor. He spent two weeks at disciplinary school for boys during high school. He got into this car crash in Prague after his last breakup. He reminds me of Tom Waits."

"My god, he sounds terrible. I wouldn't even give that kid a job, m-m-much less date him."

"You don't like Tom Waits?"

"You better s-s-stay away from him. I'm serious. Or I'll fire you."

"Jooks!"

"I'm serious. Stay away from him. He is no good. No good!"

His meddling was the first I'd felt looked out for in a while.

ALMOST RAPIST

Jooks ended our night in the den, flipping channels between the U.S. Open, the decline of General Motors, Sarah Palin's vice presidential candidacy campaign, and the new episode of *Boston Public*.

"Listen," he said, "I like having you around. I want to keep you on."

"Oh, thank you, Jooks, I'm honored."

"Alright, alright. So. I'll pay you for the weekend."

I feigned surprise, relieved that I was actually getting paid. "Is this enough?" he handed me some folded bills.

"Oh Jooks, it's more than enough, thank you so much." I tucked the bills away as if they were inconsequential. I would tally it up, like a miser, later when I left.

"Come in tomorrow. Let's say f-four?"

"Thank you so much, Jooks. I'm really looking forward to it."

"Good, and you can start to w-w-work."

CHAPTER 6:
MY FAIR SHADY

Jooks was watching *Pretty Woman* on TV. It seemed to always be on cable. Only *Pretty Woman* subdued Jooks' channel flipping. It was the part of the movie where Pretty Woman is lying on her stomach in a black-lace bodice watching television, picking over candy from the minibar. Her bare ass cheeks were illuminated by the screen. Richard Gere, in astonishment, sees her soul.

Not since I came to school dressed as Pippi Longstocking on a dare had I known anyone to internalize a film as Jooks did *Pretty Woman*.

My father was not a Swedish pirate who left me alone for months in an empty Victorian house with a monkey, horse, and trunk of gold doubloons. And I knew this. In the coming year and a half, Jooks would promote four different call girls to girlfriend, and two to fiancé.

"M-m-my favorite movie!"

Jooks set his glass of Diet Coke on top of a document.

MY FAIR SHADY

"Jooks, do you want a coaster?" I asked. "The condensation from your glass is messing up that piece of paper."

"What, this? Nah," he unfolded the letter, "I got this thing in the mail. It's a c-c-c-court summons. Some girl is suing me for s-s-sexual harassment!"

"That's so weird," I said.

"I'm an old man! How could I sexually harass someone? I can't believe it. My lawyer says since I had a stroke, maybe they think they can get my money now."

I had heard old rich guys sometimes get sued for sexual harassment because they're easy targets. I guessed everything would be sorted out fairly in the legal system if he was guilty.

Jooks lurched up out of his chair. "Hey! I wanna show you my screenplay," he told me, extracting a manila envelope from a drawer. "I want you to read the whole thing. Right now."

"You're gonna pay me to sit and read?"

"Just sit and read in the living room while I'm in the den doing my physical therapy with Danielle, and l-let me know what you think afterwards."

JÖYCE

"You don't want me to do any errands for you or anything?"

"Godammit, just sit and read!"

"Okay. Thanks, Jooks. Easiest job I ever had."

When Jooks' physical therapist came, the two retreated to the den and I sat in the living room chair by the piano, resolved to finish in an hour.

The envelope contained a script called *Struck by Lightning*. *Struck by Lightning* is about a film producer named Billy. A year after his wife surrenders to terminal cancer, Billy gets lonely and hires his first call girl, like in *Pretty Woman*. Johanna, twenty-two, blonde, confesses that Billy is her very first client, like in *Pretty Woman*. Instead of sleeping together, they spend the night talking and realize they're in love, just like in *Pretty Woman*.

Then they actually do sleep together, but for free, like in *Pretty Woman*.

The next day, they send each other text messages.

"I feel amazing!" Billy texts.

"I know! Me too!" Johanna texts back.

MY FAIR SHADY

They do date things, like visit museums and the Hamptons. When Billy invites her to move in, Johanna admits that she has a three-year-old daughter back home, in Maryland, with her loser high school sweetheart who wants her to leave New York and marry him. Billy is shocked but understanding. They seek custody of the child.

Johanna buys cookbooks and French crockery with Billy's credit cards. Billy starts looking at the best private schools for his future stepdaughter. Johanna brings her daughter to meet Billy. There's a montage of idyllic childhood activities. Happiness is wrenched away when Johanna's mom has her involuntarily committed.

Billy calls his lawyer. A page later, they track down Johanna's colleague Veronica, who isn't blonde. Veronica is the bad influence who invited Johanna to become a call girl. Billy's lawyer says to hire her services and then question her. Billy pays double for Veronica's time and confidentiality. He declines her sexual advances, seeking only to find Johanna.

The light went from sunset to dusk, and muffled laughter came from the den as his physical therapy started to wrap up. Pretty soon, Jooks would want some dinner.

Veronica is jealous that Johanna found somebody to give her the good life and becomes obsessed with Billy. She threatens to spread rumors that Billy forced her to have violent, kinky sex. The rumors reach Johanna. And just as Johanna is about to lose hope, Billy rescues her and they live together with her daughter in New York. Veronica goes to jail, and Johanna's mom goes to a mental institution. But then, in the final page and a half, there is an alternate ending: Billy fails to save Johanna, and there is nothing he can do but share his story with the world. He crouches mournfully over a keyboard before the last page of a screenplay, typing "THE END."

"Wow, Jooks. That's impressive."

"'Impressive?' It's GREAT!"

"It's wonderful, Jooks. Really, it is."

MY FAIR SHADY

"I was working on this before I had my stroke. Scarlett Johansson might play the hooker."

"Which one?" I said.

"The good one."

"The blond one."

"Yeah."

"Wow. Cool. I wouldn't even know how to write a screenplay."

"You're damned right you wouldn't," he said.

"So, like, Scarlett Johansson auditioned and everything?"

"Well, these things are always up in the air, but it was being discussed. You know, we were in the middle of casting for the brown-haired hooker when I had my stroke."

"Jooks, I'm so sorry."

"You're sorry? But you know what's incredible? The screenplay is all true. I *am* Billy."

"Really? Wow. I'm sorry you lost your wife to cancer, Jooks."

"Not that part! We got divorced. The cancer was to make the character sympathetic, so the audience doesn't hate him for buyin' a hooker. But the part with me and the hookers is all true."

"Oh, wow."

"That girl Johanna? She was the love of my life. I changed her name of course, but that's her photograph over by the TV."

He pointed to a framed headshot of a blond model/actress.

"Can you believe that when I met her, she was on her first hooker job?" he said.

"Like in *Pretty Woman*," I said.

"Exactly."

"Incredible."

"Except my version tells the truth, because we actually fucked on the first night. Do you really believe Richard Gere paid Julia Roberts just to have a conversation? No respectable businessman pays for sex without redeeming it!"

"Wow, Jooks. It's like you wrote the edgy version of *Pretty Woman*."

"Exactly. I wrote the version of *Pretty Woman* that never gets told. I loved that girl. I loved her." He put a hand on his heart.

(72)

MY FAIR SHADY

"Oh, Jooks, that's so sad."

"Broke my heart."

"What did she do?"

"She didn't do anything! It's just...she had a kid. I couldn't do it. I was just too old for another kid."

"Oh."

"I paid for her kid's school though."

"That's so kind of you, Jooks."

"I loved her. I loved them both. But I couldn't raise another kid."

He sighed.

"We should get a manicure," he announced. Since Jooks sometimes spoke in the royal "we," I dared not hope he meant me too. I had never gotten a manicure. I didn't understand why people pay to have chemicals painted onto their nails that would only peel off.

We rode twenty blocks to a nail salon. I sat in a waiting chair as women surrounded Jooks in a dainty murmur.

"C'mere." he barked. "I want you to get a manicure too."

"Really? Me? You don't have to."

"Oh, God, get in the chair for Chrissakes."

JÖYCE

"Okay. Thank you so much, Jooks." I beamed. He rolled his eyes.

"So how long have you been with Jooks?" asked a manicurist named Tiffany.

"Oh! I've only been with him two days. He's trying me out as his personal assistant," I said. She giggled.

"How come you're laughing?" I said.

"You mean you are not his girlfriend?" She dipped my fingertips into a bowl of sea glass filled with warm water.

"Oh! No, I really am his assistant." Jooks bristled in the chair next to mine as he pretended not to listen.

"Oh, oh. okay."

"Do you want polish?" asked Jooks' manicurist, Renee, his obvious favorite.

"No, I don't want polish," he protested.

"I mean clear polish." She giggled.

"I know, I know. J-just—just buff them please, thank you."

"He's a good man. He's been coming here over ten years," said the salon manager, patting him on the back and motioning for a girl to massage our shoulders.

MY FAIR SHADY

"Wh-wh-who are you seeing right now?" Jooks asked Renee.

"Oh, haha, nobody, I'm happy with me and my daughter right now."

"Why aren't you l-looking for a boyfriend?"

"I said I'm happy!" She sculpted her face into the sweetest smile.

"Even a boyfriend like me?" Jooks chuckled, half serious.

Renee sneered, half serious.

"Nuh-uh." She shook her head vigorously. Jooks froze. All the girls froze.

"Hey." He became solemn. She lowered her head, sensing the endangerment of her and her co-workers' tips.

"I sorry, Jooks. Not funny?" she cooed.

"Not funny!" he scowled.

"I didn't mean to hurt your feelings. I was only making a joke."

"Yeah, well, be careful with your jokes."

"I didn't mean it. I will be careful." She rolled her eyes up at him like a guilty child.

He examined my nails in the cab.

"What a boring color," he said.

"I got something neutral."

I'd read in a magazine that nude colors were more professional than actress red. "This was my first manicure," I said, casually.

He gasped. "You've never had a manicure?"

"No..."

"We can go and get one every two weeks."

"Oh wow, I would love that Jooks, thank you!"

Well Behaved Women Seldom Make History...but Never Die Alone says to accept gifts from men with emotive gratitude. It makes them feel strong and needed so they won't fire you. "Did the massage at the nail salon help your pain?"

"No. God, my arm is so weak. This whole side of my body. My leg. My back. My shoulder. It hurts so much."

"I'm sure it will get better with time."

"You don't understand. Before the stroke, I was a very strong man. I arm-wrestled guys for money in high school."

"What?"

"Sure! I used to go with my friend to tournaments. Don't tell anyone. I had a special way of cheating. I'd win every time."

"You can't cheat at arm wrestling."

"You can."

"Jooks, it sounds like you're not giving yourself enough credit. How is it possible to cheat at—"

"SHHHH!" he put a finger to his lips and gestured as if the cab driver might overhear us. "It's a special trick where you lift your arm. I'll have to show you when we get home."

"You mean, I'd beat you if I used it?"

"Well...it has to be a somewhat c-close match. We would arm wrestle within categories of strength. My friend was a black belt in jiu-jitsu. He'd hold the money while I'd beat everyone. I'd give him a cut."

"Wow, Jooks, that sounds like a Scorsese movie or something."

"Suuuure! I'd win hundreds... thousands! I bought my mother a car."

"She must have been a great mom."

"Meh."

"Where did you grow up, Jooks?"

"I lived in Brighton Beach with my mother. Sometimes I'd go see my father uptown. They were d-d-d-divorced."

"Huh."

"My father had more money, but my mother got me piano lessons. She had an upright. When I was two or three, I'd play songs I heard on the radio. You know, just the melody. My mother walked up to my father and asked him to buy me piano lessons. He said he didn't want to, so she stuck her finger right in his chest and said, 'Piano lessons.' So I started."

"You must have inherited your persistence from her." *And your habit of sticking your finger in people's faces*, I thought. "It was great she looked out for your talent. Not all moms do that."

"Lots of parents get their kids piano lessons."

I remembered how my mother had taken me to piano lessons every week, sometimes counting out the change at the office window to pay the fee. She also once threw my paintings down the stairs, the summer before I was going to leave for college. But by that point, I wasn't surprised. I only pitied my father. I'd tried one last time to get him to name her as a Suppressive Person in one of my final exercises for the Volunteer Minister's Course.

My mother is a black hole, but it takes a black hole to give birth to a star.

"And then you became a great musician and won the Oscar!"

"I guess so. After high school, I got into Juilliard. I didn't want to keep arm wrestling, but they only gave me a partial scholarship. I said, 'Oh, shit. How am I gonna pay for Juilliard?' I did the arm wrestling again for a little."

"Jesus, what a story. How come you've never written a screenplay about the boy from Brighton who pays his way through Juilliard by cheating in arm wrestling?"

He glowed with pleasure and leaned in secretively. "I'd be afraid that if Juilliard saw it, they'd try to take my scholarship back."

"That's nuts."

"It's not nuts." He grew offended.

"It is nuts. All you have to do is write, 'Based on a True Story,' or something. And anyway, wasn't tuition, like, five dollars when you were there? You'd make more money on the screenplay than whatever you got from scholarships in nineteen, like, fifty."

"I was born in 1938! I didn't go there in 1950!"

"They wouldn't even sue you."

"Eh, well," he shrugged. "I left Juilliard after a couple weeks."

I looked at him. His advertising jingles could make a can of coffee grounds into an overnight sensation. At the time, I couldn't help but think the stories from his life were even better.

CHAPTER 7:
THE WOMEN'S MART

The intercom bleated. "Oh, God. It's her. Would you run and get that, please? Just tell them to send her up."

"Who is she?" I asked.

"My m-m-maid."

"I didn't know you had a maid."

In the living room, dining room, kitchen, master bedroom, walk-in closet, 2.5 bathrooms, office den, and five wall closets, dust and clutter were given no opportunity to accumulate.

"Monday. Wednesday. Friday."

"Good morning, Jooks." She breezed in.

"You're fifteen minutes late," Jooks scolded. I caught sight of his tongue lolling in its marsh of bloated cereal.

"I apologize. The train stopped on my way down."

"You were supposed to be here at ten!"

"I'm sorry. I'll work the whole three hours."

"Yeah, you'll work the whole three hours. It's what I'm paying you for."

"You know I always work the whole

three hours. Sorry for being late." She smiled.

"Then don't b-b-be late," he shouted.

"I won't. Hi, I'm Alina." She offered her hand. Her long dark hair was unfastened, and she wore an ankle-length denim skirt with sneakers.

"Hi, I'm—"

Jooks interrupted. "I didn't say you could talk to her!"

"Sorry. So...I'll go and get started." She headed towards the supply closet in the corridor.

"You'll finish the work in three hours," he warned. "It should take no longer."

After breakfast, we moved to the den.

"Get outta here!" he roared at Alina.

"I gotta finish cleaning." She gave a wounded smile.

"Do it later!"

"Okay."

I watched her leave, afraid to show sympathy for fear of provoking Jooks.

"God, she's a jerk, isn't she?"

"Uh...I don't know."

"Whaddaya mean 'I don't know?'

(82)

THE WOMEN'S MART

What's this 'I don't know?' You're too nice."

On the news, stockbrokers arrived for work at Lehman Brothers to find that it had collapsed without warning. The bank survived the Great Depression and two World Wars, but the amassing of power that was too big to fail had lost the conservative values and relationship building which had survived over a hundred years of humble growth from a small town in Germany through the American cotton and slave trade and the disco years of the 1980s. Housing prices fell below the value of mortgages that had been granted without proper vetting, and people stopped being able to pay. My parents and I were only part of the first wave. Millions of people were going to lose their homes in the housing crisis. Unemployed, upwards of ten million Americans would eventually be displaced into a newly diversified class of underserved.

"God, I hope that b-b-black guy doesn't get elected because of this,"

Jooks said with a sneer. "He wants to take my money!"

I gazed into John McCain's icy little eyes and shuddered because now that Jooks had said something racist, it was my obligation to compensate by being mean to a white person of comparable stature. Obama seemed really cool anyway, so I figured it wouldn't do much harm.

"Jooks?" Alina peeked in.

"WHAT IS IT?"

"I need money for the flowers."

"Here." He thrust some bills at her. "HERE!" he screamed again when she hesitated.

"Thank you."

"Get out! God!" He stood, gesturing towards the figurative masses below. "It's really bad out there. I'm just g-g-glad I have my money. I don't give a fuck about those p-people."

I thought of my father, wasting in his chair back in Lansdowne.

"What? Don't look at me that way! Do you? Ahhhh, what do you know?"

I convinced him to let me refill his Coke. Alina was refilling three vases

THE WOMEN'S MART

with roses.

"Hi," I said.

"Hi."

"Listen, I'm sorry he talks to you that way. It's my first week. I'm sure he'll be like that to me soon."

"It's okay."

"Where are you coming from?"

"The Bronx."

"I'm actually always late too. I'm from Bed-Stuy."

"Bed-Stuy? Damn. They're supposed to have the most murders per square foot."

"I moved there for school."

Unfortunately, Jooks seemed to have a sixth sense for class solidarity happening under his roof. "STOP TALKIN' TO EACH OTHER!" came a muffled shout from the den.

I bulged my eyes, and she laughed, twirling her index finger at her temple to indicate Jooks' insanity.

When it was time for Alina to leave, she collected the prior week's pay.

He reached into his pocket without betraying any awareness of the expressions that moved across her face. "That's $120?"

"I worked more."

"Why?" He looked Alina directly in the eye. "I told you to work three hours each day."

"It took longer because I only did two days, and you made me leave the room when you came in."

"How much longer?"

"I worked one extra hour. So it's twenty dollars more. I'm rounding down."

"Oh, well...how generous of you."

I got the sense that Alina had been worrying about this exchange more than she let on. Still, she tried to sound cheerful and upbeat. "And just to remind you, three weeks from now, it's my wedding and honeymoon. So I'll be away that whole week." She beamed with excitement.

"The second week of October."

"Right."

"Who are you marrying?" I asked.

"My childhood sweetheart. We've known each other since we were kids."

THE WOMEN'S MART

"Christ." Jooks gave a beleaguered sigh. "How am I gonna clean my apartment?"

"I can ask my cousin to do it. Do you want me to put it in your calendar?"

"Not necessary."

"I can write it in!" I chirped, eager to acquire any duty.

"Shaddup! This doesn't concern you."

"Okay...well, I'll see you Friday, Jooks. Thank you," she said.

"Okay, bye." He let the door slam shut and glared through the peephole. "What a moron."

CHAPTER 8

LOVE IS A VICTORY MARCH

The occupational therapist arrived for his 3:00 p.m.

I used the hour to plan my West Virginia trip. My grandmother was making a pilgrimage from Georgia with my dad's youngest brother.

I made my tuffet on the bone-colored honeycomb sofa.

Jooks' apartment was crisp and odorless. I felt that if I could absorb its cold aristocracy, I too could become rich.

The intercom buzzed at ten 'til four. That was when I met Cora. Cora had natural, headshot-worthy red hair and delicate Irish features.

"I didn't know Jooks had a third assistant," I said.

"I was hired a month before you," she shrugged. "I also work part-time for a doctor."

"He hardly has me do anything. He bought me a manicure."

"Because you're the newest. It was

like that for me."

"And he buys meals! I always feel like I'm about to get fired though."

"Yeah...the psychiatrist is offering me full time and says I can leave whenever for auditions."

"A psychiatrist?" I was shocked, but I'd long resigned myself to the widespread acceptance of psychiatry and the shunning I would receive from my peers were I to behave as if it were anything other than completely wholesome. Still, I worried about her judgment.

"I'll probably tell Jooks about the new job soon, but I was hoping I could work nights."

"What is the hourly pay here, by the way? He handed me like $400 at the end of the weekend."

"Fifteen."

"That's good!"

"It's okay. He gets mad when I leave for auditions. A job in this city that lets you audition is gold." Her goals and options offended yet inspired me.

"I like your purse," I said, pointing

to her giant silver handbag. Metallic leather was trendy that summer. I had read so in a magazine. I didn't know how I felt about the purse, but it seemed designed to make its presence known.

"Thanks! I bought it at Bloomingdale's after a busy week. I probably can't afford it." She pulled out an economy-size container of gum. "Want some?"

"Sure. All I've done is watch TV, go in cabs, order take-out, and listen to his recordings."

"He plays his music for everyone."

"He's like a musical genius...note-wise, anyway."

"It's not my style of music. He's always saying, 'I've gotta make you see, and then you'll love it!'"

I felt a pang of envy. *Well Behaved Women Seldom Make History...but Never Die Alone* said women who admit what they do and don't like, rather than fake it for approval, are more desirable.

There came a rustling from the den. And Jooks scuffed in.

"W-w-w-what are you two talking about?" he asked.

"Acting and stuff. I haven't met Cora before." I smiled.

"Oh w-w-well, that's nice."

"Jooks—I have to tell you—well, ask you. I was wondering...if this weekend, I could visit my grandmother in West Virginia with my parents. She's coming up from Georgia with my uncle. I hardly see her anymore. I'll only go if it's okay with you."

"Ah, geez." He bit his lip.

"I can cover her shifts this weekend!" Cora said.

"Hold on, hold on...You can go this weekend, I guess, but I-I-I-I'll have to make do without you and...well...we'll see."

"I can work the rest of this week!" I said.

"Well, it's not a matter of what you want. It's a matter of what I want."

"Oh. I didn't mean for this to happen at all...it really did just come up."

"Okay. Okay," he sighed. "Well, goodbye."

"Should I come in tomorrow, Jooks?" I asked.

JÖYCE

"I'll give you a call when I want you to come in."

"Oh, okay..." I stayed confident. "Bye, it was nice meeting you, Cora."

I left the building, thinking I'd better not spend money in case I was fired. Jooks didn't like to schedule us until the night before.

The G is the slowest, smallest train in all five boroughs and the only one that doesn't go into Manhattan. I lived on the Myrtle-Willoughby stop, where it used to be red-lined. The Metropolitan platform, my transfer home, represented hunger, exhaustion, and creativity. You surrendered to not knowing when the train would arrive or went insane in the attempt. It gave the busker more time to cultivate an audience, and the most recognized busker on the Brooklyn-bound side was Joe Crow.

Joe Crow sang atonal covers of American classics on banjo and ukulele, amidst the occasional "SHUT UP!!" or admiring cluster of disciples. He sometimes told the story that his boss

LOVE IS A VICTORY MARCH

at a Manhattan deli told him to put fake dates on expired dairy products, so he walked out and kept on walking. Unable to participate in a system that required him to be unethical, he started playing music for a living. He was a nightly fixture and the soundtrack to the many joys and sorrows that were settled on the platform between trains. Patrons brought him food and coffee. Joe Crow demonstrated resistance to capitalism and the corruption that had grown synonymous with it. He may have been the one hopeful sight on a given day.

I felt like a sellout in my hipster clothes as he set up for the evening show, but I justified that I was doing it for my parents.

Much later on, Joe Crow got woken up in bed by the police for a five-year-old open container violation when his roommate became involved with Occupy Wall Street. He recorded original songs like "My Arrest," "Collecting Interest Income is Criminal," and a cover of "Tomorrow," from the musical *Annie*.

I waited on the platform, half

worried and half hoping I'd get fired. Joe Crow wasn't out yet. On the tracks, two rats fused in a vicious yin-yang over a bread crust. The beams quivered. The headlights pulsed. A stale breath heaved deep within the tunnel. One creature claimed the morsel, and they fled to separate nooks as the train came crashing down the rails.

That weekend, I boarded the Amtrak to Cumberland. Love troubles played their diabolical fugue on my tattered neurons. I texted Japetto, "HEADING OFF FOR THE WEEKEND TO VISIT MY GRANDMOTHER. SO I GUESS I WON'T BE FREE TO HANG OUT."

We'd met at The Four Faced Liar one last time. I'd expected Japetto to come alone. He brought Louis, who starred with me in *The Crucible* during college. Japetto told me his girlfriend had "flown away," but Louis disapproved.

We walked to the studio Japetto rented from his roommate's dignitary parents for $400, and Louis made hostile mention of my religion. I stared at a probable shit stain on the Indian bedspread. They improvised a tango to the record player.

"You should tango with your girlfriend, Japetto," preached Louis, then grabbed an antique rifle hanging behind the couch and pulled the trigger.

Japetto fell face-first into the couch cushion with a leathery slap.

"You didn't check for bullets!"

He erupted into laughter. The gun was real.

Louis demanded we play *Jurassic Park* on the VCR and then fell asleep.

"I can't remember, did I try to kiss you?" coaxed Japetto, over the sound of dinosaurs disemboweling an unsuspecting park-goer.

"Do you want to go get ice cream?" he whispered.

"I can't have processed sugar."

We retreated to sleep—I on the bed, he on the floor—in an ether of velociraptor screams and Japetto's final evening cigarette.

I awoke to Japetto murmuring. Not only could his girlfriend fly, she had a phone. Louis was gone, having served his purpose. I sat on the floor and put on my shoes. "Would you like me to climb under the covers with you?" I asked.

He elicited an agonized whine.

"Or are you waiting for me to pull you into a broom closet," I snipped.

He'd told me the girl had to make the first move because he'd been raped in a broom closet at church. I stalked out like a boss. I let the door slam like a boss. I deposited my rent like a boss. I refused to be tricked. Now that I'd seen how Jooks didn't put up with anyone's shit, I didn't have to either.

I had an hour transfer at Union Station and paced the shopping center. Money in my pocket was a foreign anxiety I could only calm by losing it again. I bought a notebook for twenty-four dollars with a leather wrapper fastened by a leather string. If the play about me and Japetto was going to be a success, I needed accoutrements that were so expensive they permitted no fallback plan. I bought twelve-dollar face water that the sales girl said was pure because it was French. I didn't know what face water was, but it seemed like a good idea, and more importantly, I deserved it. Nobody said I deserved to have money, but everyone said I deserved to spend money. And I believed them. I bought a hostess present for my cousin at a fancy stationary store. My parents were pretty much homeless, but no one could stop me from having class.

My parents had me after eight miscarriages, like Beethoven's Ninth. They credit a whole-food prenatal diet. My dad promised he'd live to be a hundred. His father had died when he was ten, and he was the eldest of four brothers. My cousin took us to Chick-fil-A. I ordered the Southern Chicken Sandwich. I recalled that Chick-fil-A wouldn't hire gay people, but felt it ungrateful to mention that over our meal. I found the news enturbulating and couldn't remember if Proposition Eight was for or against gay marriage. To me, more weddings meant more cake.

My father's whiskers were white and

bristled. His clothing hung on him. My mother made grandiose proclamations of paying for the meal, and my cousin repeated that it was fine.

My tranquility bordered on cruelty. I'd been the sole spectator to my parents' unraveling. A fellow witness was a relief.

I took adult pride in my sophisticated order—fried chicken on a bun with pickles. I talked about my new job with Jooks and his sexual assault summons.

"That's wonderful!" said my mother.

"I guess so."

"Do you think you'll move up?" asked my cousin.

"To what? I get him coffee and meals. He's a jerk and he's crazy, so I don't know how long I'll stay. It pays enough to support myself while I do theater and write."

"How much does it pay?" asked my cousin.

"Fifteen an hour."

"That's decent."

"Woowwwwww," said my mom.

"I have to pay student loans and rent and such."

LOVE IS A VICTORY MARCH

"How much is rent?" my mother asked.

"$500."

"That's too much!"

"It's 2008. Rent has gone up."

"Well, do you think you could find something cheaper?"

"You're telling me to get up and move? I just got a new job, mom. I just graduated."

"Just think about it!" She put on the meek smile and squeaky voice that made my reaction seem abusive.

That night, my cousin Annette and I sat at her dining room table. "Your daddy has changed," she told me.

"He's had an incredible shock."

"But don't you notice how he seems to have trouble talking and remembering words?"

I dimly sensed her navigating, rather than reasoning, with whatever ideas I had about my father's decline that might have been different from hers.

"It's been a year of repeated losses," I said.

JÖYCE

"Your daddy...he's not the same, sweetheart."

Annette's dad is my dad's fraternal twin, but she was a young adult when I was in pre-school.

"It could be so many things," I said, "I think he carried that debt for so many years, to watch it take his family down like this, the guilt made him retreat into himself."

"Sweetheart, when your parents arrived, your daddy ate like I've never seen anyone eat, and your mom seems like this terrified woman who doesn't know where her next meal is coming from."

"They got some money from selling the house," I said weakly. "I don't know why they wouldn't be eating...I've been telling my mom over and over to apply for government help and to get a doctor for my dad." I shrugged. There was little else I could do.

During her twenties, Annette nursed her mother through cancer and cared for my grief-stricken uncle while getting married and starting a household. She tried not to be judgmental about it. "However you choose to deal with the situation is fine."

"I want to know what you want me to do."

"Well, my vote would be to go home and take care of them."

"It's just that growing up, I was blamed for maladaptive behavior that should have been a clue to family distress. I didn't have a happy childhood. I spent years planning my escape. And now that everybody else has figured it out, that my parents are a wreck, I'm responsible for going home to take care of them? I could never live with my mother and be effective enough to help them. She's not like other mothers. Her identical twin sister avoids her!"

"Sweetheart, it's whatever you want."

"Whether they meant to, my parents raised me to be a type-A achiever with sociopathic tendencies. If I moved home to live with them, I'd be undermining everything they've sacrificed."

I saw her mouth gape open a little.

JÖYCE

The next day, I sat and talked with my grandmother. The whole family ate at Ponderosa. I loved Ponderosa's all-you-can-eat buffet for $8.99. New York delis cost $8.99 per pound.

That night, the Amtrak countryside rolled over me. I pictured my mother weaving down the highway with my father struggling to wait for the next bathroom.

I hoped I hadn't lost my job with Jooks and the familiar dysfunction it provided. I wasn't meant for jargon like "proactive," "moving forward," and "please dress appropriately for an office setting."

Jooks was a fading tyrant, but I was worried corporate America did everything Jooks did, only streamlined.

CHAPTER 9:
PANTS MACABRE

It's hard to pinpoint when Jooks and I began to wear on each other. But I was convinced that I'd gotten hired by Jooks on the fumes of love alone.

Now, I was rictus grins, stunned silences, and secret tears. The disaster with Japetto made me fall ill. The old assurance of being fundamentally cast out both comforted and starved me like a parasite.

Some girl had written on Japetto's Facebook wall that she was sorry he'd been sick all week. Our twin infirmity was comfort that I hadn't fabricated our bond.

"My boss is psychotic. But he can't be suppressive," I told a Scientology staff member, "because he's an artist." We were standing on the curb in front of the New York Org by Times Square and all the Broadway theaters. I felt a sense of loss for our times on staff together, rushing to the subway stations with carts and folding tables to sell copies of *Dianetics* on muggy summer weekdays, the adrenaline of saving mankind mingling with the humiliation of potentially being spotted by my fellow classmates.

"An artist can be suppressive," said Adam. "They can become a suppressive if they get low-toned enough."

"Right," I said. "But I don't have other job opportunities, right now. My parents just lost their house, and I need to save a little more money."

"Okay. Well, get that handled, and then come back on staff," he said with welcoming encouragement. I knew that they all believed in me and wanted me to succeed.

"I want to be an artist. I don't know if I should be on staff."

"Then, route out properly and come back on course."

"Okay."

"That was a cool video by the way."

"Oh. You saw it?" I had made a YouTube Video skit in comedic mockery of self-pity and spite following romantic rejection, as a secret way of purging my grief over Japetto's betrayal.

"Yeah. I liked it. Was it about anyone in particular?"

"Oh." I thought for a second. "No." I wasn't sure if this was a lie. I had never lied to anyone in the Church, but because the video was a work of art that I intended as fiction, I did not include the identities of real people. It was therefore not about anyone in particular. It was my creation.

"I see," said Adam. I sensed he knew. He was pretty high on the Bridge to Total Freedom, so I would have to watch out for his psychic abilities.

"Wh-wh-wh-wh-what was your name again? I'm sorry. I forget because of the stroke."

"Oh, I'm not offended."

I strained to be the same shimmering girl Jooks had hired and prepared his breakfast. He'd start padding around near dawn with a glass of Eli's fresh-squeezed orange juice and the New York Times. On arrival, I fixed his bowl of Rice Krispies with one-and-a-half Splenda packets, one glass of Organic

JÖYCE

Valley one-percent milk, with another glass of orange juice and one banana sliced into thin medallions on the side. Sometimes I'd microwave the glass of milk in three-second increments because the cold hurt his teeth.

"Can you believe another girl is suing me!" he chuckled, skimming the latest summons. "So w-w-what have you been up to?"

"I made an internet video."

"You wanna see me on the internet?"

"Sure!"

"Patti Smith sang my song on a t-t-television show for children. My twins are in the audience!"

"That is so cool!"

"I was on a tour bus with her for a week. She smelled terrible. Terrible."

It was then I learned that smelling terrible couldn't stop me from being famous.

"You smell," he said. He went to his supply closet and pulled out a stick of Dry Idea roll-on deodorant. "This is for you. You'll buy the next one." It was the best antiperspirant I'd ever used, and after stealing the next couple from his supply closet, I did buy my own. If I died of armpit cancer for not using the aluminum-free deodorant my parents had always advised, I'd be the freshest smelling corpse.

The next day on my way to work, I bought a shirt at American Apparel in case mine stank. Jooks yelled at me for being late, which conditioned me to be later the next day. Juggling time and hygiene right out of college was hard.

"It's good I never hire assistants I'm attracted to, I'd never get any work done—no offense, honey."

"Oh, none taken." I laughed in his face.

"Remind me to have you clip my nose hairs."

"What?"

"The maid does it, but she's not here. You'll r-r-remind me?"

"Okay."

I snuck past his chair, the day nearly done.

"Go and get the nose clippers," he bid me. "It's the Tweezerman on my dresser!"

I marched slowly there, thinking that I would give the universe time to intervene, and walked even slower back.

"C'mahhhhhhn!!!!" he rasped.

I arrived with the clippers flaccid and a pensive frown.

"Well?" He flickered his eyes at me.

"Shouldn't your hairdresser do this?"

"Wh-wh-why? You can do it!" he encouraged.

I sighed.

"Dooo iiiit..." he growled. "Just do it!"

Maintaining two feet of latitudinal clearance, I probed the clippers into one nostril and made a snip. A scale of mucus fluttered down. I flinched.

"What?!"

"I don't want to hurt you..."

"Keep going."

I clipped a few hairs—some real, some imagined.

"How's it look?"

"Fine."

"Good. Now do the other."

PANTS MACABRE

I circled behind the chair.

"Where the hell do you think you're going?"

"To your other nostril."

"Why?"

"So I'm closer to it."

"Can't you reach it from that side?"

"I'd prefer to be closer to it."

"You're crazy," he said. I reached the clipper into the right nostril, feeling sick. I couldn't seem to hold still.

Snip.

"Ow!"

"Sorry!"

"Goddamnit!"

"I didn't mean to!"

"Goddamnit!"

"Are you OK? Is it bleeding? You're not bleeding. I don't see a cut. Thank God. Do you want me to try again?"

"No."

"Oh, okay. I guess I'll just go and put these back then."

"G-Goddamnit."

In a moment of reckless benevolence over Italian take-out, I asked, "Jooks, how was your day today?"

"Oh, shut up. You don't care about my day."

"I do, or I wouldn't ask!"

"You'll never believe it. We brought my underwear to the doctor. I have the strangest discharge!"

"Well, I'm sure it's—"

"Here, lemme show you." Jooks popped up and disappeared chuckling around the corner. "Boy, it's the darnedest. Dr. Gordon couldn't make heads or tails."

He re-emerged, untying a plastic grocery bag and heading toward me. "You'll be amazed!"

Sometimes the body reacts before the mind. I began tingling all over. On sheer adrenaline, I stood and shouted, "NO!"

His jaw dropped. He stopped in his tracks, a hand upon his chest.

"What?"

"It's just that...I'm not a doctor," I sputtered. Now I would stand stalwart beside the institution of Western medicine.

PANTS MACABRE

"Not a doctor? What the fuckareya talkin' about?"

"I think that's something a doctor should look at...I wouldn't be qualified to help."

"Fuck you!" he bellowed, consumed with insult.

"Jooks! Why would you say that to me? I haven't done anything wrong!"

"Fuck you!" he cried, returning his sullied knickers from whence they came. "Fuck you!" He stabbed his finger in the air at me. "'Not a doctor,' horseshit!"

"I'm not..."

"I don't feel like talking to you!"

The leather cushion hissed as he sank.

I froze while Jooks glowered at the television. After ten minutes, he chortled at Boston Legal. "Heh heh heh, Shatner." He looked at me, extorting the new mood.

I widened the corners of my mouth in what some consider a smile. Jooks' underthings were safe in their bag.

My job was starting to alarm me.

JOYCE

My face lost feeling from suppressed emotion. I winced at the sound of Jook's voice.

At breakfast, he probed his tongue into his molars.

"There's something spongy growing in there..."

I spun away to microwave his milk. "Should I call the doctor?"

"Go in the den and tell me if I have any email."

I was glad to be out of his sight.

"Well?" He followed me in.

"Jooks—I just sat down."

"Don't I have any email?!"

"Let me check," I said, refusing to make a mistake and excuse his yelling. "You have eTickets for '*Mamma Mia!*'"

"Lemme see!" He leaned on the desk with his arms on either side of me like in a sexual harassment training video. I angled my body forward. He returned to his breakfast.

There was a voicemail on my phone from Japetto, with just the phrase, "Let's weave some webs. Oh, the tangled webs we weave," which I googled.

PANTS MACABRE

It was from a poem by Sir Walter Scott.

"What are you d-d-d-doing?!" he demanded a moment later.

"Checking my email."

"Did you print the tickets?!"

"You didn't tell me to. So, no."

"WHY NOT!"

"BECAUSE I'M NOT A MIND READER, JOOKS!"

"Oh, you're not, are you?" He looked at me long and hard, plotting how to get rid of me.

CHAPTER 10

GREAT ARTISTS STEAL

Even with a life of ease, minutes from the best doctors, staving off decline was an occupation. With characteristic industry, Jooks packed in doctor visits as he'd once done conference calls and power lunches at The Four Seasons. When the waiting period was a month, he'd demand that Friday. As one appointment ended, I scheduled the next, with Jooks barking telephone-assertiveness coaching on the cab ride home.

"Get Dr. Gordon on the phone. Tell them I need to speak to him immediately."

"Hi, I'm Jooks' assistant, and I was calling because he needs to speak with Dr. Gordon."

"IMMEDIATELY!" Jooks bellowed.

"I-immediately," I added.

"Dr. Gordon is in an appointment. I can take a message," said the receptionist.

"Jooks, she says she's in an appointment, and she can take a message."

GREAT ARTISTS STEAL

"Tell his secretary I'm an Academy Award winner, a Grammy Award winner, and I need to see the doctor today!"

"He says to say he's 'an Academy Award winner...'"

"We know Jooks well here at the office, but the doctor can't take more walk-ins today."

"Jooks, they're aware of your importance, but he's with another patient."

"UGH, just give me the phone." He snatched it from me.

"H-h-hi...Good...How are you...Listen. I need to see the doctor today. I still have the spongy thing in my mouth, and it's not going a-a-a-away."

He redirected the cab to go to the office anyway.

The waiting room was filled with elderly people. Jooks went straight to the receptionist, who rolled her eyes at a nearby colleague. He leaned in with his best stance.

"H-h-hi, I'm here to see Dr. Gordon!" He never allowed uncertainty in his negotiations.

"Jooks, take a seat. We'll call you when it's your turn."

"I n-n-need to see him now."

"I understand. There are people here who made appointments. We'll get you in."

Pretty soon Jooks was seen by the doctor and returned with a prescription.

"I can't believe you!" Jooks muttered as Dr. Gordon saw him out.

"See you next time, Jooks. Make sure he gets this prescription," he said. Dr. Gordon was a slender man with nicely trimmed chalk-white beard and hair. His careful demeanor abstained from effusive cheer, and he tended to observe Jooks from a place of concern rather than ornamental social exchange. Jooks had about ten doctors, but Dr. Gordon was his general physician.

"You'll never believe it," he whispered as I hailed a cab. "The doctor says I have th-th-thrush."

"What's thrush?"

"N-n-never mind. That jackass says I need a female suppository for my throat."

"A what?"

"A suppository! It's what a woman uses! To put inside her vagina!"

"Oh, dear Christ," I choked.

"Don't tell a soul." He stifled laughter. "Where's lunch?"

I handed him soup and napkins from Dean & DeLuca. Beef stock sloshed down his knuckles when the cab turned. I dabbed the seat while he paid the driver.

"Don't go to Semmelweis. I don't want those girls gossiping about me! Get it at the Duane Reade." He handed me his prescription.

"It's not for me, it's for my boss," I assured the pharmacist. "He's like seventy. It's not sexual—dear god, no. It's just some mouth infection old people get. He's supposed to take them in his mouth. And see! The name on the prescription? It's a man's name. So it couldn't possibly be for me."

She lowered her eyes to the keyboard and said the prescription would be ready in fifteen minutes.

JÖYCE

I brought Jooks one dose on a bread and butter plate.

"Hmm, tastes minty..." I fled to the kitchen, away from the sounds of his contented suckling. Alina was doing the dishes.

"You know what that means, don't you? He's been eating some girl out."

"Sweet Jesus, no," I gasped.

Jooks burst through the double doors and shoved a warm canister of urine into my hand.

"Here, take it!"

He had seen three different doctors regarding a posterior discomfort and was sent to the hospital for tests.

"Jooks, I'm going to need to wash my hands, and then I'm going to need a rubber glove if you expect me to hold your piss jar." I set the container politely onto an emergency firehose cabinet.

"Shut up, you! What if I have ass cancer!?"

"I don't want that to be the case, Jooks."

GREAT ARTISTS STEAL

He sent me to Zabar's for chicken salad, egg salad, creamed herring, crackers, and relish. Jooks was doing speech therapy for an hour with Phoebe, a woman in her early thirties, slender, with carefully trimmed bangs and hair that grew several inches past her shoulders, so I walked one way and used some of the fare I'd saved him to buy myself a miniature meatloaf.

"Guess what!" he declared.

I stepped in hoping he wouldn't notice the plump loaf sticking out of the grocery bag.

"Yes, Jooks?"

"Phoebe has a date tonight!"

A German otorhinolaryngologist had recently declined his overtures. He'd made three out-of-pocket appointments with her in two weeks, courting her with mix CDs of his jingles and songs.

"Where do you live?" he'd interrupt in the middle of a glottal exercise.

"I just bought a house in Staten Island."

"You bought a house?"

JÖYCE

"Yes! It has seven marble fireplaces!"

"I-i-it's your husband's house."

"No. It's my house."

"What? H-h-how is that possible?"

"Because I bought it."

"Nah."

"Yes."

"Aren't you worried your husband will be intimidated and leave you for another woman who stays home to take care of him?"

"No."

"Don't you want to date a man who has his own house?"

"My husband has a house in Germany. We go there when we visit. So, what were you hoping to accomplish from these appointments?"

"You know, I-I usually don't go for women in their thirties."

He made me wait outside when he realized I wasn't playing wing woman and dismissed her as a "jerk" and a "terrible doctor" on the cab ride home from his final appointment.

Phoebe was his speech therapist.

She often dressed in demure fitness attire. Like me, her defense was to stifle all emotion and sexuality around Jooks.

"I don't get this guy Phoebe's seeing! It's their third date, and they didn't even fuck!"

"I see," I replied from the kitchen, swaddling the stolen meatloaf in my purse.

"What's the point if you're not gonna fuck?!"

"Well, we're still getting to know each other," she said.

"Where did you meet him?"

"Online."

"Online? Ahahahah! And you haven't fucked? Why else would you meet anybody online?"

"Let's talk about your speech exercises, Jooks."

"Yes," I chimed, carrying his dinner tray.

"I gotta meet more girls. Ever since my s-stroke. This stutter. If I don't get rid of it, they won't talk to me! I've gotta practice my speech every day for fifteen minutes! You..." He stopped and shook his head.

"Why are you mad at me?" I asked.

"I'm not mad at you, I'm mad because I can't t-t-think of the word!"

"It's okay Jooks, just finish your thought," coaxed Phoebe.

"Go get my calendar," he demanded. "Write down every day, from 9:15 a.m. to 9:30 a.m., 'Speech Practice,' and I'm gonna read to you out loud. A n-newspaper, a p-poem. For fifteen minutes. And you CANNOT be late."

"Okay," I smiled sheepishly.

"Please, honey, please. Don't. Be. Late." He wrung his hands.

"Okay." In all my life, nothing had fixed my lateness except acting school, and that had been taken from me. I could not trust my own psyche, but I gave him the honest loser's promise.

CHAPTER 11

OFF BRANDO

I was addicted to pathological charisma before I got to acting school, but Japetto had cured me of that. I decided to make the fictional version of me in *The Unloveables* become a prostitute. She'd say, "When my love was free, I only got cheated. So I decided to start charging."

In October, I started rehearsal for *Canaries*. I bought a refurbished black Macbook. I could stalk Japetto online and work my way to YouTube stardom in the privacy of my room. Once I had some savings, I would leave my job.

After a disorienting four weeks with Jooks, the theater welcomed me again.

Late one night, I took to the bed in a posture of torment before my handwritten manuscript for *The Unloveables*. Fictional me was living under the stairs in fictional Japetto's apartment building to see if he'd notice.

JÖYCE

Near 1:00 a.m., my phone rang. Fulfillment of all fulfillments, it was Japetto's number. On the third ring, I answered.

"Hello?" said a female voice, and I jolted with horror that it might be Japetto's girlfriend.

"Uh...hey..."

"It's Thalia!"

We'd once bonded in the student lounge over astrological signs. She was from Florida and had dated our first-year speech teacher.

Japetto had confided during our summer flirtation that Thalia's posts on my Facebook wall indicated that she'd become obsessed with me because of her obsession with him. I avoided her after that. Three years later, as my roommate, Thalia would claim he'd written her love letters from Prague, professing an urge to stab somebody.

"Thalia!" I imagined them together in bed.

"Japetto is in the bathroom, and I stole his phone. We're at The Four Faced Liar! Oh, hi Japetto—look who

I called on your phone! Japetto and I were talking about how awesome you are!"

"That's so funny, we were just there," I said. This call was her dominance tactic.

"It's so weird, I walked in and Japetto was sitting at the bar."

"That's funny." I faked a chuckle. "Wait, but I thought you didn't drink."

"You don't either, do you? Talk to her!" Thalia's voice receded as she shoved the phone into his hands.

"Hi."

"Hi," I smirked.

"How are you?"

"Good. How're you?"

"Can I...call you later?"

"Okay. Bye."

"We should all hang out!" Thalia's voice gaily returned.

"Yes. Definitely. Well, I'd better go."

"Okay, talk to you later! Byeee!"

I laughed aloud. A glowing relief came over me. Thalia was welcome to him.

JÖYCE

An hour later, he called back, frantic.

"She came into my bar! I had no idea! I swear!"

"That is so strange..."

"I did something terrible." His breath pumped with every footstep.

"What did you do?"

"We watched YouTube videos at her apartment. She lives right across the STREET from the bar. It's so ODD. She tried to kiss me."

"Why did you go to her apartment if she's obsessed with you?"

"I don't know."

"Did you kiss her, too?"

"No. I sort of...went...limp," he snorted with laughter, "and told her...I was incapable of intimacy."

I laughed. I had never been so amused by someone's misfortune before, but nothing felt wrong with Japetto.

"I'm an idol," he said.

"You are an idol," I agreed.

"What?"

"You just said, 'I'm an idol,' didn't you?"

"No, Mi Idolo. That's the name of the

Taco Truck. It just left."

"You should come over."

"Oh, I'd better not, it's so late. I'm sorry, honeybear."

I froze. He called girls on Facebook "honeybear." It was then that I knew he was trash.

"Well, goodnight."

"Goodnight."

"See you later. In the week."

"Yes, yes, we'll be seeing you."

"Put that down! We gotta watch the game." Jooks slapped my script away without removing his eyes from the screen.

I was in a ten-minute play called *Canaries* about three coal miners who exchange monosyllables of working-class stoicism and then die. I played Coal Miner Number Three.

"Jooks, why is it a problem if I memorize while you watch TV?"

"If you're not watching with me, then what am I payin' ya to do?!"

I faced screenward but ran lines in my head.

(127)

JÖYCE

"Ohhhhhhhh!!!!" Jooks raised his fists at a touchdown, then looked at me. I pursed my lips in congratulations.

To Jooks, fifteen dollars an hour meant that he could rent one hour of my entire human potential for fifteen dollars. To me, it meant Jooks would receive no more than fifteen dollars' worth of my potential for no more than an hour. We'd never specified the terms.

I had a lot to learn from how he got his start in advertising. Jooks was hired as a jingle writer in the 1960s, a struggling musician with a wife, a dog, and a record that hadn't taken off.

"The agency was a bunch of losers," he said, "but then so was I. I went from making fifty dollars a week to $500 a week. I was the only person in their music department. So my wife went to the hardware store and got a brass plate that read, "Jooks, Music Director," for my office door. Then I sent about twenty letters to the most important advertising people in town, saying, 'I'd like to introduce myself, I'm the music director of such and such agency, would you like to have lunch?'"

"Did any of them say yes?"

"Sure! They all said yes! What's the big fuckin' deal asking somebody to lunch? God, I'm afraid for you. I managed to become acquainted with most of the big advertising men in New York. Meanwhile, I spent all day in my office using the agency's equipment to create music for my portfolio without doing the work that I was paid for! A few months later, the art director checked in. I had no assignments done. Not one! So he fired me, but by that time, I had the connections to get hired at a better agency."

"Weren't you worried the agency that fired you was going to ruin your reputation?"

"Nah, it was so small. Buncha losers. They had no idea."

Whenever I criticized myself for losing my work ethic or taking Jooks for granted, I remembered his inspiring tale of pulling himself up by the bootstraps.

I had to leave and risk my parents for a better job.

CHAPTER 12:
CRÈME FRAÎCHE PRINCE

The master bathroom was a forgotten shrine of half-used shampoo.

Jook's first wife was the mother of his eldest twins. The second was a Playboy cover girl and Will's mom. The last had been his massage therapist, who he caught funneling money from their joint bank account to her mom's mortgage and had escorted out by the police. Each toiletry told a story. There was Paul Mitchell Platinum Blonde, Kérastase for curls, Oribe Shampoo for Beautiful Color.

One afternoon, he demanded I unclog the jacuzzi tub of grey washwater from his Epsom Salts bath. I wrapped my arm in a trash bag and made fruitless attempts until he called maintenance.

Then, he sent me to a shop near Central Park, called Petrossian.

"Get three small tins of their cheapest caviar, with two crème fraîche and blini."

CRÈME FRAÎCHE PRINCE

Like everywhere Jooks sent me, Petrossian was the nicest place I had ever been. A counter on the right sold caviar and smoked fish, and a counter on the left sold coffee. You could enjoy the seating area that extended beyond whether you spent six dollars or $600.

I sidled up to the fish counter.

"Hello. I'd like to buy some caviar."

"Okay...what kind of caviar?" said the bearded man. His tattooed disdain and my reluctance with authority betrayed us to one another.

"Three...2.7 ounce tins...of American... with crème...fraîche? And three...blini?" Shaking visibly, I sauntered to the coffee bar for a café au lait and financier.

I figured the tip was fifteen percent, or about eighty dollars, just like a restaurant check.

"Have you ever had caviar?" Jooks asked.

"No, I haven't."

"Set one up on a plate. We're gonna have some for lunch."

JŌYCE

"Oh my gosh, Jooks—you don't have to share that with me! It's so expensive!"

"I want you to try it."

"Okay—I'll set it up on a plate for us to eat."

It was good, but I couldn't dwell on the fine points of caviar when I could only afford canned sardines and occasionally salmon.

Around six, Jooks said, "Listen, go ahead and take an hour to get coffee."

My face fell. *So this is why he fed me caviar,* I thought. *He's going to start sending me away to save money.*

"I'm still going to pay you!" He rolled his eyes. "I have an appointment at seven!"

"Sure, Jooks. Whatever you want." I slumped with relief and flashed a caviar-fed smile.

"I'll call you when I want you back."

I sat at the Hot'n'Crusty and ordered a black coffee. I'd read people of character prefer black coffee. Forty minutes later, he called. I headed back, feeling conned because he'd said a whole hour.

"Bring me a Diet Coke and y-y-y-y-you can go home."

"How was your appointment?"

"Great!"

"What was it?"

"That's not your business!"

"Jooks—is there something I did wrong to annoy you, or..."

"No.   Wh-wh-wh-wh-what's   the matter?"

"Are you trying to fire me?"

"Not at all. I had a visitor."

"Like a lawyer?"

"I saw a girl," Jooks said.

"You were interviewing another assistant?" my voice thinned.

"I WAS SEEING A HOOKER, OKAY? THERE, N-N-N-N-NOW YA KNOW! Now get out. I'll see ya tomorrow."

He started having a visitor every week. When the doorman called, I stood in the service stairwell with the garbage.

"I don't want her to think I'm seeing another girl or she'll get jealous!" he cautioned.

I'd hear someone step out of the

elevator and depart about five minutes later.

Sometimes, he'd reserve dinner for two and Broadway tickets. When Masha came, he bought caviar.

"God, she was good," he said, shirtless. I tried not to breathe the humid air. "She's in school. Her boyfriend owns some delis. That poor guy has no idea she's a hooker. What an idiot," he laughed.

"Isn't she a call girl?"

"Yeah, a hooker!"

"I thought a call girl is someone you call to come to your place, and a hooker stands by the road."

"Same thing. Her relationship will never work. Masha wants, you know, things."

"What things?"

"Boots, scarves, handbags. Louis Vuitton. Those things. She's the one I love but says it's just business between us." He waited for me to reassure him, but I never did. Because giving the impression that I believed his love was mutual would have been a lie. I didn't want to invalidate his beingness, so I listened, though I couldn't imagine anyone loving him. I also sometimes worried whether sympathetic tones of acknowledgment counted as abetting prostitution.

CHAPTER 13

THE DEVIL WEARS NEW BALANCE

For the first time in weeks, I saw Vel.

"He sends me away so he can see call girls," I told her.

She nodded queasily.

Vel was training me to mix the pharmaceutical applesauce.

"How's school?" I asked.

"It's good. Busy."

"I didn't know he had a third assistant: Cora."

"Yeah, she's nice."

"She is. Jooks is...really hard to deal with sometimes."

She nodded.

"So, what's your major again?" I asked.

"Nursing and home care."

"Ohhh, so this is right in line with what you want to do."

"Yeah, it's nice."

"Wow. Did you just find this job on Craigslist like me?"

"I got it through a staffing agency,

actually."

"Oh, huh. I kind of feel like he's about to fire me half the time."

"Don't worry, you're doing fine. He's just like that."

"Okay. Well, as long as you have school and Cora has her other job, I guess he'll need me to fill in."

Before I left, I cleaned up his dinner. I had plated each course on appropriate china from his cabinets and spread bathroom towels on his lap and over the ottoman underneath his tray and on the white carpet beneath his feet. I washed the dishes though he insisted it wasn't necessary.

I brought him his evening medication in the applesauce, watching him balance the spoon handle in the crook of his open thumb as his lips grasped for food.

"You do my pills better than Vel does," he said as if she'd been cheating him.

"All I did was make a paste with the crushed pills and a drop of water. Then I blend it with the sauce so the bitterness would be evenly distributed."

JÖYCE

One day the following week, as the leaves just began to fall, Jooks and I left his psychiatrist's office. The rain had stopped, but I paraded alongside, umbrella thrust over his head.

"Listen, I want to fire the other two girls," he said.

"What? Why?"

"Meh...." He leveled his hand from side to side for his so-so assessment. "Vel is in school and can only work two days. Cora has another job. I don't like it."

"But Jooks, you agreed that they could work for you with those schedules. That's why you had Vel hire me, remember?"

"I know. I've ch-changed my mind."

"I mean, why not let us each have a regular schedule?"

"Honey, nobody gets their own schedule. It's my schedule we're on. I want you to stay, but I want them to go. I want to hire new girls."

"Well, that's not my place." I conveyed guilt and sadness.

One way to gain Jooks' sympathy

was to let weak and illogical feminine sensibilities take offense. I felt like in hustling not to get fired, I had upset the labor standards. I wouldn't know whether to pity or congratulate them, but I wasn't going to fire anyone. In my worried silence, Jooks let the topic evaporate until one Friday, at the start of my evening shift, Jooks sat me down.

"Listen," he began, "I want you to fire Vel."

I froze.

"Jooks, I'm not doing that."

"Do it. Or I'll fire you, then I'll fire her."

"Jooks, you can't." I softened my eyes helplessly—the better to appeal to his savior complex.

"Listen, honey, I already fired Cora this afternoon."

I made a small gasp.

"Here," he handed me his ringing cellphone.

"Jesus fucking Christ," I muttered.

"Hello?" Vel answered.

"Vel?" I said.

"Hey," she replied.

"Um—I'm sitting here with Jooks. He—he just told me that I had to call you and tell you that he wants to let you go."

"Don't say that!" he yelled, then whispered, "Tell her that she's fired!"

"Sorry. Jooks is now talking to me at the same time I'm trying to talk to you—"

"Wow," she said, "I don't know what to say."

"I—I don't either—he uh—he said he'd fire me if I didn't call you, and that he'd fire all of us regardless...?"

"Uh huh." Her voice was toneless.

"Ask her where I should send the check!! And how much!"

"He wants to know where to send your check. And how much."

"It's either four hundred, or five hundred if he wants to pay for the shift I would have worked tomorrow," she said.

"I-I'm really sorry, Vel,"

"Don't talk to her anymore! Say goodbye!" Jooks hissed.

"I'll, umm, I'll Facebook you...Jooks keeps telling me to hang up."

"Don't tell her that!!"

"Yeah...we'll talk," she said.

"Bye."

"Bye, Jöyce."

She hung up.

"Jooks—you can't tell me to fire someone and prevent me from speaking nicely to them."

"Whatever."

"Can we please write out her check now? I'll put it in the mail."

"I guess," Jooks muttered.

"So. Do you want to do the $500 and pay her for the shift she would have worked tomorrow?"

"Okay," he said after a few seconds.

"Who's covering all the empty shifts?" I asked. His average day went from 5:00 a.m. until midnight. I wasn't available for all those hours of consciousness.

"We're gonna put ads on....David?... No. What's that thing I hired you from?"

"Craigslist."

"Yes! We need to find another girl."

CHAPTER 14:
JUMP FOR MY LOVE

I texted Japetto, "YOU LED ME ON," as a wounded animal would text.

There was something refreshing in making someone responsible for all my feelings.

To my surprise, he immediately texted back. "I know. I didn't mean to."

A rounded-out adult psyche might have responded with exploratory discussions yielding understanding, bittersweet departure, and the possibility of future artistic collaboration. Not mine, though. Mine was a relentless spewing of bile. The deranged verses of a mind unhinged. A divine feat of digital terror. Unsolicited text messages born of darkness.

"LIFE IN CAPSLOCK BITCH."

I would even respond to criticisms he hadn't actually made.

"OH SORRY ABOUT THE SPELLING MISTAKES I GUES THAT MEANS HOW LITTLE I GIVE A HSHIT."

For days, I wept. I had wept this way

after we first met, already knowing how it would end.

Often, I would scream at Mother growing up that *Child Dianetics* says you're supposed to let the child release all of their emotions in order to expel negative charge, so I knew the more I cried, the healthier I was becoming. Wracked with ancient grief. Keening on the planet. The shedding of a skin. My tear ducts raw. My cheeks a mineral residue.

I tumbled from bed, through subways, down streets, to Jooks. He yelled, and I numbed. I was thankful for the privacy of his self-oblivion, to turn my head when tears could not be stopped. I'd flee home, resume my figure of collapse beneath the blankets.

My job with Jooks was now no longer temporary but indefinite. I couldn't fake emotional stability long enough to make it through a job interview, much less an email query. I had no will to audition or socialize. Cartoon portals closed around me. Banished to my own dimension, I flickered from view. Without language for the shames and terrors that had eaten away at me, I drank the poison of Japetto into the final delicate bits of my character and reputation and untagged myself from every photo.

Enjoyment was gone. Sending a hate-fueled lyric to Japetto was the only time I knew myself to exist. I created misguided YouTube videos in my room. I ordered expensive take-out at work on Jooks' dime when he offered. I experimented to see if eating whatever I wanted would speed up my metabolism, or make me fat. Such were my dull pleasures.

I could work the next sixteen years for Jooks just like Pearl had done, or until he died. People would say, "There's when she broke."

In acting school, they'd drilled into us: add nothing, deny nothing. Never try to control or package or intellectualize the emotions you experience. Part of our job as actors was to permit emotion without judgment, experience it without anticipation, let it compel you and change organically. You don't manipulate when or how or what the emotion becomes, and you continue your action. On or offstage, I'd never felt an emotional pain that I thought could sink my entire life. I'd experienced the anatomy of human emotion as a frontier and could drift into the void without being engulfed, or keeping anything off limits. Everything was preparation for the next role.

Lying awake, I pictured myself getting up soundlessly and walking down Myrtle Avenue, turning down Tillary Street, the bridge I'd crossed into Manhattan many times on foot when I didn't have train fare. The footpath was suspended high over the water, and the brisk wind stoked the embers of my cheeks. On one side was the fenced-in track, the cleansing roar of the train that let me sing at full volume without hearing myself. For anyone who passed, I could blame the cold for my running nose and streaming eyes. On the other side was the giant railing, the high stretched cables, and a drop to the water below.

There was a deep dull heavy hurt slung down the back of my throat on a hammock in chains. I was an abandoned mine. I thought of what the jump could be: innocent childlike exhilaration. All my failures peeling away as I hurtled through the air, until nothing remained but love and light. And then I'd hit the water.

Except I didn't think of it. I watched myself think of it—it was only an acting exercise.

Even if my parents could handle things on their own, and they couldn't, I would have to be completely sure that I wanted death and knew how to get it. There wasn't money for failed suicide attempts or hospital stays or cries for help. If something went wrong, I might end up stuck in my mother's care alongside my father, just as she'd always wanted me to be, and then hell would truly begin.

I thought of the students who jumped to their death in the library when I was a freshman and singing at their memorial for the bewildered parents in the dim University Hall. Wouldn't they all love it if I died. But how infinitely hateful it would be for everyone if I lived. I knew better reasons to survive—but that one made me chuckle.

I rattled off another little nothing in a text to Japetto: "UR LIKE THAT BITCH HEDDA GABLER. IN THE PLAY HEDDA GABLER."

Whatever the route, I didn't want to be around people. I needed to reconstruct my ways of coping with them. For the time being, everyone who wasn't me could go eff themselves, because I had nothing else to contribute. Japetto and I were soulmates, but perhaps, one day maybe, we could just be soul friends. From here on out, it was me and Jooks—wandering together on the heath.

CHAPTER 15:
SELF IMPROVEMENT MONTAGE

> "Whose woods these are I think I know.
> His house is in the village though;
> He will not see me stopping here
> To watch his woods fill up with snow.
>
> "My little horse must think it queer
> To stop without a farmhouse near
> Between the woods and frozen lake
> The darkest evening of the year.
>
> "He gives his harness bells a shake
> To ask if there is some mistake.
> The only other sound's the sweep
> Of easy wind and downy flake.
>
> "The woods are lovely, dark and deep,
> But I have promises to keep,
> And miles to go before I sleep,
> And miles to go before I sleep."

"That was really good, Jooks."

When I was on time, I got to hear his morning speech exercises.

"Do you know what Robert Frost was talking about in that p-poem?"

"No. What, Jooks?"

"Oh god, you're an idiot."

"What was he talking about, Jooks?"

"He was talking about s-s-s-suicide."

"Oh. But I mean...it could just be

(148)

about taking a trip to the woods. On a cold, dark day."

"Please, just be quiet."

"Alright."

Jooks was hunting for a new assistant on Craigslist. He had me maintain a job listing and refresh his inbox every few hours.

Hundreds replied. We'd click through each submission for his review.

"Too old," [click], "Too fat," [click], "You can only see her head in the photo, can't risk it, she might be fat," [click]. "She's cute...it's a shame she had to be Black."

"Why won't you hire Black people, Jooks?"

"They smell.

"Really? You hired me...and you said I smell..."

Jooks ignored my objections, entirely. "In the C-C-C-Craigslist ad, can we say, 'WHITE ONLY'?"

"No. You can't do that."

[click] "That's a guy! I only want girls!" he screamed at me. "Why does your stupid ad keep getting the wrong fucking people!"

JÖYCE

"Because Craigslist doesn't work that way, Jooks. You can't control who responds to your ad!"

"I'm sure you did something to screw it up."

"I did exactly as you asked, Jooks. I posted the ad. JUST like you said."

"I HAVE NEVER HAD THIS MANY WRONG PEOPLE BEFORE. YOU MUST HAVE MADE A MISTAKE WHEN YOU POSTED IT."

"Here, look. I'll show you EXACTLY what I did. I clicked: 'POST>JOB>GIGS> TALENT>' See? Just like you told me. Then I typed:

> ACADEMY, GRAMMY AND GOLDEN GLOBE AWARD WINNING RECORDING ARTIST SEEKS PERSONAL ASSISTANT FOR HOUSEHOLD ERRANDS AND LIGHT OFFICE DUTIES. TASKS INCLUDE ACCOMPANYING TO APPOINTMENTS, SCHEDULING, LIGHT HOUSEHOLD MANAGEMENT AND PAPERWORK. GREAT PAY, IDEAL CANDIDATE IS A STUDENT OR ASPIRING ACTOR/MODEL. PLEASE SEND PHOTO, RESUME, AND PHONE NUMBER. YOU MUST SEND ALL THREE TO BE CONSIDERED.

SELF IMPROVEMENT MONTAGE

"How's that, Jooks?"

"Why do they need to send a resume?"

"Um. Because. Maybe it's good to look at a resume if you're hiring someone?"

"I guess." [click] "Who's this girl?"

"I don't know, Jooks. I'm seeing her picture for the first time, in this moment, here with you."

"Shut up! What's that thing in 'er ear?"

"She's wearing feather earrings."

Her email signature said she was an indigenous American photographer. Her picture was a self-portrait framed against a stormy sky and Western grasses, from bare shoulders up, dark brown hair peeling in the wind, a thoughtful and open expression on her face. Like me, she was presuming to be seen on creative merit.

"Call her now."

His blocked number went to voicemail as usual, so I left a message.

We interviewed three to five girls most weekdays. Watching Jooks strut his stuff to bright-eyed young artists who'd barely crossed paths with

(151)

corruption was a welcome distraction. I needed to achieve symbiosis.

Like it says to do in *Well Behaved Women Seldom Make History...but Never Die Alone*, I pretended not to be threatened, all the while working feverishly at personal growth so other girls would look like shit compared to me. At no point did I have the agency to think I could disapprove of what he was doing. Sometimes the only option is a solid self-improvement montage.

For me, this meant holding onto my present occupation long enough so my parents wouldn't suffer the effects once I got fired.

Sitting at my desk, I summoned all the Jooks trivia I knew into a small scratchpad.

After ten minutes, I got bored and started editing a YouTube video called "Halloween Cat Friend," but the exercise actually got me into a more Jooks-centric headspace. I started planning outfits for later instead of just wearing men's T-shirts with whatever pants I found on the top of my laundry pile. I

SELF IMPROVEMENT MONTAGE

became so punctual over the course of that week, it was like *Mission Impossible*. I ran from my apartment to the G train, from the G train to the L train, from the L train to the 6 train, and from the 6 train to Jooks' apartment, every time I had to work a shift.

I would watch a train pull out of the station just as I arrived on the platform in despair. Thinking that my entire livelihood came down to whether I arrived on time or fifteen minutes late.

At home, Jooks left packs of spearmint Dentyne Ice at strategic points and chewed them almost continuously, to keep his veneers fresh. The only water he drank was Fiji. Throughout the day, he'd open a bottle, take a few sips, then forget it and open another. At night, there were always five or six lying around to be thrown away.

I once picked up a white ceramic pitcher painted with little red vines. There was a $300 price tag on the bottom. The man had about thirty pairs of Cole Haan leather slip-on shoes in his walk-in closet, twenty or so khaki pants and Cashmere v-neck sweaters, along with forty or fifty long-sleeved, button-down shirts from Brooks Brothers and Bloomingdale's.

He also expected a lot from his assistants, who would be both sorely abused and severely underpaid. "Call that girl again!" he told me. "The one with the feather in her ear."

"Jooks, you called her three times this week. I don't think she's going to interview."

"Call her!"

It was the same routine with every interviewee: He expounded on his early success, the harrowing stroke, his children sobbing on the hospital floor, his miraculous recovery. I never reciprocated the conspiratorial glances designed to make applicants feel they were vying for an exclusive privilege. If someone was promising, he took her into the den for a live-narrated tour of his advertising jingles and photographs of girlfriends past. I'd gone through the same interview, but when the door closed behind them, I found myself waiting for the sound of screams or physical struggle that would send me back to fling open the door, call the police, and hit Jooks over the head for subdual if need be.

Should he like an applicant, or more accurately, sense that someone was naive enough, he would have her work a trial day.

He extended the invitation to a dancer from Brooklyn named Macy but was disappointed. "I asked her, 'What's one thing you'd buy yourself if you had the money?' and she said, 'A new bike. Mine just got stolen.' So, I handed her $200. I admire that she's a dancer—it's a noble profession. But I didn't like her reaction. She didn't seem grateful enough. I don't want her coming back."

Macy was scheduled to return the next day. He made her show up so the doorman could turn her away. She had forgotten her day planner and Jooks wouldn't let me bring it to her.

He had me spend a day training a film graduate from France who he was crazy about. I told her of his mounting rape and assault accusations while I took her around town on errands. He'd acquired two new summons.

"I can't explain it! She's twenty-seven—too old for me, and too fat for me too, but I don't want her to work for me—I want to date her!"

"It must be the mysterious allure of the French," I said. She was hired elsewhere.

An actress with bright red hair sang a song at the piano at his request.

"Can you come in this F-f-friday?" he asked her.

"I have work this Friday."

"You have work?!"

"Yes. I work at a restaurant."

"So quit."

"Quit? I can't!"

"Why not?"

"I don't know if you've hired me yet!"

"You can't come in Friday because of another job?"

"I—I didn't know you were going to ask me to be available then. I'm free Saturday."

SELF IMPROVEMENT MONTAGE

"Nah. We'll call you."

She left, confused and distressed, but probably better off.

"She was an idiot. Doesn't she know that when a big producer or director asks you to do something, you drop what you're doing immediately and do whatever they want. Screw her. I don't want somebody that stupid workin' for me."

On days he didn't meet anyone he liked, or none of the girls called back, Jooks was in an ill humor. "Maybe when we hire a new girl, we'll tell her that the pay is t-t-t-ten dollars an hour, instead of fifteen," he said. My throat clenched. As a symbol of working people's resilience myself, class solidarity was one thing I had never lacked.

"Is that so you can eventually drive my pay down to ten dollars an hour as well?" I asked.

"Maybe..." he frowned.

"So, like, a bait-and-switch?"

He ruminated, unsure how to respond, but apparently really thinking about it. From then on when we interviewed, I announced with fervor that the pay started at fifteen dollars an hour, and not a penny less.

Each day my grooming and competence improved. Job loss proved less of a threat than I'd expected, with most interviewees having a natural aversion to Jooks. I started to worry that my lack of personal standards was more unusual among my peers than I had thought. It seemed like Jooks was more interested in the process of meeting girls than actually hiring one. Jooks had power over women's livelihoods, but less power than he'd had when he was younger, to harm or to rescue. He wanted to feel like the biggest thing to come into our lives, as he may have one time been, but also, he truly pitied us.

For a while, Jooks and I were content. Although I was hugely overworked, my employment felt stable. If my rehearsal ended early enough, I'd return to Jooks afterward, and he'd insist I take a cab on his dime. I strategized his schedule so that his massage therapist, computer specialist, speech therapist, or someone would be there when I was indisposed. He was still too weak for excursions on his own. I tried to save money, but knew I couldn't keep doing sixty-hour weeks, working the job of three assistants.

For a while, he seemed to let the issue go. October lurked near the end of a prolonged summer. One day up on the terrace, he told me, "Listen, we're not finding the right girls. I would prefer an actor or a dancer type. Someone who's desperate, as you girls tend to be." His smile glimmered. "Who are you texting?"

"My friend Ryan. She lives in Queens."

"Is she cute?"

"Well," I began to think of ways to deter him.

"...So...no," he finished for me. "D-d-do you have anyone you could call n-n-now for an interview?"

"Eh—my friends, Jooks, aren't really your style."

"W-w-well, w-w-why not?"

"They have boyfriends. Jobs. You wouldn't like them."

There was no way I'd let Jooks seep into my social pool. I knew that much.

JÖYCE

I set up his cushion and beverages and made my way to a picnic table underneath the trellis.

"You don't want to l-l-lie on a chair in the sun?" he asked.

"Well, I don't like to get my skin in the sun too much."

He couldn't argue because of his open disdain for aging women. I would not occupy the same geometric plane as Jooks, even on separate surfaces. I cracked open *The Unloveables* and scribbled across the pages with bravado, to prove that Jooks could not inhibit my creativity. But my pencil wandered into a sketch of his reclining form.

Jooks was heroin chic. His legs looked like a couple of broomsticks stuck into some khakis. From a length of white tube sock, his New Balance sneakers pointed into the air. He had five pairs of the same grey sneakers, each varied slightly in size and width. He mixed and matched according to what was comfortable for each foot. I drew his melon-like skull. His features grimacing at the sky. His hair, a

SELF IMPROVEMENT MONTAGE

portabello mushroom with a wasting disease. Like the charred remains of a straw roof. From thirty paces away, I sketched, and I seethed. A helpless rage moved the pencil in my hand, scraping and digging the paper like an angry ghost who had claimed a Ouija board. I was indentured to Jooks in every way, and now he inhabited my mind.

CHAPTER 16:
ALL MY DADS

On Sunday, Jooks invited me to see *Mamma Mia!*

"I got tickets for me and a friend, but she couldn't make it," he explained. "It's the best musical! I've seen it probably a dozen times."

There were hundreds of people waiting in line at the theater.

"Watch this," he said, limping up to the ticket window as if the sidewalk were empty. A few pointed and muttered, but when someone swoops in and does the unthinkable, most people are stunned into passive spectatorship.

I slunk away as if I didn't know him while he stammered out his name to the helpless box office attendant. Tickets in hand, he shed his bashful grin and looked right at me.

"C'mahhhhn!" he shouted.

"Those suckers," he snickered in my ear, "they think I'm some retard and feel too guilty to say anything!" His willingness to cast aside vanity for

ALL MY DADS

the sake of personal gain was another lesson in marketing.

"We should've waited in line like everybody else, Jooks. There were, like, six ladies in wheelchairs out there!"

"Bah, what do you know?"

We sat third-row aisle.

"Ha ha, boy this show is GREAT! It's my favorite!"

"It must be really good then!"

As he recounted tales of his own Broadway show and how much of a jerk Ben Brantley was for reviewing it poorly, Jooks draped his arm over the back of my chair. And I made a great show of shifting to the very edge of my seat until he moved. He brushed my knee with his fingertips, and I pivoted away on a sixteenth note. He looked around the theater, I guess to check for witnesses. Or to make sure that no one had seen him embarrass himself.

Mamma Mia! was about an American girl who grew up on a small Greek Island with her whimsical innkeeper mother who is a painter. The girl, Sophie, is about to get married but had

(163)

never met her father and decides to find him so he can walk her down the aisle. She steals her mom's old hippie diaries and figures out who she was sleeping with around the time she was conceived. She narrows it down to three men and invites them all to the wedding.

The mom is shocked when they show up. The daughter tries to figure out which one's her dad. Essentially, the plot is just an excuse to sing more ABBA songs. Some vaguely fit the story. Others were incongruous musical outbursts. The audience loved it, especially Jooks.

So suspending disbelief that someone doesn't just get a DNA test, and suspending disbelief that wealthy older men everywhere are happy to take on an illegitimate adult child that might not even be theirs, the daughter says, "I like you all so much. I want you all to be my dad!"

And all of the dads are like, "Sounds great!"

Jooks wouldn't give a shit about some former fling who'd aged out of his dating pool. He would hit on the daughter, unless she was his—in which case, he'd book it out of there to go find some Greek girl who was struggling economically.

The *Mamma Mia!* playbill has a painting of a joyful, dark-haired woman in a big white poofy wedding dress, but the bride in the actual production was blond and wore a casual sundress. The name *Mamma Mia!* seems Italian, but it takes place in Greece and refers to some old hippies who aren't even from there.

"I love that musical!" Jooks cried as we left the theater.

"It was great, Jooks! Thanks for inviting me." I blinked the glaze from my eyes and remembered to be grateful. I'd gotten a $300 theater ticket for free and spent two hours watching something uninterrupted by Jooks' channel flipping. I knew to remain wary of his generosity, however, accepting only when he insisted, and circumventing any feeling that I owed him something.

On the cab ride back home, we passed Tiffany's. He turned to me with a wry smile and said, "You know, when you buy an engagement ring at Tiffany's, they have a room on the fourth floor where they give you champagne."

"That's so nice," I smiled.

"Even better, they have this great return policy." He chuckled and slapped his knee. "You have seven days to get a full refund. Sometimes, years ago, I would propose to a girl and spend the week with her. Then, if I didn't like 'er...." He waved his hand in dismissal, illustrating the next logical step.

"Wow." It was then that I wished I'd asked him to buy me that pack of Twizzlers at the theater.

CHAPTER 17:
IT TROLLS FOR THEE

The intercom from the lobby ground out its angry mechanical drill. "Hello?" I answered

"There's a letter down here for Jooks."

"Oh, okay. Thanks."

"Hey! Get in here!" Jooks shouted.

He lay on his massage table in the den. His shiatsu masseuse kneaded away.

"They said you have a letter."

"W-w-what kind of letter?"

"I don't know. They just said a letter."

"Call them back. Ask what the envelope looks like."

"If you want I can just go get it."

"NO! CALL HIM BACK."

I swung into the hallway and called the intercom.

"Jooks wants to know what the envelope looks like."

"Uhh, it doesn't have an envelope."

"Jooks, it doesn't have an envelope."

"Oh god, better g-g-g-go down and get it. Don't sign anything!"

JÖYCE

One thing I could be certain about when it came to Jooks, I wasn't signing shit.

Charles was on duty. Charles was about twenty-five. He was Dominican from the Bronx with a wife and two kids. I liked Charles because he never pretended to smile the way most people do at their jobs. No one ever smiled at the Church unless it was genuine or had a purpose.

Charles gave me a folded ten-page document, and I brought it to Jooks. He spent the last few minutes of his massage rifling through the pages.

This time, Jooks didn't laugh.

"Oh shit, we better call my lawyer."

I'd only heard people say, "Oh shit, we better call my lawyer," in movies.

He strained his memory for the name and handed me his phone.

"M-m-m-matthew Richardson. He's my lawyer. Call him."

I scrolled through the names and called.

He snatched the phone when it started ringing.

IT TROLLS FOR THEE

"H-h-h-hey Matt—it's me J...Jooks. Long time no see. I had a s-s-s-stroke. Please call. We have a b-b-b-big p-p-problem. I got a letter from the Supreme Court. The District Attorney says I assaulted several girls. She wants to put me i-i-i-in jail. This is b-b-b-b-bad."

He hung up.

"Gosh, I can't believe this. I'm an old man! How could I rape somebody?"

"That's terrible," nodded the masseuse, then took her check for $130 and left.

"This is bad. This is b-b-bad."

"Wait, what's the difference between this and the other summons?" I asked.

"This is an indictment."

"What's an indictment?"

"N-never mind, honey. It's complicated."

"I'm sure they can't get away with suing you if nothing happened."

He seemed not to understand the rationality of what I was saying. I watched his reaction. I thought if I were accused of something I didn't do, I'd be thrown into an incoherent rage, but that was then. Today, I'd stay calm and decline any statement without a lawyer present.

Jooks seemed to be not that affected by it, which was suspicious, unless he was accustomed to such attacks as a person of influence. I once played Liz Morden, a wretched convict in *Our Country's Good*, who spends the whole play saying nothing to defend herself against a false accusation until the very end, because she doesn't think anyone will believe her.

"THE DA WANTS TO PUT ME IN—ah, never mind. Go pick up my s-seafood Cobb salad."

The intercom railed again.

"Oh, brother, you'd better answer." Jooks peeled himself from the table.

"Hello?"

"Pearl is here to see Mr. Jooks."

"Jooks, he says Pearl is here to see you."

"WHAT? I don't want her here! You tell them to send her out. And if she ever comes back, to call the police."

"Uhh...Jooks says to, um, tell her to..."

IT TROLLS FOR THEE

"NO, not 'Uhhh-der-duuuhhhh-he told me to,' JUST TELL THEM YOURSELF!"

"Umm, he doesn't want to see her and he says he wants to—"

"DON'T SAY I SAID IT—TELL THEM YOU'RE SAYING IT."

"Jooks says to call the police if she ever comes back."

"Uh. Okay. Sure," said the doorman.

"Thanks." I hung up. "Jooks. Don't yell at me like that."

"You have to be strong when you talk to people or you'll never get anything done."

"Right. Who's Pearl?"

"She used to work for me. She's a jerk! She stole money from me."

"That's horrible. What happened? How did she steal it?"

"I don't wanna talk about it. Also, before you get dinner, I need you to go to the drugstore and buy me three of the bath poofy things."

"Any particular color?"

"Shut up."

"I'm not making fun of you. I'm

asking genuinely."

"NO PARTICULAR COLOR. Thank you."

"A seafood Cobb salad and bath poofs. Got it."

"And get me Thousand Island dressing at Hamburger Heaven downstairs. You can buy it from them in the little cups. Get four."

"Okay."

"And get me two large coffee milkshakes."

"Jooks, maybe you should go easy on the milkshakes with your heart and all."

"I have a pacemaker. My heart can never stop!"

"Okay...bath poofs, seafood Cobb salad, milkshakes, and dressing."

"LARGE COFFEE milkshakes and THOUSAND ISLAND dressing."

"Yes, I know."

"And I want double crab meat in the salad."

"Okay." I started writing on a post-it.

"And have them add seared scallops, instead of the other ones."

"Seared scallops, not steamed."

IT TROLLS FOR THEE

"And no corn. Or lettuce."

"Okay. So your salad will just be double crab meat, an order of seared scallops mixed in, since that's another menu item entirely, chopped tomatoes, shrimp, and asparagus."

"Have them take out the asparagus."

"Okay. And remember they charge like twice the amount for these changes. Is that okay?"

"I DON'T GIVVA SHIT!"

"Okay, geez." I waited.

"What?!"

"How will I pay for this?"

"Oh right, I forgot. Take my credit card."

"Am I allowed to do that?"

"Yes. And take cabs. Don't walk."

"Um—Häagen-Dazs is like three blocks away—"

"I SAID TAKE A CAB," he thrust some twenties in my face.

I sped through the lobby. A woman was sitting on the entryway bench and talking to Charles. "...It's just that he's been having a very hard time, and I want to make sure that he and his kids are okay. He's like family to me," I overheard her say as I passed.

I swept around the corner into Semmelweis. It was a tiny private pharmacy with high shelves and high-end merchandise. I scanned narrow aisles for mesh bath poofs in gender-neutral or traditionally masculine hues.

"Jöyce?" said a voice. "Hi. I'm Pearl, Jooks' old assistant." I turned to see the woman I had just passed in the lobby smile and stick out her hand.

"Oh, hi." The doorman evidently hadn't followed Jooks' orders. I was freaked out. I'd never been followed before. "How'd you know my name?"

"Sorry, I asked the doorman. I was just trying to visit Jooks to see if he was okay. I worked for him for sixteen years. He's practically family." Her face was a quivering pool of exaggerated concern. I wondered what would lead a person to remain Jooks' assistant for sixteen years, and what were the cognitive effects.

"Sixteen years?"

IT TROLLS FOR THEE

"I actually live in Seattle now, but even after I moved, I used to fly out sometimes to work for him. Until he got rid of me."

"What would you fly all the way out here for?"

"Oh, certain administrative tasks. Things he relied on me to do for him."

"I see." I pictured her flying across the country to pick up his meals, take him to the nail salon, and complete light office work. I couldn't imagine anything else.

"Certain times, I guess...certain times I would get...girls...for him. I guess."

"Oh." I was mildly disgusted. Whatever Pearl meant by "getting girls," it made me wonder if she'd somehow gotten wind of the rape summons and was here to see if she was going to get in trouble. "Why would you do that?"

"Because he's lonely. And depressed. And just wants to be loved."

"Like all humans," I replied without feeling. "Are you an artist? A performer?"

"Well, yes, I'm a singer. He encouraged

me to still go out for castings while I worked for him."

"That's nice of him. Why is he mad at you?"

"After the stroke, I stopped bringing girls into his life. It wasn't right for them to be around all of that...sickness. He kind of blamed me. Then he screwed me over."

"What do you mean you helped him 'get girls?'"

"Introduce him. To friends."

"Huh. He said you stole money."

"Yeah. He's referring to money of his which I gave to his son while he was in the hospital, as well as wages I was owed that he didn't want to pay."

"I figured he wasn't telling the whole story."

"You need to be careful around Jooks."

"You mean like he'd get violent?"

"Assassination."

"Like try to kill me?"

"Character assassination. Are you an actress?"

"Yeah. I just graduated."

"You're so young. You want to stay on the legitimate side of the business."

(176)

IT TROLLS FOR THEE

Heading towards the register, I accepted none of her sympathy-stricken gaze.

"I never expected this job to be anything but labor in exchange for money. I'm not chasing any carrots. I refuse to do anything but get his lunch and make his phone calls. There's no way I'd do anything dubious for that man, much less 'get girls' for him. I just need to save up a chunk of money. I plan on leaving in the next few months," I said.

Her tone switched to the world-wise condescension of a 1920s Times Square hustler. "Honey, have ya seen the ads on Craigslist lately? He's already looking for a new girl."

"I have. I'm the one who put them there," I said.

Her face fell carefully back into that quivering pool as she tried to think of what to say next.

"I have to go run these errands," I said. "He's gonna call and scream at me if I take more than three minutes. As I'm sure you know."

"Well, we should exchange numbers, in case you run into trouble or ever need to call me." She took out her phone.

"Sorry, but I don't see why I need your number. I'm not involved with you any more than I am with Jooks, and if he ever tried to do anything to me, I wouldn't call you, I'd call the cops. I'm just here to run errands." I headed out of the store, shaken but intact.

An hour later, Jooks and I were eating. I told him Pearl had followed me to the pharmacy, and he was startled but thanked me for my honesty. I didn't want to be accused of secrecy later.

When he turned on the TV, the news showed an apartment one block up on 64th Street, where I had seen a news camera perched on a tripod for the past few days. Somebody named Bernie Madoff lived there. Madoff's fifty-billion-dollar Ponzi scheme had just imploded. A sixteen-second video clip of a reporter shoving Madoff on Lexington Avenue had gone viral on every channel.

Madoff was disgraced as the classic

model citizen who scams everyone. Jooks was the opposite type of offender, too predictably obnoxious for his rape charges to register as a shock. As stock values avalanched, brokers quietly leapt from windows, opened internet cafés in Costa Rica, bought farm land in Siberia, or became trailer-park moguls. Articles were written about why the finance industry seemed to incentivize narcissistic and sociopathic tendencies.

That night, I noticed an article open on Jooks' computer: "THE DATE RAPE 'DOCTOR' THEY COULD NOT CONVICT." It was about an unemployed ambulance worker who would go on a date with a victim, drug them, sexually assault them while they were unconscious, then act like they were both waking up from a perfectly normal night together the next morning. Just like in *The Twilight Zone*, the victim would dismiss her gut feeling, unable to place what was wrong. Sometimes a victim would go on more dates with him to try and make sense of the bizarre nightmare, but no matter what the FBI did, nobody could convict him. I read the whole article, but didn't tell Jooks I'd even noticed it there.

"How do you s-s-send somebody an article from the internet?" he asked that evening.

"Oh, it's easy. You just cut and paste the link into the email."

"There's an article there on the computer already open. Can you put it in an email f-f-f-f-for me."

"Sure, Jooks. Do you need me to read it?"

He thought for a second.

"N-n-no!"

"Okay."

He sent the article off to his lawyer with the message, "Hey, what do you think of this?"

Meetings with Jooks' lawyer became common. On such occasions, he'd break out the aluminum cane. At that point, he still had the choice.

Once out of the cab in midtown, Jooks would leave me in the waiting room and vanish past the reception desk with his legal team. I drank styrofoam cups of coffee and tea from the break room while I feigned deep focus, learning lines, jotting out more of *The Unloveables*, and reading Aristotle's *Poetics*, barely able to grasp anything beyond caffeine and text messages as I dangled over a canyon of loss.

After an hour, Matthew Richardson would deposit Jooks, waving his hands in the air and chuckling, "But Matt—the craziest thing is," he'd say, "I didn't do it! I don't understand! Who are these girls?" as the elevator swallowed us again.

"Jooks, I don't get it. Where did these accusations come from?" I asked on the way out.

"They said I raped them during an audition!"

"What? When?"

"Last year sometime, in the spring. It happened before I had my stroke, so I can't remember the girls they're even talking about!"

"You mean like the auditions happened, and you had the stroke that night?"

"No, no, no, it was a few months after. Remember that movie I wrote? You read it. The script about the hooker?"

"Oh, yeah. *Struck By Lightning.*"

"We were in the process of making that movie, back when Pearl used to work for me. A few months later, I had the stroke. And now this! I can't believe it. I just can't believe it." He held out his hands in disbelief. "How could anyone think I did this?"

"Oh, Jooks, that's so unfortunate. I'm sorry."

"You're sorry? Imagine how I feel!"

I could not imagine how he felt.

Even Jooks' own lawyers didn't trust him.

Jooks popped his head into the waiting room one morning and beckoned me through the carpeted maze of cubicles. "C-c-come into the office a moment," he said, leading me to the corner office filled with pictures of Matthew Richardson's wife, and the people on Jooks' legal team. One was Danielle, a younger partner with a chestnut-brown bob who wore knee-length brown skirts and off-white blouses. She was intelligent, unassuming, and a good listener.

"Do you have Jooks' passwords to his email account?" she asked.

"I c-c-c-can't remember it!" Jooks threw up his hands, embarrassed.

I logged them in.

"We need to see if Jooks has anything he overlooked so we can build the strongest case."

They found nothing. Jooks' email box was kept tight and emails got deleted as they were dealt with.

"Matt I-I-I told you, I didn't do it!" Jooks chuckled and looked at me for affirmation.

"You guys never posted Craigslist ads?"

"Oh, we posted bunches of them!" I volunteered.

"Shut up!" cried Jooks. The team of lawyers gasped.

"What? Just for those job interviews. For the assistant position. The same way I was hired," I said.

"Oh r-r-right. Sorry, honey, I forgot."

The legal team released a sigh.

"Oh my god, I would never help him pick up girls," I assured them.

"Well fuck you then!" he bellowed at me.

"Do you remember if you guys posted anything for the auditions?" Danielle asked.

"Oh, I wasn't even working for Jooks at the time. That was another assistant. I had nothing to do with that time period. I'm probably not even relevant to this case."

I wanted it to be quite clear that I was not, and would not be, involved in Jooks getting in or out of trouble. I had not arrived at any personal conclusion on Jooks' guilt. It was possible a slew of girls he might have treated like shit or slept with or both were descending upon him in his medical catastrophe. He was, after all, a major fucking asshole, capable of inspiring rage and indignation. It was possible he was so obviously an asshole that his douchery was being exploited for the easy assumption that of course he'd be a rapist.

But I really didn't know.

CHAPTER 18

A DECEPTIVE WOMAN AND A STONE-FACED MAN

It was my birthday, but no one could know. I was twenty-three. I was too old for Jooks. Japetto had vandalized my soul, so I disabled my Facebook wall. Those who cared would have to find me in real life. I shunned digital gratification and idleness.

After a noonday manicure, Jooks had his massage. I waited for a package in the living room. Jooks had just subscribed to the Meaningful Beauty Anti-Aging Skincare line by Cindy Crawford.

I examined the framed print of his Vogue spread from thirty years ago on the hutch. His eyes were vacant. His face stretched slightly askew.

To treat myself, I texted Japetto: "THERE'S JUST TWO KINDS OF PEOPLE I DON'T UNDERSTAND: THAT'S A DECEPTIVE WOMAN AND A STONE-FACED MAN. UR BOTH. LOL."

Jooks didn't have many explanations for a twenty-three-year-old companion when the two of us went out together in public. It was one thing for his acquaintances to assume I was a prostitute, but there was also an entire unspoken economy. Once I'd seen it, I was marked. Strangers insinuated willingness to barter or pay for sex. My understanding became their expectation. A Ukrainian bar regular at Atlantic Grill would glare at my body with entitled hunger and annoyance, as if I owed him much more than my formal greeting. A businessman on the late-night train turned my answer to his casual inquiries, that I was leaving work as a personal assistant, into some lewd request to hire me for some "personal assistance." The kindly old bartender at Jooks' favorite Italian spot invited me to his beach house in Florida. The ancient gentleman in the waiting room of Jooks' accountant gave me his card in case I was looking for "work," but never responded to my resume.

I would act oblivious—and mostly I was—to this hostility for my youth. Men reacting to my body would

A DECEPTIVE WOMAN

register vaguely and stoke confusion. It did not matter whether I was sexually attracted to them. There was no safety in which to figure it out.

CHAPTER 19:
I HEARD THERE WAS A SECRET CHORD

"Watch this!" Jooks improvised a shimmering series of chords.

"Jooks—that's fantastic. I can't believe you can play with both hands! Pretty soon you'll be composing again."

"Well, I don't know if I'm ready for that just yet."

"Either way, it's just going to be better from here. I'm so happy!"

"It was Masha," he chuckled.

"What do you mean?"

"We fucked last night."

"Oh."

"I gotta get a g-g-girlfriend, so I can recover."

I nodded.

"What do you know! I'm tellin' you it was Masha. I'm sure of it. This changes everything. I need that girl."

He clenched and unclenched his reanimated hand in wonder.

As Jooks' body recovered, so did behavioral patterns, which were as old as his psyche.

He ployed Masha with Fifth Avenue shopping trips, Broadway shows, and fine dining. She stipulated that any gift he gave her was his choice. He would still pay her hourly rate, and things would not move into a relationship. Devoid of addictive ambiguity, his passion receded, but his propensity for romance was resurrected.

On the way to rehearsal, I stopped at Garden of Eden for yogurt and an apple. There was Mimsy in a short black pleated skirt and cardigan, black ballet flats, her downy hair and purified complexion, clutching a diet soda as I clutched an apple. Opportunity bent towards her Ivy League blood like a dousing rod to water.

I had not seen her since our theater apprenticeship two summers prior. I got lucky and was cast in a role that put me on the map among my peers that season. Then she asked me to do an independent project, saying she liked to surround herself with successful people. She would hint about how my working-class guilt held me back. "You need to know when it's okay to break the rules," she told me. Her wealth forced her to be on guard against grifters but granted her other kinds of innocence. Once she had a dress stolen from her dorm room, and I could tell she had to try hard not to suspect me of doing it while we'd been rehearsing together. I kept asking her to start rehearsals right away and suggested we do a scene from *Phaedra's Love*. She kept making me read other plays that she bought with her parent's credit card, and I felt obligated on account of the expense. I even wrote a script for us, which she rejected, and then another, which she also rejected. Then, she said, "You know what? You're right. Let's do *Phaedra's Love*."

By the time we finally started rehearsals, I was so exhausted and overbooked, I barely got to work. So my performance in our project was weak, while she was showcased—as if she'd planned my whole downfall from the beginning. Since Mimsy's Aunt Dill was on the festival board, she got their family friend, the star auteur Floyd Lumber, to bring the whole acting company of *Gory Gory General Grant* during their thirty-minute break from a week of twelve-hour tech rehearsals, to watch me fail. At the end, Mimsy treated me to ice cream. She ordered a small vanilla soft serve, and when I ordered a small vanilla soft serve but with peanuts, she glanced at me suspiciously, like I had taken advantage.

It just isn't easy—bridging social divides for the sake of friendship. We had equally valuable lessons to learn from one another, but Mimsy could afford tutors.

I would need to greet her in the Garden of Eden before she saw me hesitate.

"Mimsy!"

"Oh my god. Hiiiii! How arrrre you??" She gave me a hug.

"Mimsy! How are you doing? What have you been up to?"

"Well, I graduated last spring. I've been living in the West Village and auditioning."

JÖYCE

"Oh wow, do you have an agent?"

"I, yes. I do, I've been working with an agent." She took on a sober look of humility and said the name of the agency.

"Oh my god. That's amazing. They're one of the big ones. How did you get signed?" Mimsy detailed connections, introductions, trips, dinners, meetings, auditions, friends of friends, colleagues of parents of friends, and a summer of toil and uncertainty, meticulously following leads that lacking start-up capital, a driver's license, and stability, I would have fumbled. Advantages aside, Mimsy had abilities and parents who schooled her in shameless hard labor. Or rather, smart labor. Her industry savvy made me certain she would become a professional actress. She had a kind of resilience that usually only poor people have. While Mimsy stayed hungry, I stayed malnourished, hoping to leverage the chip on my shoulder as an integral component of my brand.

"So what are you up to?" she asked.

"Well, it's been interesting," I began

my pitch. "My parents lost their house, and I had to get a stable job on really short notice."

Her openness in describing her great fortune gave me openness in describing my misfortune.

"Oh, no!"

"Yes, well...I'm sure it will be extremely valuable in my personal mythology as an artist."

"What are you doing for work?"

"I'm this crazy guy's personal assistant. He won an Oscar and a Grammy and stuff for this song he wrote in the seventies."

"I want to be a personal assistant."

"Really? We actually need to hire another person. But Mimsy—he's horrible."

"Horrible how?"

"He's a narcissist who sees prostitutes fifty years younger and is getting sued for sexual assault." Her eyes narrowed. "He had a stroke last April. It could be someone looking for a payout."

"Right, people do that. How do you know he sees prostitutes?"

"He sends me away for an hour to get coffee and says, 'I'm seeing a prostitute.'"

"Oh wow. So you'd refer me?" Mimsy wasn't much better than Jooks, but now that she was here, I could think of nobody else.

"Do you have a survival job?"

"I do catering."

"I've been wanting to get into that!"

"It's been really hard. A family friend owns the company. I pass hors d'oeuvres to childhood classmates who make six figures."

"That's really hard. Can you refer me?"

"Well...yes, I could," she hesitated, ever the dutiful gatekeeper.

"What do they pay?"

"Nineteen an hour."

"Jooks pays fifteen. Your job sounds better. If you refer me, I might leave Jooks for that."

"I need to leave for auditions on short notice."

"Jooks will try to guilt you into staying. You're a great negotiator though. You have nothing to lose by applying."

SECRET CHORD

"We can commiserate about him together!"

We agreed to get in touch over Facebook. Mimsy went to parties at Harvard with the founder Mark Zuckerberg after all. She never followed up on my catering referral.

CHAPTER 20:
YOU CAN'T TEACH A PIG TO SING

When the Estrogenius Festival was over, I was free to spend all my time with Jooks. He planned a Tuesday dinner with his entertainment lawyer, Newton Wash.

"Tell them I'm an Academy Award winner. Grammy Award winner. People's Choice Award winner. I want the BEST table. The BEST waiter. Say EVERYTHING'S gotta be PERFECT. This is a dinner for my friend. He's my lawyer AND an investor on Broadway!"

"Jooks, I can get the same things without being a jerk to people. It's just not necessary. It makes people hate you."

"Be a jerk!" He jabbed the air with his finger inches from my collarbone. I thought how funny it would be if I snapped it off and threw it in his face, but I restrained myself.

"Tell them I get the BEST!"

"Got it."

Fig and Olive was a Michelin-starred

farm-to-table. I entered through a thick velvet curtain. Servers wore ankle-length bistro aprons among reclaimed wood, aromas of Chanterelle mushrooms, and seasonal offal. One stood at the maître d' podium shuffling through menus.

"Hi, what can I do for you?"

"So, my boss is crazy. He won an Oscar, plus the People's Choice Award. And a Grammy. He's old now. He wanted me to tell you about his awards and get 'the best waiter, the best table, and the best service,' so that's what you'll be dealing with. He's nice when he feels taken care of."

"I understand completely. I can give you a reservation for three at seven."

"Jöyce?" I stopped and turned. It was Gaelyn from the one-act festival placing candles on the tables with the other staff. Usually actresses would invalidate my beingness, but Gaelyn had none of the typical dominance or extortive flattery. She was in a play about three female astronauts. My focus had been drawn straight to her onstage during our tech rehearsal before we even met. I felt like

JÖYCE

I was watching a professional actor and not someone just trying to pull off a technique.

"Oh my gosh! Gaelyn! Hi!" My joy surprised me.

"How are you?" she asked.

"I'm good—I'm booking a reservation for my crazy boss."

"I overheard! What's the deal with him?" She leaned in with a glossy smile.

"He won an Oscar and stuff for his song back in the seventies and did a lot of advertising. I think he made a movie."

"Do you think I could give him my card?"

"Oh, yeah...the thing is...I don't think he has a lot of business activity. He had a stroke."

"Oh, no!"

"Also," I lowered my voice, "he's been getting summons for sexual assault charges and even rape. It's possible they're just preying upon him now that he's had a stroke. He sees prostitutes."

"Oh, wow. No, you're right."

"Apparently the girls accusing him

were at some auditions he was having. He's been interviewing a lot of girls for a second assistant position, but it seems like he just wants to sit and talk with them. He'll probably get a creepy crush on you."

"Huh."

"His friend coming with him is a Broadway investor. He's probably more worth your business card."

"That would be great. I know what those people can be like. I once hung out with this older actor when I was eighteen. He kept saying he'd get me roles and auditions. I eventually figured out he only wanted to sleep with me, and I left. I don't have much to lose if I give him my card, but I also know when to step back."

"Yeah, your judgment is probably better than mine. Anyway, I'd better get going. He, like, screams at me if I take more than three minutes."

"That's horrible! It sounds like you should be looking for a new job." Her concern made me sad that I hadn't felt the same for myself.

"Yeah, well...you're right. Good luck

with the business card."

"It was really good seeing you, Jöyce! We should get coffee soon."

"You too, Gaelyn! I'll probably see you soon."

Jooks didn't notice Newton's eyes well up seeing him cling to the door for balance.

"I was this man's first client!" Jooks slapped his arm around Newton, a timid, optimistic Sancho to his Don Quixote. "Then I said, 'How about you be my lawyer for the year?' and I gave him $100,000. Do you remember?"

"I remember."

"Now he's my lawyer for th-thirty years, with a firm of over a hundred! Remember when we w-w-went down to sue Lily Tomlin?"

"Jooks, you sued Lily Tomlin? Why? She's awesome," I said.

"She was using my song in her show, but she changed the lyrics, and it was not nice."

"I remember."

"We went in there and sh-shut it down!"

CAN'T TEACH A PIG TO SING

Jooks took Newton's wife to look at photographs in the den.

I stood in the living room with Newton, strategizing how to indicate that I really was Jooks' assistant and not a hooker.

"I really am Jooks' assistant and not a hooker," I smiled fetchingly.

"So how is Jooks?" asked Newton, like I'd said nothing at all.

"Well, it's hard to tell his gradient of improvement since I see him every day. I think he is getting better. He's remembering names and places. He even played the piano with both hands again."

"Wonderful. He's such a gifted man."

"Yeah, I know. He said his other hand started working again because of the prostitute he had sex with."

"You know, I remember this quote he used to have on the brick wall above his piano in his old apartment. It went, 'Never try to teach a pig to sing; it wastes your time and annoys the pig.'"

"That's...what? Is that, like, inspirational?"

"It was an interesting quote I remember."

"I can see Jooks connecting to a saying like that. I love quotations. I keep a Häagen-Dazs lid thumbtacked to the bulletin board above my desk at home because of the quote inside, about using just a few simple ingredients to make something extremely well. Their business ethos is inspiring."

"Oh really, that's wonderful. So what else has Jooks been up to? How's he doing other than physically?"

"He chases girls my age and spends shitloads of money on them."

"Well, do you say anything to discourage him?"

"Well, you've known him for a few decades. What's your experience been like trying to regulate his... appetites? I'm his lowest employee. I make less than his housekeeper and am continually about to get fired. His psychiatrist costs $500 an hour. Has he been doing anything to discourage Jooks? It's a multi-week process for him to add more fruit to his diet. I'm pretty moral and uptight. I care when people around me do unwholesome things. When I've even tentatively suggested to Jooks that he shouldn't, you know, buy a Chanel bag for some random woman, he gets offended, because to suggest this is to suggest that he's not in a romantic relationship filled with complexity. Which he's not. He's just paying for sex. There's just layers of delusion."

"I see, I see." Newton smiled. Jooks returned with Mrs. Wash.

"Hey Newton, you could give my assistant an audition, couldn't you?"

"Jooks..." Newton shifted.

"C'maaaahn!" he prodded.

"An audition for what?"

"One of the Broadway shows your friends are doing!"

"I'll see what I can do."

"See?" Jooks said. "I do look out for you."

I waited for them to leave, so I could order dinner with his credit card and try to learn a monologue. As always, Jooks returned too soon.

JÖYCE

"Boy! Your friend is stupid!" Jooks pulled out Gaelyn's comp card. I hoped he meant that she was stupid for interrupting his dinner.

"I told her to come up here, and she didn't!" he cried.

"Must have been because she was at work."

"If a big producer wants to meet, you stop everything."

"Maybe she was wary that you invited her up so late."

"What?! I was just gonna talk with her."

"I'm sure it's not you. It's just so late."

"If she's too stupid to come up, I don't want her. Ah well. Too bad for her, man. That's sad."

"Yeah."

"Wait a minute...I know. Call her."

"She's working."

"I don't care. Call her..."

"Jooks—"

"...and don't say I told you to call her. Tell her that you're calling her."

"Umm."

"If you won't, I will." He punched in her

number then thrust his phone to my ear.

When voicemail picked up, I disconnected.

"We'll call her first thing tomorrow then."

I avoided the task until noon the following day, suggesting Gaelyn might sleep in. My voicemail recorded Jooks scolding, "Don't ask her to call! Tell her to call!" in the background.

"You'd be there too! I want her to read me some poetry."

An hour later, Gaelyn didn't call.

"Call her again."

"Jooks. She knows you want her to call."

"How about you call on your phone."

"Why?"

"I want her to pick up!"

"It's you who's trying to reach her."

"You're so stupid!"

"No."

"Look, I just want her to get the phone call."

"She did already, I'm sure." I smiled.

After work, I passed Gaelyn taking a cigarette break.

"Hey!" she greeted.

"Jooks keeps pressuring me to call you. He says he wants you to read poetry for him."

"Yeah..." she said, "what do you think?"

"I feel bad I put you in this position. I didn't want to discourage you since he was at dinner with a Broadway dude, but now it's obvious that this is totally weird."

"I feel bad I put you in this position," said Gaelyn. "He seems really demanding and now I've created drama at your job."

"Nah, he creates the drama. If you want to check out how totally creepy he is, I would be there. I'm sure he'd just...talk about himself, play a bunch of jingles, and text message stalk you. I don't think it's going to result in any auditions though."

"Okay, I'm starting to get the picture. I really don't have time for those kinds of people. My boyfriend and I are saving up to move to LA at the end of the month."

"That's awesome! I'm so glad for you guys."

CAN'T TEACH A PIG TO SING

"Your boss sounds like such an asshole. If you want, I can tell him off for you."

"I'm just worried he's gonna make me call you again. Maybe if you give a blatant 'No,' it will nip this whole thing in the bud. And he won't blame me for sabotaging him."

"Okay..." She settled on me with a firm and even gaze. "You should really think about finding a new job. Like, really, Jöyce."

"I know. I need the money. Have a good night, Gaelyn."

"We should get coffee."

"Okay. I'll probably call you tomorrow...from his phone."

"Don't worry. I'll make it clear he has to stop," she said, gazing at me down the sidewalk as I continued towards the train, her cigarette and watchfulness contrasting oddly with her childlike face.

The next day, I called as promised.

"This is Fig and Olive, how may I assist?"

"Umm, Hi. I'm...calling for Gaelyn."

JÖYCE

"What is this regarding?"

"My boss wants to reach her."

There was a muffled change of hands.

"This is Gaelyn."

"Sorry, Jooks had me call—"

"—DON'T SAY 'SORRY'—"

"Listen," she said, "contacting me at work could be considered harassment. I know it's not you, but tell Jooks he is never to contact me—"

"—What's taking so long? Tell her to come up—"

"Great, I'll tell him. I am so sorry—"

"—If she says no, Hang up!—"

"It's okay, Jöyce, I totally understand. He is such an asshole. You really need to find another job."

"I know—"

"—HANG UP!!—"

"Jöyce, are you okay? It sounds really bad up there—"

"—HANG UP!!!!—"

"I have to go. Talk to you later."

"Okay...bye..."

"—HAAAAANGGG UPPPPPP!!!!—"

"She'll report you for harassment if you call."

CAN'T TEACH A PIG TO SING

"The thing is," his tone switched to mild coaxing, "I want her to try out for my movie."

"What about me? Why can't I be in your movie?"

"I have another film you're right for, but not till later. If she won't meet with me, I can't cast her!" He threw up his hands. Then a new idea came over him. "Wait, I know...call her."

"You said you wanted her to read poetry. Why all of sudden do you want to cast your film."

"That's not your business."

"We need to let this go. I only met her in the one-act festival and then bumped into her downstairs. Nothing you can say will convince me to contact her."

"Oh. I didn't realize you weren't f-f-friends."

I got Mimsy an interview. She was the only person I knew who could out-asshole Jooks.

"Your friend is a jerk!" Jooks laughed. "You know she actually claimed she went to Harvard?"

"She did go to Harvard."

"I'll have her work when you're not around," he chuckled.

CHAPTER 21

ROYAL WE

It was the best of times, it was athleisure time. Jooks had expressed interest in firming up his physical condition. "I want you to buy me a gym m-m-m-m-membership," he said. "Get me a p-p-personal trainer. Female only. And I want the p-p-prettiest one."

"Uh-huh."

"Tell them I'm an Academy... Grammy...People's Choice..."

"I'll tell them everything."

"Right. See you soon."

The glass office of the sales representative at the gym overlooked a black marble and walnut lobby with its circular distressed aluminum reception desk, a macrobiotic cafe, a retail area for $250 duffle bags, hobo-chic gym-to-cocktail frocks, and disposable thongs. It seemed complicated to have a whole other wardrobe for yoga, so half the time I wore any old clothes to class, to prove you didn't have to pay a retail company before being allowed to use your body. Not that I had time to exercise between working for Jooks and having a boyfriend, anyway.

Riff was an account manager with four-hundred-dollar frosted tips and an unsettlingly well-tailored suit.

"So...my boss had a stroke. He won an Oscar and Grammy and Academy Award, back in the seventies, and insists I announce these things with great importance. They are important. But I'm sure there are people at this gym who don't feel the need to list their awards."

"Right."

"Another thing that concerns me is he wants a female trainer—'the prettiest one.' He has a few rape and assault accusations. They're just accusations... but...I need you and any trainer he works with to have this information. He's still a human being, but he definitely presents as 'crazy asshole.'"

"Well, we can't assign trainers by gender, however our employees are equipped for the discretion needs of elite clients. I can try to provide a trainer that he'll be 100% satisfied with."

We called Jooks on speakerphone.

"D-d-d-did you get a pretty girl?" he asked.

"They can't request that."

"I have a match," Riff chimed in. "She's experienced with recovery training."

"Okay. W-w-w-we'll meet with her." He meant the royal "we." "W-w-w-what's her name?"

"Baila," Riff answered.

"When would you like to meet with her and how many sessions should I buy?" I asked.

"W-w-w-we'll meet her first. Then I'll buy."

"You buy a session in order to meet her," I said.

After Jooks haggled for the next morning, he settled for the next week.

That afternoon, he purchased a grey Nike tracksuit and dragged me to Solstice gym, where I sat on a bench outside the glass-walled aerobics room that was twitching with limbs.

(213)

JÖYCE

I cut a bulky figure in my I. Goldberg grey wool Civilforsvaret jacket and oversized red buffalo-plaid mad-bomber hunting cap lined with rabbit fur from L.L. Bean that Jooks begged me never to wear.

Jooks rode the elliptical and looked around the gym. It was a weekday morning with only a few silver foxes and Upper East Side moms. I stared chastely into my phone, texting atrocities to my ex-boyfriend Japetto.

CHAPTER 22

GUESS I'M THE UGLY ONE

Mimsy let me in with a tender smile. Jooks had changed the lock.

"Jöyce is here!" she cried. "Need anything else, Jooks?"

"When are you coming next?" he croaked warmly.

"Well...Thursday I have an audition, and Saturday I'm going to the park with my roommate. I can come Monday. Could we write it on the calendar?" cooed Mimsy.

"I'll g-g-get the calendar."

Jooks floated out. He never fetched anything for me.

"Hey! How are you! We're finally seeing each other!"

Her glow exhausted me.

"I know! Our schedules are opposite!" I tried to lament. "Was the interview okay?"

"He was like 'Do you have a boyfriend?' and 'C'mon, you didn't go to Harvard!' He asked what I make in catering, and I said nineteen dollars. And he was like 'No, no, no...' "

"'No' is his favorite thing to say."

"I'm so glad I'm seeing you!"

"Yeah!"

"He hasn't mentioned paying me."

"Ask now. I'm here, so it's less painful."

Jooks padded in.

"Here!" he shoved the twenty-two-by-seventeen-inch desk-pad calendar in her face with affection. "She tried to bring this thing with us in the cab today!" Jooks chuckled while she kneeled at the coffee table and engulfed every desirable shift with her name written in magenta marker.

"So we can say Monday through Thursday nights next week? Saturday and Sunday during the day? Jöyce is that okay? I have auditions."

On weekdays I edited weird YouTube videos that I make alone in my room. And I reserved weekend evenings for weeping and shaking in my bed.

"Sure!" I said. Since everything had been taken from me and my family already, I had a more flexible schedule.

"You're. Amazing. Umm, Jooks?"

Mimsy glanced at me.

GUESS I'M THE UGLY ONE

"Yes?"

"I was thinking, since it's Friday, I could receive a paycheck."

"Paycheck?" Jooks appeared baffled.

"If it's not too much trouble before I leave. I wrote down my hours." She handed him a tiny square of paper. "Or was this an unpaid internship?"

"Sure, ya jerk. Go get the checkbook," he told me.

His cheer dimmed. I brought the three-ring binder of perforated LLC checks.

"You write it," Jooks waved his hand.

"You want me to write it?" she repeated.

"He'll need to sign," I cautioned.

"What's fifteen times twenty-eight?" she asked me.

"Umm, $420," I said, wary as always of those who delegate arithmetic.

"Yeahh, four-twenty," said Mimsy.

"What?" I said.

"Nevermind. So that's okay, Jooks?"

"Oh, would you just write the thing!" he said, enjoying our sideshow.

"I want to write 'Personal Assistant?'

Only there's no room—I only got as far as 'Personal Ass.'"

Mimsy's modern charm was a welcome contrast to my fearful peasantry. "Okay, I guess I'll be going now, byeee!"

She gave me a hug and then gave Jooks a hug.

"Goodbye, sweetheart."

My inability to perceive Jooks as a sexual being left me unable to evaluate his nearly backing Mimsy into a coat closet.

I felt remorse that I couldn't muster a hug. His affection for Mimsy seemed paternal but would mean a rollercoaster of instability. I preferred the golf cart of function. That Sunday, and every Sunday thereafter, Mimsy took my place at the nail salon.

Early the next week, I came over to find Mimsy rushing out the door already.

"I fixed your fruit plate for you!" she said.

"Aww, sweetheart, that looks wonderful."

"Great! I'll just get going for my

audition."

"Okay! G-g-good luck, honey."

"Thanks, Jooks! Have a great day guys, I'll be back at six!"

Mimsy let the door slam shut.

"Wasn't it so great of her to do this?" he said, admiring the fruit.

"Umm. You realize I do that for you every morning, right?"

"Oh—can you take the garbage out?"

"I'll let Mimsy do it when she gets back."

"She's too stupid to do things like that. It should be someone smart, like you."

"She was here all yesterday. It's strange you didn't have her change it then."

"I know...but...I'd like you to do it."

I stood there.

"Now," he finished.

"We have to get her trained soon, so she and I can share the workload," I remarked, pulling out the garbage and gagging at the stench of rancid duck.

"You let me worry about that."

Jooks sucked down chunks of kiwi and papaya.

JÖYCE

Soon, Mimsy was half of what Jooks wanted to talk about. "Mimsy started eating omelets at lunch because she says she needs to lose weight," he marveled, eating an omelet. "She has an audition today. She won't get anywhere without somebody in her corner. I keep telling her if she wants to do film, she should go to L.A."

At the next dinner with Newton and Mrs. Wash, Jooks had me reserve for four.

"Mimsy has to come too. She doesn't want to stay up here while we're downstairs."

"Are you sure you don't want me to do anything for you?" she'd ask him when our shifts overlapped.

"No, let Jöyce do it. I'd like you to sit here and talk to me."

I started ordering turkey burgers with no bun, thinking I could slim down to upset Mimsy.

Autumn arrived. The leaves, who'd whispered kindness through the harsh winds, peeled into the next life and left the trees to claw the sky in grief.

"I was thinking I'd go home for Thanksgiving," Mimsy said.

"I'm trying to save money, so I'll stay and work," I said.

"Really? Are you sure? You don't want to go home?"

"I'll go home some other time."

"Oh my gosh, you're amazing, thank yoooou."

"No, it's fine. I mean, I need to work anyway."

I became semi-conscious of being not just personally screwed but societally screwed. Jooks and Mimsy strengthened their bond by using me in a mild game of psychological abuse and labor exploitation. Since I lacked their ruthlessness, I figured I should give up on success and just be okay with failure and getting fucked over. Like mother would always say to comfort me when I was upset with her: there are children who get treated much worse.

CHAPTER 23:
MAMMA'S VOID

"I need to get another girl," he muttered.

"Why, Jooks?"

"I wanted Mimsy to come home and wait until you got here, but she says, 'Oh, I'll miss my plane to Boston!' and gets out of the cab in the middle of traffic."

"Well, she can't control that."

"I need to get rid of her."

We were at Cole Haan on 57th and Fifth.

"You can pick something!" he said.

The salesgirl, tethered to the earth by her five-inch pumps, gave a congratulatory smile.

"I wouldn't know what to pick," I lied in breathless confusion.

"Would you just pick something?" He rolled his eyes.

"Those riding boots are practical," I said.

"How about these?" He pointed to a pair of $300 black suede high heels.

"Oh...those look nice..." I smiled,

cursing him. There was no way I could run around the city doing errands in those.

"I have this shoe," said the sales girl. "It's extremely comfortable."

Jooks traced her with his eyes as she rung us up.

"W-w-we gotta go to Chanel. I gotta get Baila a purse."

"Baila? Your gym trainer?"

"Y-yeah. She never had a Chanel bag. I told her 'I'm gonna get you one.' She doesn't believe me."

"Why did she make a point to mention it?"

"I asked her."

"Oh."

"I took her to a Broadway play and dinner."

"Really? Like a date?"

"Nahhhhh...she's thirty! Too old. It's just n-n-nice to go with someone."

Inside Chanel, they offered me champagne, which I regretfully declined.

"She wants the black one, with the C on the front."

"Such a pretty bag," I grimaced. I

liked the plain black quilted one myself.

"A-a-and I'm gonna get her a watch from C-Cartier."

"Like Edith Piaf gets her lover in the Marion Cotillard film."

"What film?"

"La Vie En Rose."

"That was boring. I shut it off in the first five minutes," Jooks boasted.

He chose a platonic, $5,000 titanium watch.

"Let's go to Viand," he said with an air of mischief.

"What's Viand?"

"It's across the street. Famous, famous place. Everybody goes there."

It was a tidy nook diner with inexpensive food and a long-time staff.

I ordered split pea soup. Jooks pushed away his tuna sandwich after one bite because it wasn't like the one from Hamburger Heaven.

After the gym, we thought of movies to rent from Video Room.

"Ummmm, *Gladiator*?"

"...no..." he said.

MAMMA'S VOID

"*Braveheart.*"

"Nah."

"*The Illusionist...*"

"I like that one...but not tonight."

"*Pretty Woman*? *A Beautiful Mind*? *Erin Brokovich*?"

"Meh, I don't wanna watch anything!"

"What about the *Mad Men* boxed set your older son got you?"

"Too boring."

"Have you seen *Angels in America*?"

"Tony Kushner was a jerk when I met him. He acted like he was the best writer."

"He won the Pulitzer."

"I know what we'll watch."

"What?"

"My movie!"

"*Pretty Woman*?"

"No, my movie."

"You were in a movie?"

"Starred...wrote...directed...scored. Didn't you see in the hall?"

"I didn't know that was your movie poster."

"You think I hang fuckin' movie posters that aren't mine? My god, you are dumb."

"By the way, never call me dumb."

"We're gonna watch my movie!"

"Yay!"

"The movie is called *You Fill Up My Void*. It should be somewhere by the TV."

"But that's the name of your hit song."

"I wrote the song for the movie."

In *You Fill Up My Void*, a comedian meets a producer who toys with the idea of putting her in a movie, but then decides not to after they sleep together. She's heartbroken and records a song called "You Fill Up My Void," which tops every chart in the closing credits montage.

"I was one of the biggest people in advertising—but in movies? I was nobody. When I found the lead actress, I knew she was the perfect girl, but she couldn't take off work. I said, 'How much would you need to live on?' and she said, '$500 a week,' so I said, 'Okay.' Except for her and a couple people, none of us were actors!"

I applauded Jooks' frontiersmanship and moxie. The story of someone trying to succeed at anything was enough for my tender sensibilities.

"I finished the movie in two months. I spent all my money. Every studio rejected me."

"Impossible!"

"Every single one. Finally, I called a friend of a friend who was an entertainment lawyer and begged him for a meeting with an executive at Columbia who he vaguely knew. The executive said, 'Well, unfortunately, while we like your movie, we just don't see a way to sell it.'

"I couldn't take it anymore. I stuck my finger in his chest and I said, 'Listen you stupid fucker, you're gonna take my fuckin' movie whether you like it or not. I've worked too hard, I poured too much money into this...' and he said, 'Okay, okay, if I had known you were gonna get that upset...' They agreed to play my movie for one week in Seattle, Portland, and Austin.

"In the meantime, I drove to every radio station around Austin, Seattle, Portland. I gave them a copy of my song to play—bribed them sometimes! That's what you did with radio!"

"You knew advertising."

"I knew advertising. The song played on the radio, it got a Billboard ranking. I went into record stores and gave them boxes of the single to sell. When the movie came out, the song was playing everywhere—"

"Whoa."

"The theaters were packed. I was back in New York. It was snowing at eleven o'clock at night when they called and said I was getting a nationwide release. I ran out into the street and dropped down on my knees and screamed up into the sky."

Jooks raised both fists, intoxicated with victory. When the sky unlocked, it swallowed whispers and engulfed futures, and snowflakes vanished into him. A god pinned to the earth by skyscrapers. "You can't be weak with anyone. You can't be meek," he explained. "You have to force your way in, or else have very powerful friends. That's how it works. The song won every award. Then I had to tour."

"You were famous!"

"Of course, I was. But I didn't like it."

"I wouldn't like it."

"People would recognize me. I would see them and run. I moved to London. I composed for the musical *Metropolis* on the West End. You heard of it?"

"No. I'll check it out."

"It did okay. Best of all, I married a Playboy cover girl."

"You mean centerfold?"

"She was on the cover."

"Nice."

"Will's mom. I got a second movie deal back in the states. This one I directed, wrote, composed, and starred in. That's the other poster in the hallway, *I Will Probably Never See You*."

"You acted? Cool!"

"I didn't want to! The actress I wanted had just finished *Charlie's Angels*, a huge movie at the time. She had a screen test for our f-f-focus group."

"You mean where an audience turns a little knob if they like the actor?"

"Yep, so they can see if it will make

(229)

money. I asked to read with her because I wanted her to feel encouraged. I just read from the script but she was totally prepared. The studio called and said, 'We have good news and bad news.' I said, 'Oh, no—did she test poorly?' They said, 'She beat out every girl.' I said, 'What's the bad news then?' They said, 'You beat out every guy. You've gotta play the starring role.' I didn't want to cause I was fuckin' exhausted, but they wouldn't budge! They wanted me to be like Woody Allen."

"It's cause you weren't trying."

"Huh?"

"In school, they say sometimes the best acting happens when you're not even trying. The Actors' Studio rejected Dustin Hoffman like a dozen times. Another actor asked him to be their scene partner. He said yes as a favor, and they accepted him."

"Amateur bullshit. I always try when I succeed. Anybody can be in a film."

"Oh."

"You're a goddamn know-it-all."

"Did the movie do well?"

MAMMA'S VOID

"It did terrible. I thought it was good. Then, I didn't do anything for a long time."

"Oh, no."

"Let's watch the film! It's great!"

I Will Probably Never See You begins with Movie Jooks getting dumped by his college girlfriend at a snowy ski resort. Many years later as a successful film composer, Movie Jooks bumps into her again. "You know how I always brag that I conducted the New York Philharmonic two times?" Jooks interjected. "Well, that's because I hired the New York Philharmonic for this scene! That's them on the screen! We did two takes!"

Movie Jooks and his college ex are in bed together. She goes, "I'm not a forever person. Never have been, never will be. Let's just share our love while we can." Sadness lingers.

Then they ride down the highway in a red convertible with the wind blowing in their hair and white sweaters tied jauntily around their shoulders, jog around a track wearing 1970s tracksuits, share an ice cream cone, sail on a yacht, and ride horses on a beach.

"That was my yacht!" he interjected. "And guess what? Those were my horses!"

"That's so resourceful," I said.

They pull up to his hotel, and they speak in broken whispers and long close-ups.

"Well, it was nice knowin' ya. Lotsa luck," says Movie Jooks.

"Please!" she begs him.

"Goodbye."

"Goodbye...."

Movie Jooks is sad. Then it's Christmas. Carols mingle with children's laughter. Someone knocks. Movie Jooks answers. The ex bought a plane ticket to New York. Now she's on his doorstep.

"You're here!" says Movie Jooks.

"I wanted to come." She is holding a present wrapped in jolly paper.

"I thought you weren't a forever person," he says.

"I'm not," she assures him, "but I'd still like to try."

END

"Wasn't it great?"

MAMMA'S VOID

"Yeah!" I said. "Great!"

I walked fifty blocks to Union Square. At night, the city was a cheap light fixture installed over a cosmos with no frontier. I flitted along the anesthetic storefronts.

My parents would receive a turkey dinner from Whole Foods. I could help from afar. The year before, we ate rotisserie chicken from PathMark in their motel room, surrounded by things from the old house. They'd rented me the adjacent room for the night, where I scribbled out song lyrics in order to become Bob Dylan and lift my parents from adversity. Stage lights silhouetted my gaunt frame, harmonica rack, a puff of untamed curls. At breakfast, the lobby had a folding table of coffee and powdered donuts. I would need to grow accustomed to life on the road once the band started booking tours.

"Oh friend, friend, where have you gone?" I wailed into the abyss of Hazel's voicemail. "Everything is terrible, and I have nothing. Nothing!" But Hazel was studying in Thailand.

JÖYCE

The all-night Tower Records was plastered in banners that said, "Going Out Of Business" and "Biggest Sale Ever." I picked *Small Change* and *Orphans: Brawlers, Bawlers & Bastards* by Tom Waits. I read Eminem's whole autobiography in the cafe and replaced it on the clearance shelf.

I clutched my exquisite $300 heels and studied the album cover of Tom Waits in a dressing room in front of a stripper and thought how much it would suck to still be that stripper.

CHAPTER 24:
NEGATIVITY SCENE

December marked holiday tidings. Jooks brought Mimsy and me to Daawat with his daughter Maya. I sat pecking at the paneer and tikka masala while Mimsy slyly referenced Jooks' call girls, giggled with Maya's boyfriend, and demonstrated the different styles of cutlery etiquette.

Maya's twin brother, Mark, was visiting the next Sunday.

Mark's daughters were Molly and Gale. Jooks put a hand to his heart.

"I just love Molly, the youngest. She's three. We went to a restaurant after I was released from the hospital. I was walking for the first time since my stroke. Molly took my hand. She's this tall." He marked the air somewhere below the table. "She led me from the chair so carefully and said, 'Don't worry, Grandpa, I'll make sure you don't fall.' Can you imagine?" Jooks chuckled. "The older one, Gale...meh. I don't like her so much. She made a face when her parents told her to sit in my lap. Nine years old. What a jerk. Anyway, each of them gets three books."

"Any particular kind, Jooks?"

"Whatever—just not too expensive."

"You might have fun picking them out."

"Nah."

For Gale, I chose *Encyclopedia of Faeries, A Light in the Attic,* and *A Wrinkle in Time.* For Molly, I got *The Diary of a Wimpy Kid, Calvin and Hobbes,* and *Where the Sidewalk Ends.* I flipped through *The Gashlycrumb Tinies,* an alphabet book about children who die, thinking about my situation in this world, and grateful I'd stopped imitating Jooks and text-harassing Japetto. "M is for Mimsy," I hummed to myself, "Too pure for this world...J is for Jooks who assaulted twelve girls."

I presented the books to Jooks already wrapped in paper that was covered with drawings of books.

"Great. I'd like you and...what's her n-name?"

"Mimsy."

NEGATIVITY SCENE

"Right! I keep wanting to call her s-sponge.' I'd like you and Mimsy to be there."

Assigning wrong words was an effect of the stroke called aphasia. Still, I envied her for evoking porous absorbency.

Mimsy forced a gentle smile when she saw me at the house a few days before Christmas. "I had no idea you would be here!"

"Are we getting paid for this?" I asked.

"I'm definitely charging him. I'm so happy you're here!"

"He sent me to buy books for his grandkids and probably felt obligated."

"I'm so glad! How has it been?"

"He's crazy, but the hours are good."

She reached around me for her diet ginger ale.

"How are auditions?" I asked.

"So-so," she said. "I'm auditioning for amazing people and projects, and I get called back, but then the role goes to someone else. I almost got a feature guest role, but the casting director told my agents she didn't have enough examples of previous work, so they went with someone more experienced. I'm talking with them about doing more non-union and student films."

"I wish I was in your position. I've done student films but an agent seems unattainable."

"I thought you were, like, a theater person."

"Why? Doesn't everyone kind of need both? I mean...you're incredibly savvy so you must know it's impossible to get theater gigs without film credits."

"So, to do that, you need to, like, know all those people. So things with Jooks are okay. Does he seem to like me?"

"It's weird...he alternates between loving you and threatening to fire you," I said.

"He said he wants to fire me?"

"I'm sure he talks about firing me. I think he does it as a way of pitting us against each other to maintain power."

"I think you're right. We can't let him do that. He sometimes says he wants to fire you," she admitted.

NEGATIVITY SCENE

"That fucker! I refuse to fucking stroke his ego! I can't stand humoring his delusions whatsoever."

"I know you can't." She sounded worried for me. I couldn't fathom why.

"He talks about hiring a third girl. Then he'd probably let one of us go."

"We can't let him. We have to juggle him and keep each other from getting fired."

"I know. To be honest Mimsy, I mean, I need this job now because my parents lost their house, but if I had a safety net, I would never. I wonder why you stick around someone so toxic."

"It's hard to get a job where you can take off for auditions. I need the structure. Plus, it's kind of interesting."

"I don't get how you handle him so well, without seeming to absorb the negative emotion."

"I just don't put up with his bullshit. I hate to say it, but you kind of mother him. If he asks me for something ridiculous, I say, 'Do it yourself.' If he freaks out over something idiotic, I fucking laugh at him."

"Fuck," I sputtered, nearly in tears, "he treats me like shit. It's like you get paid to go to dinner and get your nails done. Why do I always get groceries and empty trash? I've let the ball drop with auditions because I work here all the time..."

"You can't say that. I'm here all the time, and I audition. I try to do chores and errands, but he won't let me! It isn't easy for me always. He calls me for advice. He asked his trainer to marry him. It was this whole drama where she cried and told him about sleeping in the subway her first night in New York. He was so mad at me when it didn't work out, I had to suck up to him for a whole week. You? You're indispensable."

"I did kind of make that my strategy. I'm pretty much incapable of faking any admiration for him, so I acquired enough tasks where it's too inconvenient to fire me." I flinched at how easily Mimsy appealed to my vanity.

"Scheduling, phone calls, groceries, you're really good with those details... and I'm just not." Her tone became sickeningly sweet. "Like you're the real

assistant. I'm, well, more of a friend."
She shrugged, accepting her lot. "Oh,
umm, can you open this for me?" She
held out her soda can. "I don't want to
mess up my manicure."

"Sure," I said, as entire generations
of coal miners died inside of me.

"They're coming up from the lobby,"
Jooks said. "I gotta get you a job with
Mark so I can fire you."

"Jooks wants his son to cast me in
a commercial," Mimsy said. "It'd be
$10,000 to survive on while I look for
other work."

"Any idiot can be in a commercial,"
he muttered.

If anyone would be rewarded for
Mimsy's negligence at her post, it was me.

"Ooh, I want to be in a commercial
too, Jooks. Can you tell your son to cast
us both?" I said Mimsily. "Maybe Mimsy
and I could be in one together. How fun
would that be?! Please, Jooks?"

Mimsy snapped her head to glare at
me but I held my bright-eyed stare. He
looked worriedly between the two of us.

Mimsy ducked into the bathroom

just as Mark and Liz ushered in their two little girls.

"This is J-J-Jöyce..." Jooks introduced me as they dropped an Eli's smoked fish basket off in the kitchen. "My other assistant is much younger."

"Actually, she's just one year younger," I corrected him cheerily. "It's confusing since she's two years behind me in school."

"Nobody a-a-asked you," Jooks said.

"Dad, do you have plans for Christmas?"

"I might see a friend."

He was petitioning Masha to duck out from dinner with her boyfriend's family to spend an hour at the River Cafe for double her usual rate.

"Who's this 'friend,' Jooks?" Mimsy mocked.

I froze in horror. She would stage her audition, here and now. The family seemed briefed beforehand not to ask questions about Grandpa's "special friends."

"It was so nice of you to bring the basket from Eli's," Mimsy continued as if welcoming guests into her own home. "I always feel you can tell a person's background by how they eat. I'm also Jewish." She gazed expectantly at Mark and his wife.

"I'm Episcopalian," Liz offered.

"I was born Jewish," said Mark, twiddling his thumbs and shrugging, "but we do Christmas/Hannukah type of stuff. Not actually religious, just..."

"...for the aesthetic!" I finished, enlivened by the spectacle of Mimsy's failure. "I just love the food you brought too! I'm not Jewish as far as I know...I mean my mom was secretly adopted so...you never know. Good food is non-denominational!"

Mark and Liz smiled, and Mimsy furrowed her brow.

"What do you both do?" asked Liz.

"Well, I'm an actress," Mimsy admitted.

"Yeah, me too..." I sighed.

"How is that going?" Liz asked, trying to sound positive.

"I mean, it's so difficult," said Mimsy. She had a mature sense of the odds, in contrast to my clownish certainty. Even in defeat, watching Mimsy negotiate was quality training.

"And what about you?" asked Liz.

"I've done a ton of independent, off-off...off...Broadway, downtown, Brooklyn, no-to-low pay, experimental sort of theater. Some of it's been good, most not so great, but I've padded my resume. And now I'm interested in writing more and choosing what I act in more carefully. I figure if I'm going to do something that's badly written, it might as well be my writing."

Liz chuckled. Mimsy held her angelic glow.

"I mean, I went to school for acting so I over-academicize things," I continued.

"Where did you study?"

"NYU," I mumbled with Kurt Cobainian self-deprecation.

"I didn't have any formal training... my parents made me go to Harvard," Mimsy said reluctantly. Mark smiled at us both with glassy exhaustion.

"Want to sit in Grandpa's lap?" Mark said to Gail. She inched over to Jooks and sat stiffly on the edge of his cobbly knees. Jooks smiled. Her eyes seared into her mother.

"Mommy can I sit with you now?" she squirmed.

"Sure, honey." Gail flew into her mother's lap as I exhaled. Molly smiled sweetly at Jooks. She was decked out in bohemian striped knee socks, chunky wool knits, a breezy ragamuffin skirt, and little canvas Mary Janes.

"Molly dresses herself," Liz smiled, wearing crisp earth tones with her thick hair coiffed back into a tidy ponytail herself. She was practiced in deflecting glances of inquiry to buy a daughter a few more years of nonconformity. Molly fiddled with a rhinestone button as they all said goodbye and left.

Jooks started laughing as the door closed.

"Mark pulled me aside and said, 'Dad, couldn't you have picked girls a little older?' He thought you were both hookers! So much for the commercial."

He screamed in laughter and slapped his knee.

JÖYCE

We lined up before the bagels, cream cheese, bialy, smoked salmon, sturgeon, sable, and herring. On the loveseat built for two, Jooks' femur dug into my left with Mimsy on my right. I hoped the football game on TV would end soon.

Mimsy fumbled the serving fork under a clingy sheet of lox until Jooks grasped the scrap of flesh in his fist and shook it off his hand onto her plate, eyes still fixed on the TV. "There," he squawked.

We glanced at one another from the corners of our eyes, bodies quaking with silent laughter.

CHAPTER 25

THE OLD MAN AND THE C

Mimsy returned to New England for Christmas. She mitigated Jooks' mistrust of her refusal to endorse his pursuit of another gym trainer, to her great professional risk in favor of the general good. At least he craved her daughterly warmth that shone like an Exxon station on the barren highway of his existence. Mimsy texted him occasionally. "Hi, Jooks! How are you! Hope you are having a great day!!!" Her exclamation points exhausted me. To Jooks, they were tender keepsakes.

"H-h-h-hi honey!" he cooed. "H-how are you?"

Her plush rasp wafted from the phone, and he slipped out of the room for privacy.

"She doesn't know when she's coming back!" He shook a fist at the air. "Of all the rotten...She's no good."

Mimsy had fallen ill. Her parents were taking her to the doctor.

"I wanna show you something." Jooks

rifled through the drawer. "I once made an album. It didn't do too well. I thought it was great. Take a look."

He handed me a cardboard record sleeve.

Jooks sat on a bale of hay in the middle of a barn, ukelele on his knee. A wheat stem dangled from his mouth. Standing all around him were seven or eight dwarves holding musical instruments.

"Huh," I said, "so is surrounding yourself with much smaller people a sort of...statement...about other musicians... in relation to you?"

"Yeah, something like that," he said.

"Wow, you look so much like Will in this picture."

"Oh, I'm MUCH handsomer!" he laughed.

Jooks handed me a stack of hundreds and the list of building staff that had been slipped under the door of each apartment.

"We gotta tip 'em," he muttered, "or there's gonna be trouble. They've got a union...it's terrible."

THE OLD MAN AND THE C

Named and stuffed, I handed the stack of envelopes to the doorman in the lobby.

"He give you a tip?" Robert asked.

"I wasn't expecting one. I'm getting a ton of hours this week."

"You ain't even get off for Christmas? Wow. Hard worker. You should definitely be getting a tip."

Jooks was at Prada trying to talk Masha into Christmas dinner. I hung out with Alina in the kitchen on her housekeeping shift.

"Where is that from?" I asked.

"It's guava cream cheese coffee cake. I got it in the Bronx. You want some?"

"Sugar makes me break out."

"Where's Mimsy?"

"She's away. I don't know how long. I think she's sick."

"One time, Mimsy stood in the doorway and held out her empty soda can like this. Asking me to throw it away! She stood there going through her cellphone, with her whole arm up in the air dangling the soda can until— no joke—I put down the dishes, turned off the water, took off my gloves, and walked all the way across the kitchen to take it out of her hand for her."

"Are you serious?" I laughed. "She could have thrown it away in the time that it took for her to ask you. Without interrupting her cellphone."

"I know."

"It seems like, sometimes, people who were raised with housekeepers and maids and stuff seem to think—"

"—that every housekeeper is their housekeeper?"

"Exactly. It's really weird. I don't even think she knows."

"Yeah, like...she's actually a nice person. But then she'll do stuff like that," said Alina.

"I honestly don't know how to deal with it."

"Are you going home on Christmas?"

"I have to work. My parents lost their house."

"I didn't know that," she said, her amazement overwhelmed the usual show of sympathy. "I'm sorry."

"No, it's fine."

THE OLD MAN AND THE C

"So, you get a bonus?" Alina searched me with her eyes.

"The doorman asked that too. Should I? I'm getting a ton of hours."

"He's supposed to give you a Christmas bonus."

"You should get one—I mean, your commute is ridiculous."

"Yeah. He not gonna give me one, though."

"Really? He gave one to the doormen..."

"Cause he's gotta see their faces every day."

"Okay. Damn, I didn't think about it, but now I feel bad if you're not getting one."

"We should both get a tip. Also, he asked me to work Christmas Eve, but I gotta help prepare a big meal for my family."

"What'd he say?"

"He said 'If you don't like it, I can hire someone else.'"

"Like Scrooge in *A Christmas Carol*."

"I know but he's Jewish, so...."

"Doesn't he celebrate Christmas? His movies all have Christmas stuff."

(251)

"You didn't know he was Jewish?"

"No. What does being Jewish have to do with tipping, though?" I said.

"Never mind. Nothing. Can you ask if he'd change his mind?"

"Sure."

"I'm gonna ask him for a raise after Christmas. If I don't get it, I think I'll quit. My friend Adele cleans the penthouse upstairs. She'll get me another job."

"That's good. I'm happy for anyone who doesn't have to be around him."

"He treats you badly too. I hear the way he yells at you."

"I know. I should leave. I'm going to, eventually."

"When?" she asked.

"I should figure that out."

"Umm, Jooks," I said the next morning, "Alina was wondering if she could have off Christmas Eve and come in the day after Christmas."

"NO!" roared Jooks.

"I see."

"Did she ask you to say that?"

"She said 'See you Christmas Eve,' so

I asked about it."

"Well, no need to mention it yourself," Jooks sneered.

"Sure. But you're paying her holiday hours?"

"NO, goddamnit!" he bellowed.

"Okay. That's an interesting way to say it."

"Would you shut up!"

"Okay," I said.

"If she doesn't fucking like it, there are people who would do anything for that job."

I texted the whole exchange to Alina, as promised.

"Oh well :(see you Christmas Eve..." she texted back.

Jooks was feeling foul because Mimsy hadn't given him a return date.

"She'll 'let me know.' What does that mean? If this was a real job, she'd be fired," he muttered.

A few cheerful texts from Mimsy later, Jooks had a change of heart. "Go to Chanel. Buy a bottle of Chanel No. 5. I want you to mail it to Mimsy. She MUST receive it Christmas Day."

JÖYCE

Deep within my marrow, something ruptured.

"I don't know her address."

"Ask her!"

"Okay."

"Don't ruin the surprise! Say it's so you can send her a Christmas card."

"That will sound weird. I'd never do that."

"Did she text you back?"

"I actually haven't pressed send yet."

"Why the fuck not?"

"I haven't finished writing the text."

"Well, why?"

"Because you're talking." I pressed send, then spun away and strutted into the kitchen.

"HEYYYY!" cried Jooks.

"She hasn't written back. I can go to Chanel in the meantime."

Devoid of urgency, I sucked down a glass of Diet Coke.

"You better fuckin' have that thing mailed on the right day!" he shouted.

"I'll bring you the carbon copy." I routinely mailed things for Jooks, like Will's college ID or envelopes of cash to his Mexican butler.

THE OLD MAN AND THE C

To spite him, I stopped into Petrossian and used his cash to buy a coffee and financier. I heaved open the massive double doors to Chanel and stepped inside like the place ain't shit.

I thought of suggesting that I pick up some Chanel No. 5 at Macy's, alongside the Jessica Simpson and Beyoncé perfumes, or buy it on Amazon.com, alongside holy water. I ignored his blocked number while the cashier rung up the shit. Instead of letting me go straight to UPS, to ensure the package would arrive on time, he texted me to stop home so he could personally sign the card, even though he had never handwritten anything else, since I'd known him, unless legally required. He dictated his message to Mimsy, "Dear Sweetheart, Merry Christmas. You won." Whatever the fuck that prize was, I didn't want it. He carefully added his own signature, which he usually made me forge.

Maybe it was a plot between Jooks and Mimsy to falsely accuse me of forging my paychecks and present the holiday card as proof of his real signature, I thought, half serious and half questioning.

Jooks talked his psychiatrist into an extra appointment before the holiday.

"I don't get why he can't see me until the day after Christmas. He's an atheist!"

"Even atheists need a day off," I replied.

I chatted in the waiting room with Karen, who nannied a client of the child psychiatrist occupying the adjacent office. Karen was from the islands and had the deep focus and melodic speech of somebody who hasn't spent the majority of her life urban multitasking while feeling like shit. We usually started the conversation by saying how tired we were, and I'd ask Karen about her three kids, who got all A's, fixed themselves dinner, and drank homemade organic juice.

When my friend Ryan went to Barbados, she said nobody had credit cards. Instead of getting a whole house and paying off a mortgage where you lose everything if you fall behind, people saved money to build their house one piece at a time, only paying for what they owned. Living in an unfinished house was normal.

Karen's charge emerged from her appointment. She had waist-long hair and black Chuck Taylor high tops. "Don't you love my beautiful new iPod?"

She sang and danced.

I liked the child psychiatrist because she gave her clients snacks and eyed Jooks suspiciously.

After his appointment, Jooks tasted the five different soups from Hale & Hearty and selected "chicken and rice" for lunch. Around three o'clock, he shoved two $100 bills at me.

"Here. Go Home."

"Oh, thank you so much! I really wasn't expecting—"

"Ah, shut up. Have Christmas Eve to yourself."

"Well, thanks Jooks—I really wasn't expecting anything—Merry Christmas!" I smiled.

"M-m-m-merry Christmas." He put a hand on my shoulder. "Please be here on time."

JÖYCE

I had forty hours to myself. I felt so fine, I thought I could afford to buy a few things.

I went into Diesel and got two pairs of jeans, one on sale for $150, the other for $170. I'd never spent that much even on a winter coat or shoes. The freedom to buy clothes could replace my actual freedom. Then I went to The Guitar Center and bought a microphone for making internet videos because the internet was like freedom to me. I shot a video in our living room about someone who puts a teabag in a mug full of whiskey to hide their drunkenness.

I called Hazel.

"Oh, Boggis," she proclaimed in holiday goodwill, "will you partake of my Christmas Eve family dinner?" She had made a video montage of feasts, snowball fights, and bellowing holiday carolers set to festive mandolin. Hazel's table of cheer was the only cure.

My Shame of All Things lifted in light of our Great Friendship.

"I would love nothing more,

THE OLD MAN AND THE C

Cottswald. I'm tired. I only have a half-day to decide. I'm editing a video."

I heard the clamor of music and cooking utensils. In a rush of holiday euphoria—for how do holidays happen?—I returned a video celebrating that I, Spud, was coming!

I boarded a Chinatown bus the next day, and by 6:00 p.m., set foot in four inches of Philadelphia snow. The fir-branch-draped marble arches of the 30th Street Station echoed with greeting. I took a train to the suburbs. Hazel and her brother made lone tire tracks as I waited under a cone of lamplight swirling with snow. My clamped-down heartbreaks were free to throb. New York City had reduced me to a caged tangle of reptilian emotion, reacting to stimulus but not actually feeling the subjectivity of my response.

Hazel presented me with Christmas dinner and a tiny ascot that she had crocheted. We all played Scattergories. Her dad eyed me unhappily, knowing he'd be the one to deposit me at the

11:00 p.m. train so I could catch my 1:00 a.m. bus. I returned to New York for a full night's sleep, invigorated once more.

"The fucking package didn't get there!" Jooks screamed, to greet me Christmas morning.

"I showed you the carbon copy of the package slip," I said.

"WELL, YOU FUCKED IT UP!"

"No. I told you they can't guarantee Christmas Day delivery."

"I KNEW YOU WOULD FUCK IT UP. CALL UPS!!"

"Hi—I'm calling about a package. Can I give you the tracking number?"

"Tell them I'm an Academy-Award Winner."

"Jooks, she informed me, once again, that they don't guarantee Christmas delivery."

"TELL THEM I'M AN ACADEMY-AWARD WINNER."

You could catch a plane to Boston and hand deliver it, like in your movie, I thought.

"YOU... FUCKIN'..." he sputtered.

(260)

THE OLD MAN AND THE C

"Sorry about that—I have two people talking to me at the same time—" I was approaching tears and my voice squeaked. "Jooks, it's already there. Looks like Mimsy failed to notice it on the doorstep."

"It's not her fault. Hang up and call her."

I dialed lackadaisically.

"She's not answering."

"Call 'er again!"

"It's 10:00 a.m. on Christmas morning."

"I KNOW AND I WANTED HER GIFT TO BE THERE!"

"P.S., you know she's Jewish right?"

"I don't care. Call her!"

In a couple hours, Jooks' phone rang.

"H-h-h-h-honey h-h-h-h-have you got it?"

"Thank you, Jooks...so thoughtful!" I could hear her. His phone was on max volume.

"Sweetie, you're welcome. Merry Christmas. I miss you."

"Um...the card says, 'You won.' What did I win?"

"Aw, honey, you know. You know you won."

"I don't know."

"You know."

"No, really I don't! Did I win the perfume? That's what you meant, isn't it, Jooks? I get it now! Yay, I won! I won the perfume! SO thoughtful! Again, thank you."

"M-m-m-merry Christmas, sweetheart."

"Merry Christmas to you too, Jooks...!"

"I miss ya'!"

"Awww...so sweet! Miss you."

"Wh-wh-wh-wh-when are you gonna c-c-c-come to your senses and get b-back here??"

"I'm not sure Jooks...I haven't seen my family in a while."

"Aw, honey," he sighed.

"Oh, Jooks, some of my cousins who I haven't seen in years just got here. Can I call later?"

"Okay, honey. C-c-c-call back later."

"WHAT WAS THAT!!!!" Mimsy texted me.

"I. Do not. Know." I replied.

THE OLD MAN AND THE C

"CREEPY!!!!"

"Yes. Yes, indeed."

Jooks acted like the past twenty-four hours of my hazing hadn't occurred. He became increasingly irritable. The violent flu further delayed Mimsy's return. The New Year golden ball dropped on TV. I amassed a record number of billable hours.

Jooks flipped off *Grey's Anatomy*. I'd rewritten my hours the night before and thumbed the sweaty square of paper, working up the courage to ask for my money.

I was afraid that if I waited for Mimsy to return, he might decide it was more convenient to fire me.

"You can go." He stared straight ahead.

"Umm...Jooks..."

"What is it?"

"I, uh, was hoping to be paid."

"What?"

"I have my hours from the last two weeks."

"Two weeks?" He scanned my

arithmetic. "No," he shook his head, "this is wrong."

"What?" I gulped.

"Eleven hours a day? Twelve hours a day?! That's a lie! You never worked that long!"

"I did." I held his eye.

"You were never here that long!" His voice rose.

"Yes, I was, Jooks!"

"You were late!"

"I wrote when I was late, see?"

"This is all wrong!" he shouted.

"Jooks, it is exactly right, rounded to the closest fifteen-minute increment as you requested."

"Boy, was I wrong about you!"

"I triple checked the math!"

"I'M NOT PAYIN' YOU!" His shout was deafening.

I broke into a cold sweat. "Yes, you are!" I wailed. "You're fucking paying me! I'm going to go home and figure out how to prove that I'm not lying and when I come back tomorrow: You. Will. Fuck. King. Pay. Me!"

Adrenaline hung in the air.

THE OLD MAN AND THE C

Jooks fired back, "NO!" forcefully, but distinctly pacified.

"I WILL COME IN TOMORROW WITH SOME WAY OR ANOTHER TO PROVE I HAVE WORKED THIS NUMBER OF HOURS. AND THEN YOU WILL PAY ME."

"FUCK YOU!"

Jooks shuffled to his bedroom.

"WELL FUCK YOU TOO!" I stormed out. "HAVE A REALLY GOOD NIGHT, JOOKS! SEE YA TOMORROW...ON PAYDAY!"

"Dumb motherfucker," I muttered, but with all my vocal resonance, so it would reverberate through the elevator shaft for eternity. I busted through the lobby, still quivering.

"Have a good night!" I smiled at Dorian, who had been a bouncer, a prison guard, a driver, owned properties, and worked the overnight. He had the same clean movie-star charisma as Jooks' lawyer. I had no faculties for chit-chat.

At home, I facebooked Mimsy in case Jooks tried to ban me from the building.

The next morning, he acted blameless.

"Good morning! Ah, you're on time."

"Jooks, remember when we watched *Grey's Anatomy*?"

"Yes..."

"Remember when we watched *Boston Public*?"

"...Yes..."

"And *Hachiko: A Dog's Tale*, with what's-his-face from *Pretty Woman*."

"Richard Gere? How can you forget him?"

"So the TV Guide proves I was here until 11:00 p.m. See my text messages that say 'Sorry, Jooks, I'm on the elevator running a few minutes late'? Those show my arrival times."

"Okay, okay." He turned away.

"Jooks, you blew up at me last night."

"There's lots to do..."

"Can you pay me?"

"Later."

"No. Now."

"At the end of the day."

"Alright."

"I'm an old man. I can't remember when you came and left. We need to put a sheet of paper by the door where you clock in and out or else I'm not gonna remember."

He sighed, embarrassed, so I pitied him. It did not explain his rage. I realized I couldn't always read him. But still, I wouldn't have thought he was testing my weakness for any more sinister reasons.

CHAPTER 26

THE GIRLFRIEND EXPERIENCE

"Go to my psychiatrist and pick up my Viagra. I have a date tonight," Jooks said.

I'd never been inside Dr. Shore's office. Even though he was a prominent psychiatrist, I sensed no evil about him and felt very much at ease—welcomed, even—in his presence.

"Jooks, uh, respects you, I think," he chatted, searching for the key to his desk.

"Huh. Is respect even on his emotional landscape, the way you or I might recognize it? I've been learning about narcissism online. Have you read *Malignant Self Love*? It's an eBook."

"No, I can't say I have..."

He unlocked the drawer and, instead of the prescription I expected, handed me a sack of pills closed with a twist tie, like from the bulk section at Whole Foods. No time to question the legalities, I buttoned this into my coat pocket and cabbed it back to Jooks.

The next morning, Jooks was in love. "Hannah walked into the room. I took one look, and I knew."

Jooks met Hannah through a phone number named Harvest. Harvest traveled the country and seemed to have many friends my age in search of meaningful companionship with the old and wealthy. "And get this," he continued, "I'm her first and only time working as a hooker. God, I'm in love!"

After their first night, Jooks was courting Hannah with dates, shopping trips, and spending money. They quickly became an item.

Jooks didn't want me anywhere near. I took it as a compliment that he didn't trust me to validate their relationship. Mimsy was back on her pedestal, accompanying them to boutiques, nail salons, lunches, free to come and go for auditions. She gave him just enough advice to hang onto love for the work week. When Hannah was elsewhere, I came over to do the drudgery.

"Ugh, she's Irish. You should see her when we go out! Three bottles of wine! Four bottles of wine!"

I marveled at anyone surviving a

date with Jooks on so little but also would never want to let my guard down or be under the influence around him. Now that Jooks had deregulated the hourly price of sex, Hannah could maximize profits, and Jooks could feel a woman's fake desire for the monster that he was. Paying for a pre-determined relationship, he rode his karma like a Ferris wheel, on the axis of a lesson unlearned.

The first time I met Hannah Baudelaire, she was ready to see *Avenue Q* on Broadway.

"She always says she's too tired to make love after our dates, so I'm gonna tell her the show got oversold, and we'll have a relaxing night in. You and Mimsy can have the tickets."

He waited until she arrived to tell her, so she had no excuse to cancel. Jooks had made us promise not to say where we were going.

"So what are you up to tonight?" asked Hannah.

"Mimsy and I are going to have dinner. Then I was thinking I'd make a YouTube video," I replied. It wasn't a lie since I was always thinking about making YouTube videos.

"Oh, you're an actress like Mimsy?" she asked.

"Oh. Ehh..."

"I used to want to be an actress. Then this casting director basically told me that if I didn't sleep with him, I'd never have a career."

"Oh, so what are you guys up to tonight?" My pleasantry felt like an act of violence, like making small talk with an abductee about which brand of duct tape they prefer.

"Jooks is taking me to the bank I guess," she grew sheepish. He'd written her multiple checks, canceling each at the last minute on suspicion she'd bolt. "He's giving me twenty grand, so I don't have to be poor anymore. After that, we'll grab dinner and maybe hang out."

Jooks came in like he was breaking up a union meeting.

"Wh-wh-wh-wh-what are you two talking about?"

"Telling Hannah about my video."

"Oh." Jooks grew suspicious. I might give her ideas.

Mimsy power walked from the kitchen, on a conference call with her team.

"Okay, I'm ready!" she smiled.

"Here," Jooks held out matching pink pullover sweaters embroidered with the Icelandic flag.

"Are these from Logan's trip to Iceland?" I said. Logan was the IT specialist Jooks paid every couple of months to install software updates on his computer.

"Sure are." Jooks looked at Hannah. "Logan is black, and his wife is white, so they decided to go on vacation to Iceland." He chuckled, likening their intergenerational relationship to Logan's interracial marriage.

"Wait, Iceland is bankrupt now, right?" I said.

"What an amazing sweater, Jooks..." Mimsy displayed it in front of her face in order to look at me and mouth, "Hideous."

"I like it. It's hipstery," I said.

GIRLFRIEND EXPERIENCE

"P-p-p-put them on," he said, "I wanna take a picture. Hey Logan!" Jooks summoned Logan from the den where he was checking for malware.

"You need something, Jooks?"

Logan walked into the living room in his usual business casual attire and overall pleasant demeanor. His relationship with Jooks was stress-free since he never gave him anything to be unhappy about.

"Th-they're gonna put the sweaters on to take a picture." I pulled on the sweater while Mimsy draped hers over her outfit. Logan smiled congenially next to us while the doorman Jooks had summoned took our picture.

We strolled outside. It was six o'clock. Jooks had slipped us twenty dollars for a snack.

Circling the Indian buffet at the Columbus Circle Whole Foods, Mimsy brought me up to speed. Jooks had been shopping the roster of a high-end call girl agency, never without complaint, disliking fake body parts and any insistence on a condom in spite of his vasectomy papers in the nightstand. Then he met Hannah.

"Isn't it fucked up," I said, "that we're seeing a Broadway show as the direct result of Jooks' decision to stay in tonight and pressure a girl our age for sex?"

"I mean, Jooks would probably have taken us to see this at some point."

"Right."

"We could scalp the tickets."

"It's even worse if we get direct cash. Also, I'm too cowardly to scalp them."

"Jooks and Hannah are going to do what they're going to do regardless."

"Yes, but...still."

"Hannah's a bartender. Do you know how much pretty young female bartenders make?"

"A lot, right?"

"A lot more than us. And Hannah's smart, she's not working at some shitty place. If she wants to have whatever kind of relationship she's having with Jooks, that's her choice."

"You never know people's reasons for doing stuff though."

GIRLFRIEND EXPERIENCE

"Jöyce, neither of us have anything to do with how they met, their choices in life, or how their relationship will run its course. We're trying to be actors. We should be getting these tickets, if anyone."

"I see, I see."

Beneath her refinement, Mimsy had a worldly intellect that far outpaced my quaint moral righteousness.

Two orders of macaroni and cheese, potato salad, and sweet potato fries congealed in a still life of the evening prior. "Clean this up," Jooks snapped, slamming the bedroom door. "Here! Text her: 'Why don't you give me back the $20,000 if you're so mad at me?'"

Hannah called while I stared at the blank TV.

"I was fucking trying to eat, and you grabbed my arm!" she said.

"You're supposed to be my girlfriend!" Jooks whined.

"You don't grab someone's arm in the middle of dinner and order them to have sex!"

JÖYCE

"Okay, Okay. I'm sorry, honey." He shushed her tenderly. "Wh-wh-wh-wh-when are you coming over next?"

CHAPTER 27

FEAR AND LOATHING IN LAS RAPIST

"You need to get us to the airport as soon as possible. Two articles about my trials got on the i-i-internet!" He was whisking Hannah off for a romantic week in Cabo San Lucas. It was Friday morning in mid-January, less than a month since they'd met.

I was to come in every weekday from nine to five. "I don't want Mimsy here while I'm gone," he warned.

We gathered in the den to coordinate the pre-departure errands. Hannah wore a Prada coat. Her face hung puffy over the mandarin collar with raven hair piled in a bun. Between her fingers gleamed the silver casing of an iPod Jooks had bought for her. Her nails were a rich red lacquer, upkept regularly thanks to Jooks.

"Ugh, I'm so hungover," she sighed, as if to make it up to Mimsy, Alina, and I.

Jooks chastised Mimsy for ordering an extra lunch for 'the maid,' like it would give her strength to lead the uprising, or ruin her taste for cleaning his apartment.

"Jooks was really mad at me," Mimsy fretted as we ate in the kitchen.

"Jooks is an assmaster," I said. "He's from a fucking Dickens novel."

"It's okay," Alina said. "Good thing he'll be gone soon."

I accidentally sighed with sincere longing, and we all laughed.

"It's good that we'll get to come in without him here," I said.

"Yeah," Alina replied. "Are you coming in too?" she asked Mimsy.

"No," said Mimsy, "I don't get it, he won't even give me a key. I only started a month after Jöyce did. It kind of hurts my feelings."

"Maybe you could ask him if we could split the week," I offered.

"I mean, he's still paying me," she admitted.

"He's paying you?"

"He said he wanted to pay me for the week, so I don't find a new job."

"Huh." It was necessary for my voice

to split from my body so as not to betray the shock and pain registering deep within my nervous system. Mimsy would be paid simply to exist while I would be required to both exist and complete tasks for an identical sum.

Jooks was taking Hannah and Mimsy for manicures while I was sent to The Sharper Image for a noise machine with an internationally compatible electrical plug.

When I returned, Jooks was there.

"There's a book Mimsy told me about—I'd like to read it on the plane."

"That's cool. So you're paying Mimsy for the week even though she's not coming in?"

"Yes. I want you to go and get the book."

"You. Want me. To go. And get. It?"

"Call her and ask the title."

"Mimsy's getting paid to get a manicure. You want me to fetch a book she suggested."

"Don't make trouble, honey." Jooks closed his eyes wearily. I cursed aloud and snatched the phone from his outstretched hand.

Mimsy answered her phone.

"Hey Jöyce. Um, could you just redo these three nails?" I heard her say to the manicurist. "Sorry. What's up?"

"Jooks wants me to pick up the book you suggested."

"Should I pick it up? There's a bookstore on the way home."

"Jooks, she says she can pick it up."

"NO!" he snapped.

"What was the title?" I asked.

"Shaushaurs," came her relaxed and breathy rasp.

"Sorry, what?"

"Shaushaurs," she answered.

"Uh—I still didn't hear that…"

"Shaurshaurs," she said again, exactly as before.

"Yes…I…no. I'm sorry. Can you say that…one more time?"

"Shaurshaurs," she spoke again. Perhaps it was a control tactic.

"Okay…this is unbelievable but…the phone must be a little fuzzy…I still can't hear the word. Can you, um, spell that?"

"'Out', like the opposite of 'in.' 'Liers'

FEAR AND LOATHING

like a person who lies, but in the sun. *Outliers*. By Malcolm Gladwell. Can you tell Jooks we're going to be longer? Hannah's getting waxed."

I shuddered and hung up.

"Get a roll of blue ribbon too while you're out. It's gotta be blue," he said.

I got the book at Barnes & Noble and stopped at Papyrus for ribbon and bought myself a royal blue fine-felt-tipped Le Pen with Jooks' money. To this day it still has ink.

"What do you need the ribbon for?" I asked.

"It's to tie around the suitcase handles. For luck."

CHAPTER 28

EAT, PREY, LOVE

Crawley packed the trunk of the airport car service, eyes fixed on Hannah's ass.

"Hey c'mon, hurry up," Jooks grumbled.

I stood with Mimsy on the curb. The car shrank into the distance. Several knots in my back loosened. "I'm still kind of bummed he doesn't give me a key," said Mimsy. We made our way into Le Pain Quotidien.

"Yeah." I matched her tone of sympathy. "I'm kind of bummed he's paying us the exact same thing but I have to work and you don't."

"Here, how about I pour the creamer?" said the woman ahead of us. "Really inefficient management not to have the customers serve their own half and half."

Were she a barista at Le Pain Quotidien, she'd have worked her way back to executive in no time.

I returned from the restroom to oatmeal with bananas, walnuts, honey, yogurt, and brown sugar. "I wasn't sure what you liked," Mimsy said, mixing more hot water into her plain oats. The waitress brought her a ramekin of raspberries. "Oh, do you mind getting me another thing of berries? They just look like they could be fresher."

The berries were fresh, but it was possible they had denied her fresher ones. *Extract or be extracted,* I thought.

"So, what are you up to?" asked Mimsy.

"I'm trying to write," I said.

"What are you writing?"

"A play. I don't know if I'm good enough to write it."

"Well," she posited, "how do you get good at writing?"

"By writing," I said.

"Right. Say, how about you write something for the both of us, then my agent can sign you!" Mimsy exclaimed, with a glimmer of a thought-just-occurred. It was generous, but I feared the realities. All I had left was the privacy of my writing, and now she wanted that.

JÖYCE

"I mean, does your agent even want someone like me?" It sounded like something a loser would say, but I decided to go with it anyway. "Writing shitty plays is just what I need to do right now. I can't burden some poor actor."

She looked at me with deep concern. I'd grown up near three different halfway homes, with the elderly and forgotten pacing past our front yard, people begging for change at the neighborhood store, preferring the cruelty of the elements to the cruelty of societal participation. This fate, I feared, was embedded in me too.

Later that day, I bought a cup of tea in a booth at a chilly, empty salad place that smelled of mildew, to work more on *The Unloveables*, which was handwritten in my battered spiral notebook. Fictional me was living beneath the stairwell of Japetto's apartment to see what would happen if I just stopped moving. My play had no real characters, just differently named excuses to make actors say fragments that had once passed triumphantly through my mind. For a long time, my life had been helmed by an unshakable need to protect myself against an unarticulated fear of falling through unseen cracks. Now I was there, and it was sometimes dangerously peaceful.

In the subway, a girl my age sat on the middle landing of a stairwell, caught in the rush of legs and Trader Joe's bags. She gazed serenely at a grimy rat trundling over her bare crossed legs. I had only seen the rats of New York City darting in terror: missiles of doom and disease. She'd gained its trust, coaxed it into a non-adrenal state, investing all her focus in the relationship. On the subway, I've seen a man masturbate at me in the air with his naked penis from across the tracks and a body bag pulled from beneath a train stinking of cooked flesh. But I'd never seen someone put herself in such danger for a moment of pure companionship.

CHAPTER 29

POLICE DATE

Monday morning, I hustled to work right on time.

"So, you're getting to sit around an empty apartment all week. That's great!" said Crawley.

"Ah, he'll have plenty of errands for me." I hedged my optimism. "Plus a few different people are coming by throughout the weekend for maintenance."

I added this last bit cheerfully, securing every lock when I got upstairs. Rumors were another doorman had just been fired for trailing a resident's guest into an apartment to request her phone number.

Jooks left me cash to pick up his mail at the UPS store. With no time frame, I could walk and use the money for work snacks instead of cab fare.

I passed by Crawley again with bags from the deli. Then I fixed myself a cup of Twining's Blackcurrant tea and noticed two wine glasses on the counter, side by side. One with a lipstick print as if to mock the indiscretion. My body tensed.

I swooped through the apartment bracing myself for the discovery that Jooks had canceled his trip. Maybe the handyman let himself in to fix the radiator, noticed the glasses, and moved them. The desk bore a dust footprint of the missing computer monitor. Black electrical cords splayed out. Panic leapt in my chest. Now that Jooks was vulnerable to the law, had staff robbed him while he was away?

Alina's friend Adele had once said whoever stole the antique guns from the penthouse upstairs, where she cleaned, must have worked in the building to trick the elaborate security system. If I called the doorman intercom, they could corner me, knowing that I was here by myself. They'd anticipate me on the elevator.

I grabbed my things and walked down sixteen flights.

"I'm running out for coffee but umm... Jooks' computer is gone?" I squeaked once I cleared the entrance onto the sidewalk.

JÖYCE

"Hold on a minute," Crawley directed. "Mr. DeSosa would like you to please go down and see him."

"Umm...why?"

"He'll explain once you're down there." I headed towards the elevator, resigned to trade my safety for the price of cordiality. Worried I was too polite to decline entry into a confined space, to prevent anyone from locking me in a storage unit or murdering me if there were foul play involved. Mr. DeSosa was a handsome man from Venezuela who'd studied design. His manner was more host than doorman. His office smelled sweetly of flakeboard.

"The DA came with a warrant to search," he said solemnly.

"Oh, thank god," I groaned. "I thought someone broke in."

"We had no choice. They told me I unlock the door, or they break it."

"Oh, no problem—of course, it's not your fault!" I relaxed.

"Aren't you...a little worried?"

"Why would I be worried? I didn't do anything."

POLICE DATE

"I mean, aren't you worried...for your boss?"

"Well, it's not that I agree with the prison system. But if he's innocent, I figure he'll get off. If he is guilty..."

Mr. DeSosa now looked at me with distaste."What about your job?" he said.

"What about those girls? I mean...if he's guilty of rape, why should my job matter, right?"

He became superficially polite. Between my lack of self-preservation and tone of enthusiasm, he was convinced that I was a simpleton. "They left this list of items taken for evidence plus a copy of the warrant." He handed me a manilla envelope. They took his address book, a tape recorder of musical ideas and warbled curses, photographs of girlfriends.

"This is Jooks' butler speaking."

"This is Jooks' assistant—I was calling to talk to Jooks about something urgent."

"Yes, certainly."

"H-hi." Jooks answered.

(289)

JÖYCE

"Jooks, someone came in your apartment with a warrant and took your computer and a whole list of evidence. It happened before I arrived."

"Y-you'd better go home for the day," he said quietly, so Hannah wouldn't hear. "Drop off that list to my lawyer and b-b-be b-b-back tomorrow."

"Okay, Jooks. Talk to you later." I used Jooks' petty cash to buy myself his signature tuna sandwich with one slice of tomato on white toast and the crusts cut off at Hamburger Heaven. At the time, I had no doubt the law would take care of everything, whether Jooks was guilty or innocent. Not then knowing what I do now...

That week, I started rehearsals for an experimental *Wizard of Oz*. It was my first sustained interaction in months outside Jooks' household, Mimsy, and my roommates, who only saw that I had a glamorous assistant job while everybody else scraped by on unemployment.

I arrived at Jooks' apartment,

POLICE DATE

unwrapped *Orphans: Brawlers, Bawlers & Bastards* and fed it to the Bose player. One table lamp glowed as the sky dimmed. Tom Waits' voice blew like rusty bellows and creaked like wooden ships as I sank into the couch.

His song "Bottom of the World" is about hopping a freight train to run away from home and wander the countryside. I had nearly begun to grasp this urchin freedom right before I started working for Jooks. I wanted to "dine last night with scar face Ron on tilapia fishcakes and fried black swan." Now, I was tethered to an Upper East Side sex offender, dutifully protecting my parents, singlehandedly supporting the family that in better circumstances would have been supporting me. I was fucking hurt by that, and by Bob Dylan and Jack Kerouac and Thomas Wolfe, and all the intellectuals from those late nights at the NYU library. How dare they sing their songs of boyish freedoms and ragged overalls? Why should I be stuck in this bullshit with some douchebag while they sit in some all-night diner inventing fantasies about the waitress's shitty life, so they can write another song? Well, guess who writes the songs now? I write the songs, motherfuckers!!! I write the songs!!!

Mimsy and I saw a movie about a girl whose vagina has teeth, and Mimsy got jealous when one of my favorite teachers appeared in the cast talkback afterward and said hello.

When Jooks returned, I heard the elevator approach like death's carriage. I arranged myself, hands folded, skirt smoothed, to greet them as the door flung open with uncommon force.

There he stood a minute later, his coattails billowing, his teeth clenched and translucent. The blood rushing to his head accentuated a healthy tan, earned, I'm sure, jealously trailing Hannah in the Cabo sun. She shoved past him, eyes a-roll.

It wasn't a quarrel. Hannah gathered things from the master bathroom and left with her luggage.

"D-d-do I have any email?" he growled, eyeing the new laptop he'd sent me to purchase from Best Buy to replace the one that was confiscated by the police. I had chosen a red one.

"Umm. As a matter of fact, you did get an email from your older son, Mark." I gulped.

"Did you have to get r-r-red?"

"I—I thought it was cheerful."

"Read it."

Dear Dad.

After hearing about your recent accusations in the news, I am officially withdrawing my support and want myself and my family to have nothing more to do with you. You have been predatory with women for as long as I have known you. I guess I shouldn't be surprised. I deeply regret you've chosen this direction with your life, but at this point, I consider it out of my hands. My primary duty is to protect my wife and two daughters. There is nothing else to say but goodbye.

Your Son,
Mark.

"'Protect his family'—hmph. Write back: 'Mark, I am deeply disappointed in you. Of course, you know I could not have done these things. But if that's how you feel, I have no need for you anymore. Jooks.'"

"Uhm..."

"WRITE IT."

Mimsy took the night shift. As the door shut behind me that evening, his voice rose up in alarm over Hannah's desertion. I didn't hear from him for three more days.

CHAPTER 30

THE RAPIST OF OZ

I was busy memorizing Dorothy's childhood-neglect monologue when I was summoned to rehearsal, delirious for interaction. *The Wizard of Oz: Lord I'm Coming Home* was in tech.

Out of duty and a vague desire not to lose my job just yet, I left a passive-aggressive voicemail. "Hey, Jooks, I'm in a play opening next Thursday. Just wanted to let you know my availability so we can figure out when I'm coming in to work for you next. Thanks so muuuuch."

Around 9:30 p.m., my phone rang.

"Hello, Jooks."

"H-h-h-hey! How's it going?!" he spoke several pitches softer, like Eric Cartman on South Park trying to charm his mom.

"Goin' gooood...how are you?"

"I'm okay...l-l-listen honey, I need ya to come over, now."

"Umm, I can't do that, Jooks. Ask Mimsy to come over."

(295)

"B-b-but I couldn't ask her! She's already at home!"

"Jooks. I am also at home."

"Oh..."

"You do realize this."

"Yeah..."

"My time being no less valuable than Mimsy's."

"Uh-huh, listen. I-I-I-I need ya to return the stuff I bought for Hannah!"

"Well, here's what I'll do for you. Ummmm..." I drew a long pause as I pretended to look through my day planner. "It looks like I am able to come in at 9:00 a.m. tomorrow."

"I need it now..." he whined. "I gotta return that stuff I bought f-for that... bitch..."

"Well, even if I was willing to come in, and I'm definitely not, it should bring you comfort to know that all the stores are closed now."

"Are ya sure you can't come now?"

"Nah."

"O-o-okay. Okay, honey. So I-I'll see you tomorrow."

"Yes. I can come at 10:30 a.m. Okay?"

"Bye."

Mimsy was already there the next morning.

"Hey," she whispered.

"Oh, good, y-you're here. We got plenty to do!"

Jumpy with terror of abandonment, Jooks led us into the den. Halfway down a miniature foam stairwell that led from the carpet to the couch stood a downy grey and tan Yorkshire Terrier puppy, not six inches tall at the shoulder. She stared at me with big black marble eyes and elicited a yip.

"Mila, down!" snapped Mimsy. Mila pitter-pattered to the floor. Thumb-sized evacuations peppered the far side of the cream-colored carpet, interspersed with silver-dollar urine spots. "Christ. Now we gotta get the carpet cleaned every week."

Jooks sat down, and Mila scampered up the stairway to loaf her little body along his thigh. "H-h-hey little doggie," he raked his fingers along her back. "Prada, Chanel, Bloomingdale's. And I gotta return the watch. Ugh. I stayed up all night with that dog on the couch, so she wouldn't cry. Now I gotta return her to the pet store. I feel so bad, after she thought she was gonna have a home... but I can't even look at her. It breaks my heart. It reminds me too much of Hannah."

Mila locked eyes with me from beneath the cave of his hand.

"D-d-d-do you want her?" he asked.

I hesitated, and Mimsy opened her mouth to speak.

"Sure, Jooks," I snapped. "I can take her...for the night at least. I'll see what my roommates say."

"I'll pay for everything—her food, her vet bills, the grooming. I just want someone who's kind to take care of her. That's what's important. Now you gotta go to the stores, and I'll stay here with the dog. Then after that, you gotta go home and take all the dog's things. I'll pay for a cab. You'll still get paid for the hours."

Mimsy and I split the errands and reconvened.

"Prada only gave store credit. I think

Jooks is giving it to us. It's $3,400," Mimsy said, none too impressed. "He feels guilty because he screamed at me yesterday."

"He screams at me all the time," I said. My face did that downtrodden, working-class thing.

"I know...but it was a first for me. We were at Chanel. He wanted me to go have coffee, but Hannah insisted I stay. So he was already annoyed. Hannah kept trying on this cropped red moto jacket that Jooks refused to buy because he thought it was tacky. I only chimed in that I thought it looked good, and he screamed, 'NOBODY ASKED YOU!' All the saleswomen heard, Jöyce, and like they all know me because my uncle works there. It was humiliating."

"That's so terrible." My voice was hollow. I could not relate. Nothing humiliated me.

"Hannah said if he ever spoke to me like that again, she'd leave him. I told him I can't be a go-between for them anymore. When things don't go well, he inevitably blames me, and since his relationships are destined to fail unless he makes some huge changes, I'm not putting myself in that position. He's really mad. Hannah's friend sent her the articles about his rape accusations. He went on a buying spree for three days to convince her he wasn't a rapist, but she couldn't stand him."

I stood gauze-eared and marveling at Mimsy's thought investment in the illusion of Jooks and Hannah's love.

"Girls!" Jooks interrupted a call with his lawyer. "I'm gonna give you the $3,400 credit to Prada. Figure out a time you can go together. Maybe around lunch tomorrow? How is 1:00 p.m.?"

"Sure, Jooks, I can do that," Mimsy conceded.

"Thank you so much, Jooks!" I said, hoping Mimsy would appear ungrateful in comparison.

"Hey, I'm working in the morning. Do you want to work together and then go?" Mimsy suggested.

"Sure," said Jooks.

"Sounds good," I answered robotically.

Mila cowered behind my ankle, as if

she knew I was going to take her home at the end of the day.

"So are you excited to have a dog now?" asked Mimsy.

"Yeah—I want to make sure she gets the best situation. We'll see what my roommates say."

"Here, Mila!" Mimsy whistled. Mila froze and began quivering.

"Oh, no! She's shaking!" I said.

Jooks paced into the den.

"Hey, Jooks. Look what we've discovered about Mila," cried Mimsy. She whistled again. Mila resumed quivering.

"Then stop doing it!" Jooks scolded.

I was taken aback by Mimsy's absence of sentiment towards the helpless creature as much as by her aptitude for Pavlovian conditioning.

Jooks gave me cab fare and Mila a tender pat on the head.

I took a car to Brooklyn loaded with Mila's belongings. Her breeding papers showed a $4,500 adoption fee from the pet store where puppies frolicked in a window, overlooking occasional puppy-mill protests on Lexington. At six months and 3.8 pounds, Mila was incapable of self-sufficiency. She settled on my lap, swaddled in a pink fleece blanket the size of a hand towel. She was so sad. She knew she had been rejected. I set her little donut bed next to mine. After a while, she livened up and wandered into the living room.

Jooks and Hannah had chosen from a book of baby names. It seemed a bit stereotypical for a $4,500 pet. I decided to name her Lemon, my favorite fruit, bright and versatile. Lemon's face was the shape and size of one as well with a little nubbin snout.

She would play Toto.

CHAPTER 31

FAUXLITA

I woke at 11:00 a.m.

"Sorry for this morning. I was kind of wrapped up with the dog," I said cheerily.

Mimsy smiled. We walked ten blocks to Prada.

It was sunny in January.

"Who's this fuckin' idiot?" Mimsy gestured to a girl walking slowly in front of us talking on her cellphone.

"We can just walk around," I said.

"I know, but we're in a rush. I mean... come on."

Mimsy scuffed along and glanced down at her Tory Burch-clad feet. "These are my sister's shoes, that's why they're kind of big."

"I hadn't noticed," I assured her.

"Oh look, there's my Aunt Dill. I told her to come say hi to us outside the bakery if we were passing by. Hi Aunt Dill, this is my friend Jöyce."

Aunt Dill was taller than average and slender with long dark hair. She was dressed casually.

JÖYCE

"This is my Aunt Dill. She's published a lot of books for teenagers."

"Oh wow," I said. "It's an honor to meet you." I awkwardly reached out and gave her a firm handshake, because someone told me this is the way to greet people if you want them to take you seriously.

"Aunt Dill wrote a book based on me and my friend when we were little. It's about two girls who overcome their economic differences for the sake of friendship," Mimsy said.

"Oh, I heard about your boss. I really want to write about him," said Aunt Dill.

"I'm already writing a book," I said with a glare.

"Oh," said Aunt Dill.

My book had begun with an insulting sketch of his singed mushroom haircut. From there, it had only gotten more vindictive.

"Are you writing today, Aunt Dill?" asked Mimsy.

"I'm going to drop the kids off, after we finish breakfast, and then work."

Aunt Dill faded back into the world

of adults, careful not to draw too much attention from myself or Mimsy—one entitled to family obligation, both exasperating in youth. Aunt Dill got her own TV series satirizing the wealthy a few years later, anyway. I hadn't put it together that this was the same aunt on the Williamstown Theatre Festival board that Mimsy told me had stuck her in the program last minute when I met her two summers before. To think I'd lost my chance at holding court with Aunt Dill, or writing something starring Mimsy to honor her and the family dynasty, or naming a constellation after them, to secure their patronage.

"So, I guess we each get $1,700 each to spend?" I kept the desperation out of my voice.

"It's whatever we want," she breezed. "If you find something for $1,900 and I find something for $1,500 then great, as long as we each get something that we love."

She featured a scenario that was to my advantage, like a private school featuring diversity on their brochures.

But I knew the score. Rich kids have been trying to pull the floating interest rate on me since the playground.

I silently vowed to obtain my precise fifty-percent share.

The floor of Prada was slabs of incandescent resin set into a metal grid. Each tile was a big enough pedestal for one person. I looked at my shoes, childlike and protected on a private square of light, and postured upright as I beheld the place with admiring eyes. Altars of white lucite rose up at staggered intervals, each displaying a different purse or handbag. Some were fleshy leather that dipped and overflowed. Some were bright, tight, sparkly clutches that winked maddeningly, oblivious to their fragility. There were strict black leather bags, a parody of self-denial, flayed against the unforgiving purity of the architecture. To my shame, to be desirable was often unaffordable. My peasantry was vivid in its pockmarked ignorance.

Mimsy engaged the savviness of

multigenerational wealth and an Ivy League education. We began shopping. She used her *this is how we instruct the staff* voice to see the fall 2008 collection. I hunched and grimaced at the associates, trying not to burden them. Demonstrating I was one of them, more or less, but less. They were kind, almost pitying my lack of fierceness.

I found $300 powder pink patent leather heels. I bought them a half size off, afraid to send the store employees on another trip. For $1,400, I found a navy blue pencil sheath tailored into a silent threat. I secured the merchandise with early human adrenaline, then located Mimsy upstairs, modeling a black frock of chiffon strips for three avid associates.

"Is it weird how my butt pokes out here?" She spoke with the intimacy of a lady to her governess and ate a piece of gum, eying me slyly as she let the wrapper fall onto the cushion of a nearby chair.

"I'm a terrible person. I always litter," she confided. "What do you think of this dress?"

"It's nice."

"It's the dress Jooks bought for Hannah. Nothing else fits. It's $2,500, though."

"Oh, wow."

"Did you find anything?" the sweetness in her voice intensified.

"Yep. Shoes and a dress."

"How much?"

"$1,700."

"Perfect," she whipped out her Blackberry.

"Jooks? Heyyyy! We're at Prada...I did find something...It's the dress you got Hannah...It's like the only thing that fits...It's $2,500...That's the thing, I wanted to call and see if it was okay for me to get the dress and charge the difference to you...Jöyce spent hers already...she already rang it up...So it would cost $800 extra...Too much? Okay, thanks Jooks...I'll call my parents." It could do no wrong to ask as long as she asked graciously. Money was everywhere, waiting to be born. She wasn't "buying clothes" or "asking her parents for money." For Mimsy, she was doing business and phoning investors.

I knew money by selling myself, but Mimsy knew it as a sport.

Mimsy's parents declined her request. I pictured them shaking their heads and smiling. She got Jooks to pay the difference for a $2,000 black leather motorcycle jacket.

"The moto jacket is the one thing that fits me," she lamented to the cashier. "I need to have it tailored. Can you recommend?"

I dawdled along with a pleasant smile, hoping to blend in. I understood something to fit when I could physically get my body inside of it, and be affordable until I ran out of cash.

"I'm getting my pits waxed, so I have to let the hair grow," she giggled in the cab. "Do you wax?"

"Should I? I shave. Waxing seems expensive."

"It lasts longer. Shaving gives you bumps."

"How much does it cost?"

"Like thirty dollars. Do you dye your hair?"

"No. Do you?"

"I got a keratin treatment to keep it straight. But I don't dye. My manager says most leading female roles are brown hair."

My hair was frizzy and cowlicked, not glossy like hers.

"Are we taking your jacket to the tailor?"

"I'll do it later."

"Jooks will probably make me drop it off."

"It's such a pain for me to buy clothes."

"That's why I just grabbed some basic things that won't go out of style."

"But you have that body type and bone structure that these dresses are made for."

"I'm not a model. You're smaller than I am. Petite actresses dominate the film world," I said.

She rolled her eyes.

"Jooks, do you want anything?" Mimsy phoned. "We're at Pinkberry... Jooks, I was being polite. If you don't want Pinkberry, you can't ask us to walk to Häagen-Dazs."

"I mean, we're still working," I interjected. "I can go grab Häagen-Dazs."

"No, he is so annoying."

"I mean, he just bought us Prada."

"No, Jöyce, he didn't. He just couldn't return it after Hannah dumped him."

"He could have bought something for himself."

"Jooks doesn't like Prada. Look, if you want to get him an ice cream cone, feel free. I'm going upstairs."

"I don't want to get it for him if you're not going with me," I fretted.

"Exactly. So let's go upstairs," she huffed.

At Mimsy's urging, I modeled my new dress and new shoes. Jooks could only muster up a "fuck you." He looked me over. "Fuck you," he said again.

"Wowwww, look at yoouu..." Mimsy patronized.

"Why don't you try on yours?" I said.

"No, thanks. It's not ready."

"But you made me try on mine." I

smiled with a joy so forced, I nearly fainted, then clacked to the bathroom to change.

"Must be nice," said my roommate's girlfriend when I got home carrying the bag. She had just been laid off from her $70,000 salary job. "Yeah, must be nice," said my roommate, cuddled beside her in the glow of the large-screen television we'd salvaged for free somewhere. His family was suing the state for the unlawful death of his father.

"My boss had a store credit from returning some gifts," I explained, "after one of his prostitutes dumped him because she found out about the rapes in the newspaper."

We all laughed as we all knew ourselves to be doomed. The feeling I had wasn't nice, exactly. I was clutching a bag that suggested beauty and craftsmanship were near, but that I mustn't show my curiosity or longing, lest it be snatched from me as quickly as it was bestowed.

Two years later, Buffalo Exchange

FAUXLITA

paid me thirty dollars of grocery money
for the shoes, hardly worn because they
were too small.

CHAPTER 32

ROBERT BURNER PHONE

Jooks was despair's own mistress. Hannah was gone.

He sat like a bombed-out building, surveying the empty landscape for relief. He couldn't sleep. He couldn't eat. Wild eyed and unkempt, his gaze scanned his options in the air. Hannah picked up a call from his burner phone because she didn't recognize the number.

"H-h-hi, honey!" his voice warbled. "Y-y-you picked up! Haha! Great!"

"Liar! Rapist!" came her sobbing shouts from the other end of the line, then disconnection.

"Honey, please," he whimpered to voicemail. "We can sort this out, and everything will just get better."

I offered little more than the void itself: a comforting monosyllable, the facilitation of a text message. At Jooks' acupuncture, I sifted through the wreckage.

"Call me," read a 3:00 a.m. text to Mimsy. "Hannah and I are talking about moving to Aspen for good. You could come and live with us."

While Jooks' love life dwindled, mine was on the rise. My loaf-sized Yorkshire Terrier had restorative effects. Contact was not uniformly hostile. My needs and desires were darting shadows on the bottom of a lake. I wanted to see if I could develop a thing I read about online called an "internal frame of reference." I lowered my resistance and waited for whoever approached. A couch-surfing artist didn't show up for the frozen dumplings from Chinatown I'd bragged about. An actor who screamed at the subway attendant the first time we met and thought we had an amazing bond because I let him talk the whole time. My neighbor, who was clearly an office worker only living among artists and freaks to save rent money, asked me to dinner but seemed completely free of pathological tendencies, so I politely turned him down.

Gabriel was a kind acupuncturist who worked for Jooks sometimes. He had the glow of a healer who served his clients well and would scold Jooks for yelling at me over the Japanese screen. Gabriel took pleasure hearing about Jooks' girl troubles, and Jooks adored Gabriel, as one of few who could relieve his pain.

One day after an appointment, as I wrote Gabriel his check, I felt myself beam up at him with a friendly smile, grateful to be near someone who wasn't unkind. He seemed to notice something in me that he hadn't seen before. At the time, I didn't feel I had the right to assume anything, especially about a man so much older. When he smiled back, it was light and friendly, not a smile that made me feel like something was being extracted. Still, something had been exchanged, and I wanted to know what.

At the next appointment, as Jooks scrolled through texts face down in a towel, Gabriel scurried over with a small, sweet smile and handed me a folded note, written on graph paper.

"The thing is..." went Jooks, "she's a drunk. Her father is too. She w-w-won't talk to me! She t-t-thinks I r-r-raped those g-girls!"

"Oh, wow," Gabriel said, disappearing behind the screen with a friendly wave. "How old is she?"

"She's twenty," Jooks said. "Which is just about the perfect age...twenty-three...twenty-four...that's too old."

The note read:

Dear Jöyce,

I didn't want to put you on the spot in front of Jooks so I left you this note. I have always felt we would get along well and would love to get a cup of coffee or dinner with you sometime if you are interested! Let me know :)

Best,

Gabriel.

I smiled a little. It seemed like a thoughtful note. I wrote back at the bottom:

Dear Gabriel,

I would definitely enjoy coffee or dinner sometime. I recently had my heart broken and am not really capable of dating, just looking for friends and good company, but if you would still like to go out sometime, I'd love to!

Jöyce.

I added my number and tucked our correspondence into the leather desk pad with two checks from Jooks. One was for Gabriel and one was for another client. Gabriel had mentioned a young woman he was treating who'd suffered a debilitating car accident. Jooks insisted on paying for her sessions anonymously. I'd been impressed but not wholly surprised by Jooks' generosity as he wasn't the total monster it might be more comforting to think him of being. As much as he was capable of cruelty, he was capable of kindness when it made him feel good. After a few weeks, Gabriel had told Jooks that she and her boyfriend wanted to meet their benefactor.

Jooks consented to Gabriel booking his session right before the woman he had helped, so they could meet in passing. On the day, Jooks emerged from behind the screen and finished dressing. Gabriel checked with the couple waiting outside the office.

A young man gently steered the wheelchair in from the narrow landing of the stairwell. There was no elevator, so I thought he must have carried her up the stairs. The woman reached for Jooks with only her eyes, unable to move otherwise.

"We would like to thank you," said her boyfriend. "She can't speak right now, but she's saying it with her eyes."

Jooks' nodded, and said softly, "You're v-very w-w-welcome. I wish you a good recovery." Gabriel prepared the table, and the woman's boyfriend lifted her onto it. Gabriel's treatment was the only thing that had helped her pain so far. Her arms were splayed slightly to each side of her body. Soft light filtered through the skylight, and tender green shoots uncurled from the ceiling plants, as she faced helplessly upward. Then Jooks took me to McDonald's.

JÖYCE

Gabriel and I had dinner and a movie later that week. It was something I would do with a friend. We met at his office and walked to his favorite ramen place in the East Village. It perturbed me that the waitress was pretty. He'd had an early passion for alternative medicine and was licensed in rare, special kinds.

"So, do you like working for Jooks?" he asked.

"I mean...he can be very harsh."

"It seems that way. I don't like how he yells at you. He's nice sometimes, though."

"He's at his nicest around you."

"Really? I wouldn't have guessed."

"No one else can relieve his pain, except call girls, and sometimes physical therapy."

"Well, glad I'm in good company! His stories are absolutely wild though."

"Right, well, he's being sued for rape and assault."

"Really."

"Yeah. There were some articles on it recently."

"I didn't know."

(320)

ROBERT BURNER PHONE

"Yeah, it's why Hannah left him."

"He did mention a sexual harassment suit, but I just thought...you know...rich old man...I didn't know what to believe."

"Me too."

"Well, do you think he did it?"

"I mean..."

"He couldn't have done it, could he?"

"I don't know. It's almost too obvious for him to be a rapist."

"And he had a stroke!"

"But the allegations are prior."

"Huh. How old is he?"

"Seventy."

"Wow. Seventy. I don't get it though. He dates all these women."

"I've been reading about it. Rape is a power thing."

"That's strange. And scary. Has he tried anything with you?"

"I'm very cold to him. I've got a constant wall up when I'm around him."

"Good. If he ever tries anything, let me know."

"Okay."

"How old is Hannah by the way?"

"Twenty."

JÖYCE

"Jesus. Seventy, and he dates twenty-year-olds. That's a little young. How old are you?"

"Twenty-three."

"How old do you think I am?" he asked.

He had a handsome shock of white hair with blue eyes and a strong, intelligent face.

"Fifty...two?" His expression sank.

"I am fifty-two. I didn't realize I looked it!"

"I'm good at telling age. Plus, your website shows the year you graduated school."

"Oh. I didn't know that was there."

"Why is it bad to be fifty-two?"

"It's not. I just don't want to look fifty-two."

When it was time to pay, I took out my wallet.

"No, no, no. I got it," he said.

"Why would you get it?"

"I'm older and I make more money. You'll get the next one."

The next appointment, there was a note waiting for me again.

ROBERT BURNER PHONE

I had a great time with you the other evening and would love to go out again. Broken hearts can be mended!

—Gabriel

I hadn't said anything about wanting to mend my broken heart or Gabriel being the one to do it. Since we were only friends, it was okay that he annoyed me. I could tell him to stop. That's what friends do.

CHAPTER 33

FEMMESIS

Even though I knew psychiatry was evil because of my background in Scientology, I had started reading an eBook by a self-diagnosed narcissist about narcissism called *Malignant Self Love*. My scholarship suggested Jooks actually had narcissistic personality disorder. Japetto had some adaptive traits, but then so did I. What I shared with Jooks was more disturbing: an inability to metabolize love outside a potency of the wildly euphoric kind, which involved the inevitable dehumanization of the love object in order to preserve the addictive delusion at all costs.

In his old age, withdrawn into the money and the narcissistic supply of a successful career, Jook could maintain the supernormal, discarding one fantasy for the next. My life circumstances did not allow for the bald-faced wielding of power, but I worried I had the makings of a narcissist. It slowly dawned on me that Gabriel hoped to mend my heart so he could have sex with its corresponding body. He'd absorbed Jooks' Tales of Classic American Debauchery like a ten-year-old watching *Scarface*.

Still, we kept each other company. He entertained the collective internalization of millionaire masculinity, and I sought understanding of my psychology in relation to men.

"Would you have the same interest in me if I was your own age?" I asked with the impartial tone of a documentarian. We were getting coffee at Veselka.

"Well, that's a complicated question...your character and your age are so intertwined."

I listened, but I knew that we are all immortal spiritual beings, even before entering our bodies, and certainly before the body reaches full size. His statement was therefore nonsensical, but there wasn't time to explain all this. And verbal tech is a high crime anyway.

"Do you date women your own age?"

"Oh, I have lots of female friends my own age. Are you religious?" he asked.

"Umm. Scientology.".

"Oh wow, Scientology. Huh."

"Are you?

"Not really. I grew up Jewish though. Just another Jewish boy from the projects."

"Most people think Scientology is weird."

"I don't think it's weird. I know some Scientologists, actually."

"Oh really?"

"They're nice people. Very successful."

"Really?" I said hopefully.

"Yeah. Incredibly successful, actually."

Gabriel had been married young and briefly to a Cruel Woman. Then, he had a relationship with a Great Girl, who he cheated on because his head was screwed up from the Cruel Woman. Before she left him, she trashed the whole apartment, because a Great Girl treated badly gives back just what you deserve.

I could be his Wholesome Redemption: live out my days as Gabriel's loyal, submissive young wife, retire from the theater, humbly keep house, aide him at the office, bear a child, care for him in old age, mourn him honorably when he died. The last my estranged college classmates would see of me would be the wedding photos on Facebook.

In drama school, someone told me of a classmate who wore thick eyeliner and lived, careening through the city, on pills. One night she caught a cab and married the driver, a man more than twice her age. To her parents' shock, she was healthier than she'd ever been. Acting school, with all those boys who thought they were James Dean looking for their Edie Sedgwick, wasn't good for her. What she'd needed was a Pakistani man of values and sound character.

I could devote my life to an honest man in the healing profession.

"There are reasons he isn't with a woman his age!" Hazel pleaded over Skype. "You must believe me!" She had dated a thirty-five-year-old for two years, with nothing to show for it at the end but tears and a head shaved in mourning solidarity with Britney Spears.

"He was an adult goth almost twice

your age you met at a nightclub with a fake ID," I answered.

"Gabriel is an adult Asiaphile more than twice your age who you met working for a pop-rapist!"

I paused, confused by the absence of jealousy in her tone.

"My mother's friend married a man more than twice her age," she persisted, "and she's been nothing but a nursemaid since! She pushes him about in his nightcap and a wheelchair!"

"I might not mind that actually," I moaned. "Perhaps love wasn't intended for me. Why not carry out my days bringing some small happiness to an overall decent man?"

The other line rang and a sly grin came over me.

"Spud. Did you give him your Skype number?"

"Yes, Nog. We've agreed to chat. He opened an account for me. He says I'm his Skype girl."

"NOOOOOO!! This cannot be! He's nothing but a filthy old man. Don't you dare pick up!"

FEMMESIS

"I'm putting you on hold for just a second."

"Oh, no, don't you dare—" Hazel was gone.

Gabriel stared back at me in her place.

"Hi."

"Hey," he said. "What's up?"

"I was just talking to my friend. I'm trying to work on a play. What about you?"

"Oh, just changed into my pajamas. Getting ready for bed."

Lemon was cupped in my arms, standing on her hind legs to lick my face with a tongue the size and color of a bubble gum stick.

"I wish I was that dog," he said. "Then I could give you lots of little kisses." Back when I'd had confidence, this comment would have banned him from my screen, if not my life. Having tasted dispensability, an idle dysfunction seeped from my pores. His tone had a dreamy quality.

I hoped he wasn't fondling himself.

JÖYCE

On Valentine's Day, Jooks and Hannah were tenuously reconciled. He sent me to pick up her Rolex while he had acupuncture. Gabriel left me a note on his desk and a large heart-shaped Linzer cookie filled with raspberry jam.

> To My Skype Girl, I bought you this cookie at the Farmer's Market. If I could afford to buy you a Rolex like Jooks, I would.

Going right ahead, acting as if our situation were romantic, he now openly aspired to be like Jooks. I consumed the cookie at home in a series of mechanical bites. There were to be no Valentine's activities.

"So, I don't want Jooks to hear about us spending time together," I said.

"Why not? He'll have to know at some point." Gabriel had all the ingredients for an Indian dinner in little earthen bowls spread across his counter.

It was a Sunday evening and we were to cook an Indian dinner. His apartment bore, like himself, an Eastern influence.

"He'll assume this is romantic and say, 'Have you two fucked yet?!'"

"Right." He tended quietly to some cardamom pods.

His dining table was low to the ground in the Japanese fashion. We ate comfortably on pillows and a cane mat, a custom I would abide should we wed.

We finished the meal with some really good Indian ice milk, called kulfi, which Gabriel had gone to the trouble of picking up. He showed me a YouTube video of the Beatles' last performance. I watched myself perform the inevitable—but wholly truthful—inquiry about a leg muscle. I'd stopped exercising months ago. Gabriel aligned me as I lay face down on the ground. I needed free alternative medical advice, painfully aware my body was a misleading subject. It was like how I sometimes asked him for financial tips, not because I was a gold digger, but because he knew things about money that I did not. He showed me the Playbill for his friend's off-Broadway show, toying aloud with the idea of taking me.

JÖYCE

We lay on the floor facing each other, not speaking or touching, our heads on separate pillows. I felt his measured anticipation, careful not to meet his eyes. He kept swallowing.

The nearness of another body was some comfort. I was not conscious of how I should be cared for. I was conscious only of the absence of warmth. "That's my bed," said Gabriel, pointing over to the corner by the window. His bed was no wider than a cot on a thick dark wood base. "I had it shipped all the way from Japan. God, it was expensive."

I said I'd better go. He sent me off with assorted Tupperware of chutney and dal.

My roommates were throwing a party for Janus's birthday when I arrived back home. It was also Valentine's Day, and Devon's girlfriend was moving in unannounced.

Janus deserved a break from the long sessions writing hired posts for Vice Magazine's Motherboard, occasionally punctured with shouts of "FUCK" at some unseen chiptunes malfunction. Allison was long gone. She and Clark had dated.

Almost everything I touched in the kitchen—the plates, forks, glasses—belonged to Clark. I planned to go to bed. But first, I needed to take Lemon out for a walk. A guy with a guitar case on his back came toward me while I walked Lemon out the front door. He scanned the row of buildings with an expression that was peaceful and intelligent. Normally I would have dismissed him. He looked sane, nice, and tall.

He's cute. Oh well, I'll probably never see him again, I thought.

The word 'cute' seemed like something someone would say.

He spoke into his phone and was buzzed into my building.

I pretended not to notice him on our couch with Tim, the drummer. Something compelled me to change outfits and insinuate myself. Dog in hand, I soon had a shot of whiskey and a new friend. He invited me to meet him later that week.

JÖYCE

I ate a burrito at a place of his choosing. He asked if I'd seen any movies. I detailed the full narrative of *The Others*. He ordered a beer and asked what beer I wanted, so I acted like it was normal and ordered a beer. Then we went to a bar and he ordered another one, so I ordered a beer as well. He kissed me after a while and asked if I felt a connection, because he felt a connection, and I said I did. He said there was a record he wanted to play for me at his apartment.

We had beer at his apartment as well, and my stomach was in pain. He had a glass of whiskey. We sat on the floor of the loft in front of a shelf with a record player and vinyl. Then something strange happened. He accidentally knocked over his glass after he placed it on the floor next to him. I noticed he was shaking a little and realized that he was nervous. That's when I realized, I never felt nervous around boys. I wondered what it would feel like to be on a date with someone who made you nervous in a good way. But I would have to settle for being broken, I thought, and using the tragedy to fuel my art as revenge for being misshapen. I was learning a lot. One thing that always held me back from going full throttle up the Bridge to Total Freedom in Scientology was my attachment to being an outcast. Success scared me, and so did simple, honest love. I had agreed with myself not to kiss anyone, and I felt dead inside, but he choreographed us nicely into his room and kissed me, and then we were on the bed and part of my dress was down but I felt numb and sad, so I sat up.

"I uhh—" I put a sleeve back on.

"Everything okay?"

"I had my heart broken recently and I—I'm not really capable of feeling much right now."

"Okay. No problem. Do you still want to hang out again?"

"Yeah, yeah, I'd like to."

I walked from his apartment to the train and began to weep, mostly out of rage that I was numb to interaction. I felt Japetto was to blame—Japetto and any who roamed the earth seeking to exploit great spirits such as I.

In tears and rage, I wrote Japetto adaptations of the William Blake poems he'd marked in the book he'd lent me:

The Garden of Love by William Blake

My name is Japetto
I went to the garden of love
And nobody would put up with my shit
Once they realized I had a girlfriend
Now all these girls are super pissed at me
Garden of love, WTF?!?!?!

The Lily, The Sunflower, and The Rose by William Blake

There are three types of women:
The rose thinks she's beautiful and
    confident. I'll show her.
The sunflower is overly nice to make
    up for the fact that she's not that hot.
The lily will be rewarded for her
    subordination with the public title of
being my girlfriend while I secretly
    lead girls on for my ego on the side.
My name is Japetto.

When he didn't respond, I sent him an original:

FEMMESIS

You Hiroshima'd my emotional
  landscape
Baseball Bat wants to be Valentines
  with your Shins
Good job at destroying people for fun
You sociopath

He responded:

Wonderful words.
Really Excellent.
Don't threaten me.
I'm sorry I hurt you.
I didn't mean to.
Now leave me be.

I didn't like that his poem falsely accused my poem of threatening him. He sifted back into the wind, and I faced a charred crater. Japetto had presented himself at my most desperate. Some aspect of my psychology had been shattered. I wanted to rebuild it one brick at a time.

If I learned one thing, I could not trust my instincts, impulses, or perceptions. I was unable to love organically like in dreams, movies, or poems. Japetto had demonstrated that through his well-tailored program of psychological warfare. Dysfunction left me unable to experience love unless distilled into deadly concentrations for my art. Like how Jackie Chan said the Beijing Opera breaks your bones as a child so that they heal into a better dancing shape.

I resolved to form no attachment. In college, a girl I knew, named JANE DOE, told me her mom's advice was to go with the guy who keeps coming back. The guy from the party continued to seek my company, and I meditated on the reality that he could leave at any moment.

"What is your biggest sexual fantasy," he asked the next time I went to his apartment.

"Oh," I thought. "I guess getting raped." I blushed. "Not, like, the kind you see with Jooks or on the news. Like, the kind in Japanese office porn on the internet."

Now that I was seeing someone new, my interest in the potential of Gabriel and I passed on, just as my cellphone began its own slow demise. "Battery drains to zero percent every two hours," I told him. "Hard to text."

"I'll buy you a phone and pay the bill," Gabriel replied.

"Do you generally perform such duties for your social circle?" I replied.

"No, but I would for you."

"I will return your Tupperware from when we cooked that Indian food," I texted.

Gabriel had lost all perspective on our relationship, despite my saying from the beginning that I only wanted to have platonic coffee dates. He was, in the face of thousands of years of ancient medicine, succumbing to Jooks' diabolical tales, modeling behavior he had learned from the acupuncture table, wanting to date twenty-two-year-olds while paying their bills, telling himself our twenty-eight-year age difference seemed dignified in comparison—with no expectation of paying me the proper hourly rate like Jooks' "girlfriends" were getting.

For weeks, I scheduled errands to avoid him, until Jooks insisted I accompany him to acupuncture since we were heading to his lawyer immediately after.

"So you're not interested in hanging out with guys anymore?" he asked when Jooks slipped down the hallway to the restroom.

"That's not true."

"You're not interested in hanging out with me anymore."

"Right."

"Okay."

He looked sullen but didn't stalk me like Jooks stalked Hannah.

A few months later, he mentioned to Jooks, so I could overhear him, that he'd married an old friend from Japan. He emphasized the word "old," so I'd be aware that he'd known her first.

"Congratulations, Gabriel," I smiled, wondering if his offer to pay my phone bill had been strange—and if his wife would have allowed him to keep it up. I didn't understand why men bought things for women, or what led women to accept. I had no need to mention I was seeing anybody. I thought it was good not to be his one last fling before settling down.

CHAPTER 34:
SPEAK TRUTH TO FLOWER

As I began to blink away my feelings of desolation, my mother called in March to say that she'd run out of money. I transferred one month's rent and expenses into her bank account.

My time felt worthy of more respect now that it belonged to other people.

Mimsy and I had just seen Jooks and Hannah off in a cab for their second trip to Cabo.

"He's an asshole," I said.

"He's such an asshole. Hey Jöyce—do you think he's gay?"

"What?! Why?"

"I dunno," she shrugged.

"I-I can't imagine."

I was playing along as I did in any conversation that strayed outside Scientology's haven of sanity. The question of being gay was a false category, since all human beings are organically heterosexual in our native spiritual state with a high urge towards procreation, though most sexual energy is sublimated into creative thought, and only when a person descends into the lower levels of the tone scale do sexual practices become irregular.

"How could you think he was gay?" I asked. "He's literally accused of raping dozens of women."

"Oh, who knows," said Mimsy, rolling her eyes, practicing her idle mischief.

I'd never been to the Pride Parade. It seemed like an excuse for the most socially dominant girls and flamboyant boys at conservatory to give exhausting performances of fun. Parades were hot, thirsty ordeals of your parents refusing to buy the expensive funnel cake and smoothies.

On this trip, I made sure Mimsy and I traded housesitting every other day. It made no sense why I wouldn't want to get paid to sit in his fancy apartment, treat myself to lunch, and avoid meddlesome roommates, but the last time Jooks went to Cabo with Hannah, he paid Mimsy the same that he paid me to take the week off. I cared about making Mimsy do exactly what I was doing, for exactly the same money I was getting, to satisfy my spite. And that was all.

"Hey, Mimsy," I texted, "there was sixty dollars and change for errands in the living room credenza. Do you know where it went? Alina doesn't, and she's the only other person who was here. Let me know since I have to tell Jooks."

"I haven't seen it or touched it, and honestly Jöyce, I think it's more trouble to tell him it's missing than just to let it go," she replied, with characteristic abundance mentality.

"Hey, Jooks," I texted, "I hate to let you know this but sixty and change went missing from the drawer where I put your cab fare. I can walk to get the mail, but I'm telling you now in case there's any question."

He didn't respond.

I made sure Jooks returned on Mimsy's day. Then he could scream and bluster like a poltergeist and be reminded that his negative emotions were separate from me. I bet he'd restrain himself just for her. I'd become jealous that she would dare to complain about one single instance of an abuse to which I had grown daily accustomed among many. I made myself unavailable for phone consultation. Soon after, I began to notice Mimsy's burgeoning labor-rights activism.

"How is he??" I texted Mimsy.

"Um, he is testy," she replied.

"Uh huh?" I texted back. "Let me know if you need anything!"

"Jöyce, I found something out..." she texted.

"What's that?"

"He's only going to pay us each for half of the week."

"NO," I said. "Well, he still owes me the paid week off that you got during his first trip."

"I know...can I call you?"

"Yeah, call me when you can."

Mimsy called on her lunch break.

"Hey," she said. "I'm at the gym."

"Hey," I said. "So he wants to pay us for only half the week each?"

"Yeah," she said. "It's ridiculous."

"I mean, it makes sense for him to pay us each for half the week since we split it this time. I am separately concerned about my getting a paid week off, just like he gave you, while I worked the whole first trip. I don't even want the time off, just the money."

"I know," she said. "I'm afraid to bring it up. He's so over me right now."

"Well I'm definitely talking to him about my pay," I said.

"You should," she said. "And do you think, if he'll listen, you can also talk to him about mine?"

My body absorbed a silent groan. "Sure, Mimsy," I complied. "I'll express to him that you also feel you should be paid the whole week."

"Only if it feels right to you," she said. "I don't want to start a fight. I'd never nickel and dime him. You and I are such Libras. We're obsessed with being fair."

There seemed no principle in her request other than to extract as much as possible from the present moment without consideration for past or future ones. My faith was invested in my wage-labor mentality. I forget where I heard it, but supposedly equilibrium equals death. So as long as I was chasing or running from something, I must be alive.

"Cabo was terrible," Jooks told me the next day. "Hannah wouldn't talk to me, wouldn't go to dinner with me, and when I told her I wanted to make love, she'd lie on the bed with her headphones on, listening to the iPod I gave her, and give me the finger, like this!"

He thrust both middle fingers to the heavens. "She said she had her p-period," he muttered.

I wished his films had scenes like that.

"Did you talk to him yet...?" texted Mimsy.

"Not yet," I said.

"Let me know when you do, Jöyce!" she replied.

"Okay!" I said. Being galvanized as a labor organizer brought out new fellowship in Mimsy. It's true, I would be negotiating both my dues and Mimsy's separate Wall Street rate, but it was the price her savvy demanded, and I was getting a seminar in finance. Mimsy needed to maintain her standard of living in order to be the leader that she was. On the road of our shared struggle, our common sense of conspiracy was a comfort to me.

I sat on the stool across from Jooks and watched him eat for what seemed like generations of oppression. I ate nothing, lest his generosity undermine my demands.

Mimsy would not have deprived herself, taking up and setting down her utensils strategically.

"Alright," I texted her, "I'm going to ask now."

"Yeah, Jöyce! Go for it!! Do it for what you—we—deserve."

"Jooks," I said.

"Yes," he replied, silently communing with his soup.

"Mimsy said that you were planning to pay us for only half the week each."

The word *us* felt manipulative and thrilling.

SPEAK TRUTH TO FLOWER

"That's right," Jooks assured me.

"You'll pay me the whole week," I informed him. He stood up, chair legs screeching against the marble, paper towel falling from his lap.

I stood with him.

"NO!" he shouted.

"YES!" I shouted back. "Jooks!" The warmth flushed to my cheeks, and tears nearly welled up. "You gave Mimsy a week's paid vacation! I came every day during your first trip while she got the week off. Where's my week's paid vacation, Jooks?"

"Fine," he muttered, sitting back down.

"And Mimsy, too?" I asked, trying to sound equally passionate. Not passing along her request felt like sabotage, and Scientology taught me that holding back information is "suppressive," which is the religious word for "hater."

I would relay Mimsy's will without making her look like a total asshole or conning Jooks on her behalf.

"NO. Just you."

"Okay..." I said.

"D-d-don't tell her."

"Okay," I said.

I could tell Mimsy and not tell Jooks that I was telling Mimsy, but if I let either party force me into a lie, then it would be an overt, and I would have to do an Overt and Withhold write-up with the Ethics Officer at the Church, or else my relationships with both people would deteriorate and I would begin to descend on a downward spiral. But I could not return to the Church until I made my fortune in the world. So I would have to make sure I did not do anything unethical until then.

"I asked," I texted solemnly.

"What did he say??"

"He said he would pay me for the whole week, and only pay you for the time you worked. He yelled initially, so I did not want to push back."

"Okay..." she said. "Thanks, Jöyce. I'll ask again when I arrive."

"Okay," I said. "I can ask to be paid as you're entering to give you an excuse to bring it up."

SPEAK TRUTH TO FLOWER

The doorbell rang when we were in the den.

"She's here," he whispered.

"Can I get my check?"

"L-l-later."

"Jooks," I pouted, as I'd learned from Mimsy.

"O-o-okay fine, just don't tell her the amount."

"I'll answer the door."

"O-okay," he said.

Dewy and pleased, Mimsy chunk-heeled over the carpet in new motorcycle boots, a cashmere cream sweater, her head adorned with two black silk Chanel-looking flowers.

"Hi, Jooks," she said, adjusting the strap of her Fendi flap messenger satchel.

"H-H-Hello," he said faintly to the television, and through a sliver of passing recognition, I saw that he was hostage in his own home to the demonic powerlessness of girls.

"I'll write my check?" I asked.

"S-Sure go ahead," he waved dismissively.

"It's...$633...right?" I asked.

"Yes," he said.

"And for me too??" Mimsy jutted in.

"NO!" Jooks declared. "You're not gettin' it!"

How slight the shift from proactive young woman to actual terrorist, shaking a seventy-year-old man down for money in his apartment.

"Jooks!" she protested, staying connected and vulnerable.

"Okay. Go ahead and write it then. It'll be your last check."

"Jooks!" she coaxed, her eyes tearing up as she knelt before the checkbook to sign his name. He stormed out of the room. "I have an idea!" she said. "Do you want to quit in solidarity with me?"

"Um, I would but, remember how I said my parents lost their house and stuff?"

"Oh. Right."

Years later, when I realized I had been the unwitting target of a multi-interest black-ops campaign, since before I even turned twenty-one, nobody quit in solidarity with me. In fact, they all smeared my name in exchange for deals and write-ups with prestigious publications.

"I don't know what he's thinking by firing you. It's not like I can cover your shifts."

Jooks prowled back in.

"Jooks," said Mimsy, "Jöyce and I both worked together every day of the week, I swear."

I gazed at the floor, ashamed of the lie, invented on the spot to benefit herself alone. As if we'd sat patiently on his couch each day, side by side in matching uniforms, until it was time to get the mail. All he had to do was ask the doormen and Mimsy's senseless fib would be exposed. She had crossed the line between hustling artist and con artist in my books.

"Why would you come together? I told you both to alternate days!" he said.

"No, that's not true!" she cried. "You said we were both working that week. Equal work for equal pay, from now on, remember?"

"No," he said. "No."

"Jooks," her voice warbled, "you can

ask the doormen!"

However much her fraud was bloating up, she would plead innocence to the end.

"Go ahead," he smirked. "Go ahead and take it. Are you coming in tomorrow?" he asked, looking at me, "or am I going to have to replace you too?"

"Oh, I'll be here," I said. "Will you be alright alone tonight?"

"Corinne is c-coming over."

He had already booked a call girl.

We tumbled out of the building to deposit our checks before he could cancel them. Then a natural food store to celebrate Mimsy's freedom. I became hopeful her departure would motivate mine.

"I should be able to get another job," she chatted with her father on the telephone. "I'm Ivy—an Ivy League graduate..." She turned into a narrow aisle of organic sourdough mini pretzels, and I drifted into the seaweed and fermented goods aisle. My heart yearned for guidance like an underwater flare gun. Where was my advisor?

SPEAK TRUTH TO FLOWER

"My parents say I should beg for my job back," she confessed, near the canned goods section. "They said nobody was ever that good to me before."

"But—Jooks is terrible, I don't even tell my parents what he's like."

"I guess I could sell the watch he gave me."

"Jooks gave you a watch?"

"Not really. Just the one that he made the gym trainer give back after she turned him down."

"The $5,000 Cartier watch?"

"Yeah, I have my own with sentimental value."

Parents who could give their daughter anything money could buy were telling her to stay with Jooks, so that meant I should too. I wondered if I knew things they wanted their daughter to know, the way she knew things I wanted to know.

The mood of our Kombucha and vegan chicken sandwich supper was light. Mimsy's phone chimed. "Oh, it's from Jooks," she said. "Oh my god," she held the phone for me to see. It read:

JÖYCE

"Can you work tomorrow?"

The bonds forged, the battles lost and won, the scars, solidarity, and revolution in the air, all dissolved in the bitter arithmetic that I had been used to fight solely for Mimsy's pay. Her selfishness only inadvertently increased what I was now still owed. Or perhaps my cynicism had failed to grasp the beautiful design of capitalism.

Having seen Mimsy in action, I could never hope for the benefits she created with her abundance mentality, and therefore I could never advance in the world, if being a genius negotiator meant being a possible psychopath. Mimsy was Wall Street. I was wall post.

CHAPTER 35

CELEBRITY SEX OFFENDER

It never made sense to me that Narcissus could fall in love with himself until I googled it and found out that he only fell in love with his reflection because he thought it was a separate person. Narcissus didn't even recognize his own image. On Wikipedia, Narcissus' mother asks the Oracle if her son would live a long life. The Oracle replied that he would, so long as he did not know himself. I thought Nemesis meant enemy, but Narcissus only makes her out to seem that way because she's the god of balance, fortune, and redistribution.

I guess there's that saying, "Equality seems like oppression to the privileged." If that's true, then it follows that equality seems like privilege to the oppressed, which must mean, to the equal—people who get bored the most— oppression seems like privilege, and privilege seems like oppression. There are terrible people in all three categories.

It's good the internet taught me

how to spot a narcissist so I could see Japetto, Jooks, and Mimsy for their true selves. Real narcissists make up about two percent of the population. Maybe I attracted more of them because I thought the more difficult a person is, the more you have to match their behavior on the tone scale. I always found the statistics fascinating because that's the exact same percent of people considered to be a "True Suppressive" in Scientology. The definition of a narcissist isn't the person who is afflicted by narcissism, but the false self that they have created. One of my favorite acting teachers said narcissism is a tragic disease where you feel like you're the center of the universe in a world that's constantly telling you otherwise. I also read that you can acquire narcissism as a coping mechanism. I wanted to do the latter and make my false self work for me.

"Here." Jooks handed me six quarters, warm from his grasp, as he'd awaited my morning arrival. "Go down to Smiler's Deli. Pick up the *New York Post* and *Daily News*."

CELEBRITY SEX OFFENDER

He felt so alive scanning the pages for his name like a child on Christmas morning that my fifteen minutes lateness didn't matter. "Listen to this, they call me a 'sex-crazed-septuagenarian!'"

"My favorite is 'creepy-tunesmith.' The phrasing is very current," I said a little too enthusiastically. His smile faded.

"Excuse me. Excuse me? EXCUSE ME? Can I have a comment on your recent rape and sexual assault allegations?" The reporter's voice echoed like a distant rescue helicopter as we climbed out of the cab.

For that split second, Jooks' stifling power condensed from the atmosphere and our toxic bubble imploded. "Meh." Jooks waved the reporter away without answering as he tottered over the crosswalk. "Keep walking," he muttered.

"Excuse me, miss? Miss, can I have a comment from you?" The reporter walked backwards facing me. I cast my eyes downward. "Are you aware of the allegations against this man?" he said.

JÖYCE

I felt like someone in a coma being shaken.

"Just say: No comment," whispered Jooks. We headed towards the doorman who displayed contempt at the handful of reporters and news cameras by the entrance. I was queasy at the idea of ending up in a photograph with Jooks but intoxicated by the proximity of mass-media exposure.

Jooks and I used the service entrance from then on. We took the elevator to the basement, then walked down a long hall, past Mr. DeSosa's office and the laundry room. Jooks cursed and grunted up a steep, dark stairwell towards the crust of light at the end. A doorman waited by the Lexington Avenue postern, between a deli and a shoe repair, so we could scurry into the car service and speed away. Mr. DeSosa came up with the whole plan, and Dorian even brought his chauffeur business out of retirement to drive Jooks around in an SUV when he wasn't working the door overnight. Jooks was willing to pay his price.

CELEBRITY SEX OFFENDER

It wasn't all tinted windows and glamorous escape, however. Jooks kept vigil by the phone like Miss Havisham by her wedding cake.

One morning Mimsy found him after he had fallen and cut himself on the bathroom sink. The doctor bandaged his forearms. He took blood thinners, and his skin looked as fragile as the surface of hot milk. Every news mention gave Jooks a rush of fame to counteract the isolation. His claims of innocence were as religious as a child's incantation against the dark. I guessed if he was innocent until proven guilty, then so were his accusers, but all I saw up close was the mounting stack of meetings, fees, and summons. I only pieced together the story, as I would come to understand it, from the news. Jooks had posted audition notices on Craigslist seeking "Unknown Actress, aged eighteen to twenty" with Pearl as his assistant at the time. Maybe he'd been grooming me for something similar. Pearl booked the actresses expensive hotels and flights and reassured their parents on the phone. Maybe that's what she meant when she said she'd helped him "get girls," blurring the meaning in her own mind, knowing and not knowing he'd fallen and taken her with him. The audition was for the role of a prostitute—I assumed the one from *Struck by Lightning*.

He offered wine to help the actresses relax. I never saw him drink but issues of Wine Enthusiast sat atop the wine refrigerator in his dining room.

The victims felt like the wine had been spiked with an additional substance. Police speculated that a number of women were flown in from across the country, so they'd be exhausted and preoccupied with catching their flights home.

The toxicology and rape kit evidence was little and far between, if there was any evidence at all. Maybe some of the victims had never heard of a rape kit, like me, until I read the articles. Pearl was being charged with criminal facilitation. Maybe that was why she'd flown all the way from Seattle and followed me into the pharmacy on the day Jooks received his first summons. Maybe Jooks was angling for me to replace her, the Echo to his Narcissus.

One victim in the newspaper said he had shouted, "Take off your stockings! They make your legs look fat."

In the description alone, I recognized Jooks' tactical offensive sequence: insult to create self-doubt, shout to stun the defenses, warped logic to establish cognitive dissonance—against the deafening orchestra of his awards, luxury apartment, and money.

Even from a standpoint of sheer self-preservation, for Jooks to commit rape under such visible costly circumstances, with so much at stake, made no sense. Perhaps this was his defense.

Comments online said the accusations were for money and their careers, but no acting career takes off with a rape accusation, only in spite of it. Most of the time, when I've heard an actress speak out, it was after she'd died, retired, or got famous enough to protect herself. The rapist and the rapists' friends would pretend it didn't happen. Maybe I was missing the grand design of capitalism, where there can be no victims, only entrepreneurs with competing interests.

Jooks seemed to have trained his mind to bypass rejection and process everything as a "yes" in order to persist in a brutal society and industry. I wonder if somewhere along the line, he snapped and transferred this mechanism onto sexual consent.

I worried that I had taken on some of Jooks' unchecked disregard for the feelings of others, mistaking it for a superpower that could subdue my howling pain, and I reflected critically on how I had treated Japetto. I once texted him, "I can't believe I had to hear about all of your childhood shit and didn't even get to fuck you," not because I meant it, but because I'd heard men say stuff like that about women. I was reflecting the toxicity of society back on someone I once loved. I wondered if my life wasn't just a big government experiment like Jooks', or if the universe had a plan for me.

CELEBRITY SEX OFFENDER

Jooks didn't need to know about the void, he just needed to write down all the jingles he came up with in there. Jingles that tell of redemption, climax, a key change into the resplendent. One day, love came along and lit it up, so he wrote his Oscar-winning song.

The stories we tell ourselves determine most of our power. I'm learning to keep my senses up any time someone tries to tell me a story, especially if they try to make me into one of the characters. Stories are addictive. No matter how rich you get selling them to other people, you're always in danger of getting high on your own supply.

I don't know if Jooks helped make capitalism, or if capitalism helped make Jooks, but in the end, he got stuck trying to make his biggest-selling song come true on repeat. A tale told by a narcissist, full of sex and money, signifying lawsuits.

CHAPTER 36

RAPIST COPPERFIELD

On the ropes after almost getting fired, Mimsy curbed her executive bonuses and loopholing. In a climate of political unrest, she took her aristocracy underground. It was her business if she became Jooks' gym buddy. My body moving in unison with his—even on separate elliptical machines—was out of the question.

Though she adopted working-class rhetoric, her very constitution rejected hourly wage labor, conditioned from birth to leverage everything to her advantage. In my repression and inability to break rules, my resentment was a hurdle in our friendship. "Jöyce? Can you come here a second before you go? We want to talk to you."

"Yeah." I headed into the den, with the sickening feeling of a child being scolded.

"Hey. The other day when you left, I went to pour Jooks a Diet Coke, and there was only half a glass left."

RAPIST COPPERFIELD

"Uh-huh?"

"I had to go buy more while Jooks waited." Mimsy glanced at him with compassion. "He was really mad." Jooks himself, the nucleus of our oppressive social order, glanced away in embarrassment, at this last grasp for the power she once held in his court.

"Oh, I'm sorry," I said.

"In the future, make sure to replace the Diet Coke before it gets that low."

"I mean, usually, what would happen is that at the beginning of every shift, you would check on any supplies that need to be refilled, and then refill them. I was giving you the opportunity to do that. Because of the equal work for equal pay thing we just started doing."

"I mean, still. The fact that I had no warning. You could have texted me."

"We probably pour ten glasses of Diet Coke here a day. I don't see why anyone would need a warning."

"I know, but Jöyce...still."

Even Jooks couldn't keep himself from stepping in on my behalf.

"Stop. Just stop," he said, shaking his

head like a failed father.

This was why he'd discarded her as a soft-hype girl in his low-key sex trafficking ring. Mimsy had as much trouble overcoming the concept that I was her staff as I had overcoming the concept that my needs and emotions did not exist.

CHAPTER 37:
SCENT OF AN OMEN

Spring became summer. Eventually, dating became commitment. I conned my new boyfriend into becoming my boyfriend using the lessons of *Well Behaved Women Seldom Make History...but Never Die Alone*: by presenting his male tendency towards logic with a problem that he could solve. The problem was that I was sad. As a girl all by herself in this big carnival of a city, trying to be an artist while paying her parents' rent back home, I was hurt that I had purchased so many tickets of bourgeois dalliance in society's frivolous love raffle but not won a single prize. He could make the sadness go away. He could be my boyfriend, and then I wouldn't have to be sad anymore.

I was trapped now more than ever. From the outside, my boyfriend thought it was cool that his girlfriend worked for Phil Spector's contemporary. We both had automatic reverence for any musician who had succeeded at capitalism. We both went hungry for art, but the infinite doom that closed around me inside Jooks' apartment was mine alone. Still, my chances of succeeding seemed greater here than anywhere else. I sent my mom another month of rent and expenses and worried about getting fired or stuck with Jooks for sixteen years, like Pearl. I wondered if hardship could break me so bad I'd help him get girls like she did.

I wanted being followed to feel special. I thought I was paranoid to think I'd been followed at rush hour on Lexington Avenue, but when I slowed down, he slowed down too. When I sped up, I heard his polished leather dress shoes accelerate. He stayed six feet behind.

I stopped in my tracks at the 59th Street subway. He halted, then continued past me so as not to call his own bluff.

He knew that I knew that he knew that I knew he was following me. Eyes to the sidewalk, very nervous and trying to stay in character, he turned down the stairs to the train. He was an Indian businessman in his fifties, attired more for car service than subway. I hastened towards Madison Avenue and took an unusual route home in case anyone else was tailing me.

I wondered why he took so much trouble to follow me. Regular sex might have given me a certain glow that attracted creepy men more than usual. There wasn't time to think about why I usually imagined I was a Japanese porn star with giant breasts being molested by businessmen in order to climax, but maybe my sexually aberrated thoughts had pulled him in. Maybe he wanted to ask me out but was too shy. Or was I losing my mind from spending so much time with Jooks?

A week later, I sat in Matt Richardson's lobby sipping my third break-room coffee of the evening. The three elevators opened and closed like doors of a cuckoo clock. People glided across the marble floor to and from the law offices.

"Hi, I'm Randall Cornacchia."

JÖYCE

A hungry grin floated above my copy of Aristotle's *Poetics*.

"I'm the lawyer Jooks hired to defend the doormen of his building."

"Nice to meet you. I'm Jöyce."

"Jöyce. That's an interesting name."

"It means jewel or the bringing of joy."

"Cornacchia means vulture in Italian."

"Wow."

"Jöyce, you can tell Jooks he's now two weeks overdue on my fee?"

"I will tell him that."

"You do or there will be consequences."

"I have absolutely no control over his finances, but I will relay the information."

"You do that." He walked away.

The lobby was growing familiar. Jooks had received ten separate summons, and his lawyers thought the DA had a dozen more up her sleeve. A woman who looked like a senior partner passed by in a couture pencil skirt and vest showing six inches of midriff.

Good for her, I thought.

Mimsy stepped off the elevator, late from her audition, in a Burberry ruffle skirt peacoat. Mr. Cornacchia strolled back by, acting as if he hadn't just issued a vague threat.

"Hello," he said.

"Hi, how are you?" Mimsy smiled, just patronizing enough for me to notice.

"Very good. How are you girls?" he asked.

"Good."

"I'm going to a tango class tonight... I'll need a partner." He paused.

"Oh...that's nice." Her smile grew wider, her eyes darting sideways at me.

He waited a moment longer, then continued onward.

"Well, goodnight!" he grinned.

"That man is odd," I said.

"He's old enough to be my father," she grimaced. "How did your parents meet?"

"Pennsylvania Academy of the Fine Arts. Yours?"

"My dad was a civil rights lawyer. My parents both marched at Birmingham with Martin Luther King."

"Really?"

"He and my mom fell in love, just as he was leaving the country, so she brought him to meet her parents in Boston and asked permission to go with him. Her father said, 'She's not going anywhere without a ring on her finger,' so my dad was like, 'Okay.'"

"Wow," I said.

"I know."

"I texted Jooks that you're out here. How have things been with him?"

"Well," she puffed, "like I said, Jooks is mad at me. I told him I wasn't going to talk to Hannah for him anymore."

Just then, he entered the lobby. "Mimsy I-I-I need you to call Hannah. She won't t-t-t-talk to me," he said. Mimsy wilted.

Jooks was giving love one last shot with a third trip to Cabo, pending Hannah's arrival at sunrise.

"Can we do it from your phone?" she groaned.

"From your Blackberry. She won't ignore you."

"Jooks..."

"What?" He stared her down.

"Fine. What should I say?"

"Tell her to get in the cab and c-c-come over so we can talk about our trip tomorrow."

"Okay...so can I say, 'Hannah, Jooks wants you to get in a cab to come see him'?"

"NO..." he prompted.

"Hannah. Get in a cab and come visit Jooks."

"What else do you say?..."

"Hannah, get in a cab and come visit Jooks now," she sighed.

"Right," he said. "J-J-Jöyce, you can go."

I gathered my things. A man stepped off the elevator, seemed to recognize me, then wove through the crisscrossing people towards Matt Richardson's office.

I was pretty sure it was the same man who had followed me to the subway a week ago.

CHAPTER 38

THERE WILL BE LOVE

I started locking my bedroom when I slept alone. Any day, Jooks could show up demanding that I hide him or slide his scrawny self out from under my bed with one of his Wüsthoff steak knives. Hannah had been scouting his neighborhood for her dog, and I was likely to make the top of her suspect list if she really started to think where she might have gone. I made my Facebook private and told my roommates to ignore anyone buzzing for me.

For Jooks and Hannah's third trip to Cabo, I proposed Mimsy work the full week for once so I could finally get my paid time off. Despite an aggressive lunchtime phone call, she could not overthrow the basic logic of my argument. So on the morning of departure, when Hannah didn't show, I wasn't surprised. Anonymous would have to put it on their list of demands for the day capitalism is overturned, when I finally take that week of vacation I'm owed and Mimsy gets the brunch shift at the collectivist anarchist food hall. Jooks was eerily calm. He knew it was over.

Hannah recognized the number of his home phone, cellphone, burner phone, and other burner phone. So he sent me to the bank for rolls of quarters.

The bitter February wind whipped his open Burberry puffer coat about his spindly torso. Mucus froze on his upper lip. But Jooks was impervious to the cold. He clutched the phone, eyes blasted with hope, one ring closer to her voice.

"Ah, there you are!" he cried over whizzing traffic. "Aw, honey, I missed you. Come back. Y-y-y-your nails were starting to look so nice."

Then, only a click, and the dial tone.

"Damnit," he pulled the receiver away to examine it for malfunction.

"Jooks...it's cold."

"We gotta find another payphone."

"I don't know of any."

"Are you kidding? They got tons! Where are they?"

(377)

"Not on the Upper East Side in the digital age."

"Oh."

"Plus, these things are covered in germs. A bum probably peed on it. You shouldn't be out here, anyway. Jesus Christ. You could get pneumonia."

I replaced the receiver above the shrine of empty two-ounce liquor bottles.

As the cars slowed, Jooks surrendered his cement sliver of an island that curved into the tunnel. He had discovered the city anew, chasing love through the telephone cables of its icy streets.

"C-c-c-can you zip my coat?"

He fumbled sheepishly with numb, gloved fingers.

"C'mere."

"I n-n-need a hat," he mused.

"I know." I fitted the ends of his zipper together. "How come you won't wear the wool one I got for you at Bloomingdale's? You have to cover your ears when it's cold. Always."

"Because!" he growled, "I don't wanna look like that guy!"

THERE WILL BE LOVE

He pointed across the street to a man much his own height, his own build, and his own age, shuffling down the sidewalk in a black wool beanie, much like the one I'd bought him.

"Eh, y-y-y-y-you're right," he muttered. "L-let's go home."

Jooks would have happily abandoned his fortunes for a return to the glories of his youth, before his triumph in the age of advertising—in his subliminal age—which had now passed into the age of impulse. He thought that there is something more, for the battle-torn monster at the end of all their prosperous raping and pillaging, than to be left to die in a naked war zone, no freer than we are, at nature's mercy. His old body could no longer sustain the mistakes and battles of his youth.

CHAPTER 39

THE JINGLEMAKER'S ASSISTANT

In spring, Jooks had the cardiologist set his pacemaker one hour ahead for daylight saving time. He had a new crush. It was "Corinne this...Corinne that..." Then theater tickets, reservations at the Four Seasons, and forget-me-nots from Cartier.

She had been his call girl since before I was hired.

Sometimes, love finds you where you least expect it.

"I've got good news!" Jooks cried.

"Aha. What's that, Jooks?"

"Corinne's grandmother's house burnt down. She's gotta work every night this week! Haha!" He shook both fists in the air, victorious.

Corinne was still on an hourly rate. "Isn't that great!?" He searched my eyes for disagreement. "Ah, screw you!" He moved past me to breakfast, refusing to let me spoil his good mood with my negativity.

JINGLEMAKER'S ASSISTANT

I observed the light fade as we wound down a road bosomed with steep green banks.

Our day in the Hamptons waned with the battery charge on Jooks' ankle monitor. The sedan carried us from the graveyard, where I had felt watched, perhaps by a faerie landscape in an absence of buildings amidst the trees. "Corinne said she wanted to be buried next to me," Jooks thought aloud, "but I don't know."

"No, that's weird," I said. "You haven't been dating that long."

An ice-cream parlor formed in the mist. "Ohhhhh! My favorite place," he cried. "Excuse me, sir," he told the driver, "I'd like to stop."

Outside was moist and fragrant. Inside, local Hamptons teenagers worked behind the counter. A girl in a visor hat and messy bun greeted Jooks with weary hospitality.

"I-I-I remember you!" he said to the girl. "Gahhd, I miss my house up h-h-here," he chuckled. She smiled politely. There was a silent knowing among the kids scooping ice cream, about the variety of Hamptons vacationers.

"I-I-I'll have chocolate on a sugar cone. Two scoops," he smiled. The room was filled by the neon lights, pink and white linoleum, and scent of chilled sugar.

Two damp blond kids in bare feet and oversized T-shirts scrambled, giggling, from a big black SUV through the door. Their dad was in Oakleys and a shabby T-shirt advertising a local pizza place.

"I'll have banana," I said, cheerless.

"Banana?" Jooks scoffed, trying to impress the staff.

"Banana," I confirmed.

"Ugh. Who gets banana?" He rolled his eyes.

"I can pay for it," I replied.

"No, no, no...Ugh. Okay, she'll have banana."

"How many scoops?" asked the girl.

"One."

We returned to the car, where I consumed my frozen treat in business-like fashion.

"Thanks for pulling over," he said to

the driver. "I wanted to buy some ice-cream...for my friend here."

I heard him tear up on *friend*. Jooks could be so maudlin.

Since he had taken me to see his sacred burial ground, I felt obligated to do something for Jook's birthday. His psychiatrist left me a voicemail outlining how important it was to Jooks that I call the cemetery to finalize the design for his headstone. But death is a certainty. Birthday cake would be a surprise.

"Jooks' birthday approaches," I informed Mimsy. "Do you think we should get him a cake from Häagen-Dazs?"

"You know what? Yeah. The other day he turned to me and said, 'You better get me a cake for my birthday!'"

"Should we pay for it ourselves?"

"Oh, no. We should definitely use his card," Mimsy grimaced, smarter as usual.

I kept procrastinating on the grave. Finally, Jooks demanded I sketch whatever bench and headstone I thought would be good. He was happy just as long as it featured his awards and the Oscar Wilde quote, "We are all in the gutter, but some of us are looking at the stars," which he wanted faxed to Irma right away.

I ordered a cake from a man who had received his medical degree in India but would need to retrain if he wanted to practice in the United States, at the counter of a Häagen-Dazs owned by a woman who had worked on Wall Street and reinvested her money in the franchise because of the recession. It was coffee ice cream and chocolate, encircled with chocolate Pirouline cookies, tied around with a bow. Mimsy picked it up before her shift.

As we put our things down in the hall, I accidentally splashed a bit of coffee on her Burberry circle trench.

"Oh, shit!" I threw myself on the floor to blot it off with my sleeve. It seemed such a lot of fabric for such a little rain.

"Oh, it's fine..." she said, watching as I finished blotting.

JINGLEMAKER'S ASSISTANT

Mimsy balanced the platter on her palms and came into the room. I bet she wanted Jooks to assume the party was her doing.

"Happy Birthday!" she cried.

"Jooks, I wasn't sure which cake to order you, so I got you coffee and chocolate ganache!" I said, so he'd know it was I who had set things in motion.

Then, he blew out the candles.

CHAPTER 40

WAIT, I CAN'T HEAR AMERICA SINGING

Jooks was the July portrait of Corruption in Repose. His manners were almost passable. I penciled "Corinne" into his calendar for dinners, shows, and overnight stays, which I tried to block out of my imagination.

In Corinne's country, girls dated older men, my boyfriend said. Some girls had a daddy complex, he said, and prostitution was more accepted.

Jooks couldn't have been in love so soon after Hannah. He was eerily calm and Corinne was diplomatic. I was sorry Corinne was spending time with him for money, but that was my only respite from his screams and text messages.

She probably felt a hundred times sorrier for me.

I had a boyfriend too now, just like *Well Behaved Women Seldom Make History...but Never Die Alone* said would happen if I didn't bring it up. I was okay with following a book to teach myself human behavior since that is what I had always done with the Church. I did not question sex, or turn down any request for it, ever. Afterward, I would shiver in his arms, like the heat from someone else's body let me realize how accustomed I had become to the cold.

He had read many, many books that I didn't know about. He said the cult I grew up in was crazy and so was my mom. This made me feel ashamed. In conflict, I let my fractures surface and then reeled it back into soft oblivion, so I wouldn't be abandoned.

My boyfriend was teaching me to drink. Miller High Life was the champagne of beers, he said, but PBR was the assumed beer. Coors exists, but you didn't ever buy it. Jim Beam is the best everyday bourbon, not too sweet. Islay Scotch is the greatest, and Lagavulin, because it tastes like rancid barrel wood in an exquisite way. The finest of human civilization is preserved in fermentation. I learned to drink when I was happy, but never because I was sad. Being hungover at work increased

(387)

my profit, giving Jooks a lower-quality product for the same hourly rate.

I liked the cool throb of the veins around my temples. The leisurely glamor of my body humming, "Remember me?"

I was in a naked play, *Leaves of Grass* by Walt Whitman. Mimsy asked if she and Jooks were invited to the performance, I forbade her to ask again. There was a $200 stipend. Money for acting was as poetic as the craft itself.

The show was on the first floor of a Chelsea townhouse. In the chic salon, I felt an honored artist. I stayed late running lines while the designer hung sacks of colored liquid, smoked weed, and told me about his experiences with aliens.

I had always agreed, it is arrogant to assume life only exists on Earth.

Mimsy went to "meet with some people" in LA.

I felt too old for film. I was twenty-three, but no moviemaker's idea of twenty-three. My liberation was the blue sky printed on the underside of Jooks' new eighty-dollar umbrella,

CAN'T HEAR AMERICA SINGING
which he bought on a date with Corinne at the Museum of Modern Art.

With all his galavanting, Jooks was leaving cash around.

"There's $250 missing from my pocket," he told me.

"What?"

"I had $250, and now it's gone. I think the maid took it."

"Well...there were a few people who came in and out of this apartment today, Jooks...me....your speech therapist... the doorman...it wouldn't be fair to accuse Alina. Wait, are you sure it's not somewhere else?"

"Yes, it was in my pocket!"

"Should we maybe...wait and see? Or maybe we could leave some money out when she's coming in next time to check? Or...why don't you get a safe installed?"

"A safe? I'll forget the combination."

"You can pick a birthday and tell me a clue to give you if you forget."

It was installed the very next day.

"Why did he get a safe?" asked Alina.

"Jooks was missing some money the

other day. I mean, he always has so much cash around...maybe he misplaced it or it fell behind a table or something...."

"Yeah he probably misplaced it..." she said, nervous.

"Except, the thing is," I continued, wanting to see how she'd react, "he's never said he was missing money before. Nutty as he is, I think he's pretty meticulous with his money. Or at least when it's a few hundred bucks."

"Yeah, ha ha...I dunno, he's crazy."

A few days later, Jooks sat me down on the couch. "I'm missing $1,000." His voice was low and controlled.

"You didn't put it in the safe...?" I asked.

"I shouldn't hafta—" he yelled but stopped himself. "Call down to the doormen and tell them she is never coming back into this building."

"Okay, Jooks. Sorry for contradicting you. She was the only other person in the apartment so...I guess there's no other candidates, really. I mean technically you don't know if I stole that money, but

I know I didn't so...she's the only other choice."

"Please. Call the super."

"Hi...um...Jooks was missing $1,000 cash after Alina left his apartment, and she was the only other person in here today...we're thinking she took that cash...Jooks has asked me to request she never be allowed in the building again..."

"Um...well I can make sure she isn't allowed into Jooks' apartment, but I can't prevent her from working for other people in the building."

"Okay, thanks. I'll let Jooks know."

Jooks was not pleased, but he couldn't do anything about it.

"Call her," he said.

"What? Oh, Jooks...."

"Call her. Tell her she can't come back here. You better do it, because if I call her, I don't know what I'll say."

He was motionless with rage.

"Hi..." I said.

"Hi..." she said.

"Um...so Jooks told me that I'm supposed to tell you you're not supposed to come back..."

"Yeah, they told me..."

"There was $1,000 missing from the apartment...you were the only other person that came in that day..."

"Okay..." I thought how calm she was, like waiting to be let off the hook.

"You didn't take it though, right?"

"No."

"So, um...yeah...I guess that's the reason I'm calling...I don't know what else to say...I mean..."

"Stop talking. Just get off the phone with her," Jooks prodded.

"That's all, I guess." I finished.

"That's all?" she asked.

"Yeah." I could almost hear her breathe a sigh of relief.

"Okay," she said.

"Bye, I guess."

"Bye." We hung up.

"Man." Jooks shook his head, staring off into the distance.

"I guess she probably did it," I muttered. "I mean—remember how I reacted when you accused me of faking my hours? That's how an innocent person reacts when you accuse them...

but I mean Alina would have stood up for herself if she hadn't done it, right?"

Behavioral forensics was very new for me. The Hubbard Chart of Human Evaluation I'd studied in the Volunteer Minister Course wasn't helping to explain Alina's behavior at all.

"My mother got robbed by some kids she hired to clean the garage once," Hazel told me. "They took a lot of her good jewelry, and she had been really nice to them. She paid them really well and ordered them pizza."

"Yeah, I mean—Jooks is a dick to me. He talks to Alina worse, but I have to spend more time with him—and I don't lift cash off his dresser. I do allot myself portions of cab fare for coffee and yogurt and that one meatloaf—but that's more expense-account stuff. And I walk to make up for it, you know. But then—Alina is spoken to by Jooks, truly, as if she were a second-class citizen. He was such a fucking asshole to her. He deserved it, and I don't pity him. At the same time, do you think her thievery was a result of his behavior, or do you think that theft is theft no matter what?"

"Yeah...I think thievery is thievery in this case..."

"Maybe. But she would never had been driven to it working for someone like your mom. Maybe only an asshole like him. Technically there's no proof she even did it. Jooks could have spent it. Corinne could have taken it. But if so, why didn't Alina protest at all? Why did she sound relieved to be out of there? Is it possible she was so defeated by being falsely accused she wanted to stay away? If she did steal, it's too bad she didn't get revenge by recording the way he speaks to her at work and then suing his ass. That would have been hilarious."

"I bet she was just beaten down," Hazel mused.

Whenever I saw Alina's friend, Adele, in the elevator, she refused to speak to me. In fact, she stood as far away as possible, clasping her purse with her nose pointed high in the air, in full make-up and perfume. "I couldn't help anything that happened you know..." I sniveled.

CAN'T HEAR AMERICA SINGING

Eyes cast down, she shuddered involuntarily, clearing the space of my presence.

The lobster dinner Jooks ate with Corinne the night before he fired Alina was three days ripe in the garbage. "I'm not smart enough to take it out, Jooks. We'll have to wait for Mimsy to get back from LA," I shrugged, trying not to wretch.

"I can't smell anything, because of my stroke," he said.

A doorman sent his friend's wife to try a three-hour shift.

"Where are you coming from?" I asked on the elevator.

"The Bronx. I just dropped my kids off at their grandparents'."

"Oh, that's nice. They get to see family." She looked at me, confused. "Did you have, like, any questions or anything?"

"I was wondering what the pay is like?"

"It's twenty dollars an hour."

"I mean...since I'm going to be

coming down here an hour each way for only three hours...that seems a little low...should I ask him for more?"

"Yeah, I mean...you should ask for what you think is fair...I only know what he was paying his last person."

Jooks' reaction to her appearance made my body tense. "Well!" said Jooks, placing his hand on her slight, bare elbow, "How nice to meet you! What's all this?" he asked.

"We were just discussing pay, Jooks..."

"Twenty dollars an hour...it seems a little low with my commute..." she smiled. "Maybe we could discuss..."

"If you don't like it, you can go." He pointed to the door.

"Jooks, she was only asking..." I said. "What if you just paid for her monthly MetroCard?"

"YOU BE QUIET," he snapped. "Get out!"

"Jooks," I said, "negotiating pay at an interview is normal—"

"QUIET!" he shouted.

"What happened?" asked the

doorman as I left to pick up Jooks' fifty-dollar lunch.

"She asked about negotiating pay and he, like, threw her out. But the way he looked at her was so creepy she probably deserves a better job, anyway. I don't even know what to think. Honestly, I feel relieved for her."

The doorman shook his head at me, and I felt guilty.

CHAPTER 41

EVAPORATION ECONOMICS

After the third month of giving my mother $1,200 for rent and expenses, I expressed love the way I knew best: I applied Scientology technology to her low position on the tone scale. With the bravado of a mid-career stockbroker, I swooped down 63rd Street, barking orders. "Mother, I've advised your ass repeatedly to get up on the welfare and food stamps. How could you fucking do this? Please try to be more proactive re: procuring government benefits moving forward."

I saw no choice but to give her the money. Tyranny and martyrdom combined are a complicated drug.

Before I could torture myself any further about the decision to move to LA, it was made for me. I wouldn't be able to afford it.

For all her failings, my mother had only ever robbed me emotionally. She hated asking for money, always pinched pennies and paid her bills—with something stashed away if my father's finances got the better of us. She funded and drove me to every class and lesson growing up. She hadn't even asked me for groceries when they were starving.

Of course, now that she did ask, I was saving up for the biggest leap I'd ever made. Her financial duress had a real chance of derailing my career. I was so dead inside, I doubted my ability to go chasing down carrots on the West Coast anyway, with no driver's license or job lined up. I told myself that it wasn't worth it. Based on what I know today, maybe the FBI wanted to orchestrate my California suicide to use in a smear campaign against the Church of Scientology. I'd end up having to suck cock on Hollywood Boulevard for a plane ticket home once my parents died.

I forked over hours of wages worth of misery, but I wouldn't give my mother the satisfaction of knowing she'd derailed a dream. LA was sinking into the water, anyway. What did they want from me out there? Certainly, not to hire me for acting jobs. They hadn't done that here.

I would be chewed up and spit out by my wealthier, savvier classmates. I was helpless and aware of my helplessness now. I had walked away from the Church in case my parents needed help, which they now did. I didn't deserve an acting career. I could practice the ultimate acting exercise, to experience the moment fully. And every moment was an eternity of despair.

CHAPTER 42

THE LITTLE MERSHADE

The garbage stank of ocean and dream death. "Why don't we call a cleaning agency?" I gasped.

"No good. They give their house-keepers too much say. Open a window," he muttered.

The next candidate spoke as much English as I spoke Spanish. She was in her forties and had a small son, and her husband was ill. She was very short and round, and she was always on time. If I were late, she would hustle up to Jooks, so he would send her on the tasks and errands I usually did. Jooks hated to see us fraternize.

"Maybe you shouldn't shout at her," I said, "or call her a moron. You didn't even do that with Alina. Is that because of the language she speaks?"

"SHE'S TRYN'TA TAKE YOUR JOB!" he shouted.

"Well, she's not gonna get it!" I snapped. "Maybe you shouldn't talk to her like this is a fuckin' Dickens novel." He chuckled, in spite of himself. I was surprised Jooks cared who Charles Dickens was.

CHAPTER 43

UPWARD FAUXBILITY

Mimsy was still in LA. I thought, if only I had her opportunities, I could flourish and prosper in life. I felt anyone who wanted to work with me must be trash themselves. My art looked like shit compared to famous people.

L. Ron Hubbard, the leader of my childhood cult, wrote a bulletin called "Jokers and Degraders" about how certain kinds of joking was the sign of a detrimental organization member. I tried not to be funny and focused on high-stakes crying scenes at acting school. Still, if my art didn't make it on a commercial platform, it didn't fucking exist. My chakras felt like the crushed aluminum ducts from the day my father's job site got vandalized for competing with the union instead of joining it—because his three employees had voted not to—and the police didn't let him in since they were also union.

Regions of me fell outside of words and shapes...in the negative space.

UPWARD FAUXBILITY

I guess I'd rather be indoctrinated by a proven cult leader than some random family member. That way, my operating system had a manual.

"I think I'm gonna have to let Mimsy go..." Jooks told me. "You're doing all of the work...and it's not fair." Jooks handed me the phone as if he hadn't favored her all along.

Now, Corinne filled his nights and Mimsy's priority shifts.

"Write her: 'It looks like I don't need help at night. Thank you for everything... we won't be needing you here, anymore. Very Best Wishes, Jooks.'"

I typed, slow and solemn.

"Are you sure, Jooks?" I moaned.

"Yes...just send it..."

I read him Mimsy's reply: "'Wow, Jooks...I knew it was coming but I guess I wasn't expecting it today...thanks for everything. XO-Mimsy,'" she texted.

I clung to my lot with the assurance that I was exactly where the universe had intended me to be. I had chosen my circumstances, just as I had chosen my body and the parents I was born to.

JÖYCE

I was here for a larger purpose than what feels immediately pleasant.

Mimsy left artifacts in Jooks' fridge: eye serum, a green lunch tote from a meal plan company. I vaguely sensed the loss of her company and missed her. Alone, I was a coarse girl easily mistaken for a Mormon or Jehovah's witness. I'd copied her black pleated skirt, tights, and ballet flats from French Soles, but my skirt went halfway down the shins. Now her Garnier eye-puff reduction roller was mine. I wouldn't take her meal tote. I'd never eat her damn scraps. She'd taught me all I knew of a better life, and now she'd gone away.

Jooks had bullied his maid into thievery and Mimsy into uselessness.

The only ones left were me, and the suspiciously elegant Corinne.

CHAPTER 44

CODEPENDENCE DAY

I walked Lemon outside what people were calling Cracker Palace, a row of cheap brick construction on Myrtle Avenue. A girl my age sidled up to us. I'd once seen her walking with a man she called "Daddy" but who was too young to be her dad. She plucked Lemon from the sidewalk. "Hey, let's take a walk with me around the corner," she said.

Lemon twisted in her hands like a grub.

"I can't. I gotta go, actually," I said, prying Lemon from her grasp. I was worried she wanted to lure me away and hit me over the head, so she could steal my dog.

I ran back up to the apartment, hoping I hadn't insulted anyone.

Jooks decided to take me and his youngest son out for brunch that morning. It was my first time meeting Will, who had flown in from his internship at a record label in LA.

I felt the cool breeze of a hangover on

my grey matter as Jooks and I waited by the front door. The previous night, my boyfriend and I had spent the Fourth of July at a bandmate's house in New Jersey. I'd had enough margaritas that I was blacked out on the Metro-North ride back to New York, with Lemon in my lap in her carrier bag, apparently eating Carr's table water crackers out of my limp hand. My boyfriend told me that while I was blacked out, the train had also blacked out for a moment.

"He steals my socks!" Jooks growled. "And that's not all! That boy is a thief!"

"Why, Jooks?"

"The day I went to the hospital, he told my a-a-assistant he needed $2,000, and sh-sh-she g-g-gave it to him!"

"What did he need it for, Jooks?"

"I don't give a fuck! I was dying! He c-c-coulda waited!"

"Wow, Jooks," I shook my head. Stealing is wrong.

"Okay, Dad, I'm ready."

Will traipsed from the den with his jacket.

"L-l-let's go."

CODEPENDENCE DAY

The cook at ATE flashed me a look of hatred. In my tight jeans and ribbed tank top, I could only be a looter shaking old men down for money with unchecked sexual anarchy. If Mimsy hadn't been fired, Jooks would have brought her. Her silverware etiquette matched her girlishness.

Will was a modern version of his father. He inherited the tall stature and a lanky frame, magazine-worthy good looks (from his mother), and the unassuming posture and dress of a charming slacker on hiatus from state university. If the interior resembled the exterior, his father's intellect, and all it's accompanying burdens, were passed down to him as well.

"This omelet tastes weird," said Will, respecting his father's practice of rejecting restaurant dishes.

"S-s-so order another one." Jooks eased into a sip of tropical orange juice.

"Thanks, Dad. I'm just hungover."

I gazed at the omelet, knowing not to suggest I take it home. I was learning the art of leisure and fine dining, like that *Eat, Pray, Love* book that just came out.

"My assistant also celebrated the Fourth of July last night," said Jooks, brushing my knee with his fingertips.

I bent from his touch like a fishing rod.

Will sipped from his water glass and glanced away.

CHAPTER 45

SWINE FLU OVER THE CUCKOO'S NEST

A Republican thing I did—well, fiscal Republican—was spur my mother into pulling herself up by the bootstraps. I removed her privately funded welfare, which was providing financial incentive to fail and draining my bank account. For motivation, I told her I didn't have the money and that in one month she'd be on the street if she didn't apply for benefits. I decided the only way to truthfully claim I had no money was to have no money. So I spent it.

Since I'd never had money before, I'd never had any idea how to spend it on anything except rent, groceries, and my phone bill. Since I'd been working so many fifteen-dollar hours, I'd had no time to spend it and saved everything.

It felt like nothing to drop a couple hundred dollars on clothing. Clothing just gets better as it gets more expensive.

I could afford to dress like rich kids, or go to their school, and for once in my life, I was choosing looks. I'd backed out of the apartment I was supposed to rent with two other students in LA. I figured I hadn't suffered enough, in the right way, for my art not to be crappy. Film and television were migrating over to New York City anyway. I had a boyfriend now. I could build a life. Also, whenever I had got near a dream, someone snatched it away. You had to either be born rich or make people feel like you weren't too threatening to rescue.

Thanks to my initiative, my mother and father managed to get back on their feet the following month. It's possible she borrowed money from another family member and didn't tell me. I may have been harsh, yelling at her on the phone to apply for social security and food stamps. You had to be sixty-three to get it, and she was waiting for that birthday.

Jooks and Corinne went to Cabo for a week. Corinne was demure as a pop diva ten years her senior and tall enough to be a runway model. She looked like this one extra in the Remy Ma music video for "Conceited." She couldn't have been with Jooks for reasons beyond the occupational, but she was so even-tempered that you really couldn't tell. For a while, Jooks found the emotional distance refreshing. By now, I was also his travel agent, securing the restaurants, airport wheelchair, and Roberto to butler for the week.

Upon return, they were practically engaged. In the glow of the big-screen television, he confided that Corinne was already married—for citizenship, but also for real. Jooks' lawyers wanted an annulment in case her husband wound up being a shitty cousin and tried to claim half her assets.

Corinne's grandmother's house, which had made Jooks so happy when it burnt down, was a mansion she'd purchased with her family in her home country. Jooks' housekeeper had seen it in a picture when Jooks sent her to clean Corinne's multi-family home in Queens.

"She say, 'No tell anybody Mar!' and

she show me a picture of her house in the country where I'm from—it was so beautiful!"

Jooks stared long and hard at my Prada boots, purchased for $400 at half-price and one size too big in an overstock store on the Lower East Side.

"I'm paying you too much." He shook his head as if we'd failed each other. He'd soon have wedding expenses.

News came on about the swine flu. An H1N1 virus originating in Mexico had broken out at a school in Queens.

"Jooks...you just came from Mexico..." I said, inching further away than usual.

Jooks cleared his throat and raised his fingertips to his larynx. "I don't feel well."

He emerged from his check-up with Dr. Gordon triumphant. "I have it!" he said, jabbing a thumb into his chest.

"Jooks—shhh," the eyes of ten or so elderly patients shifted about the waiting room.

"I'm the first one in Manhattan to

SWINE FLU

have the swine flu!" He covered his mouth with a giggle.

"Come on, Jooks, let's go."

"I have this prescription for...Tammy... flu?" he said, trailing after me.

I molded myself to the opposite side of the cab. I was so pissed at him for getting swine flu. Everybody else had stayed home from work. The only ones out were martyrs and criminals. "Where's my prescription?" I asked. "You did get one for me, too, didn't you?"

I did not ask but informed him that he would be purchasing a dose of TamiFlu for myself and a plus one. I knew that only the mind and not some drug could save and heal the body, and that a being could only become sick when there was a Suppressive on the comm lines, but it was the principle of the thing.

Getting doses for my roommates would be greedy. I blocked out images of them all clawing at my door.

"I got yours here...and one for Corinne," he said, handing me the slips of paper.

JÖYCE

"DEADLY VIRUS INFECTS THREE IN QUEENS," read the Post as I strolled past the newsstand to the pharmacy talking to Dr. Gordon on the phone. "Did Jooks give me swine flu? Should we take the TamiFlu?"

"Well, normally I say not to take the TamiFlu because if everyone does, it could breed a superbug, but in Jooks' case..."

"...his psychological response is a greater burden to the City of New York than a superbug," I finished.

"Right. He's in his seventies. I mean, there was some kind of germ in his test—probably cold germs. It's too soon to tell. He can take TamiFlu."

"Is Jooks gonna die from this?" I didn't really believe in death. I was just making conversation.

"Listen, Jooks is surprisingly hearty. The amount of Trazodone and Klonopin he takes on a nightly basis, just to get three hours of sleep, would cause you or I to pass out for two or three days. He's unlikely to die from this."

I concluded that his illness must be

psychosomatic.

Jooks took the TamiFlu twice a day and was bedridden for a week. I made a great show of putting on rubber gloves every time I took his temperature with the oral thermometer.

"Oh, for god's sake, do you really need those?"

"Swine flu can be deadly," I said, snapping the fingers one by one, to ensure proper fit.

"Why did Dr. Gordon charge me so much on the last three visits?" he asked, looking back over his medical records. After two doctors and a specialist, someone had finally figured out that Jooks did not have a mysterious cancer but hemorrhoids. When I called, the receptionist said the extra cost was because Jooks had been getting his bandages changed there, for which a specialized fee was added. From that point on, he gave the duty to Corinne, since she was already getting $1,500 an hour.

CHAPTER 46

BANK(RUPT)SY

After his recovery, Jooks and Corinne decided to take an Italian vacation to Positano and the Amalfi coast.

"Maybe you could come with us!" Corinne said.

"Don't say that to her," he scolded. But I was only disappointed by how much they both thought I wanted to go.

"Oh, I'm thrilled to have the time off and stay here with my boyfriend!"

I gave a blistering smile.

Corinne was majestic. She had perfect golden skin and long black hair, on a screen-ready bone structure.

"She's so big!" Jooks whispered when he signed her up with a trainer at his new gym. She showed us photos by a world-famous photographer of herself wearing a swimsuit, fashioned from bands of white lycra, like in *The Fifth Element*.

"I used to want to model...but... see...I started eating cheesy poofs... and...yeah..."

BANK(RUPT)SY

Jooks threw up his hands in exasperation.

Corinne was the same age as me. I didn't know what to think of sleeping with Jooks. Maybe my undiagnosed religious-compulsory heterosexuality made it seem more revolting, the way pregnancy makes bad smells overwhelming. Around the time he asked her to change his hemorrhoid bandages, theirs had shifted from a gig economy to a gift economy, and Jooks started to tell me about the different ways Corinne dodged sex.

They stayed at the Hotel Victoria. A song someone had written about it played while I was on hold. The Grand Suite wasn't available the whole time, so Jooks had me book the second best for three days, the Grand Suite for four days, and another suite for three days. They would have to switch rooms three times. Excellence is a muscle. I booked restaurant reservations on the Amalfi Coast and a boat tour of Positano's beaches and ruins.

Before their departure, he opened a bank account for $1,000,000 in her name. "I don't know what's going to happen," he fretted. "If I go to jail...I want you to take care of my errands...I'll pay you $500 a week. I'm giving Corinne $1,000,000. I feel so bad...I want her to be able to take care of herself when I'm not there. I'm also gonna give you $9,500."

"Why?" I asked.

The want was too much for me.

"Because you're a jerk," he laughed affectionately.

"Thank you, Jooks." I allowed my eyes to become soft and warm, trying to think of the money as Mimsy would have—with an abundance mentality.

"You don't have to."

Once Jooks mentioned the sum, however, I felt I must have it whether or not he went to jail, so my incentives would remain pure. It was less than what he owed me for overtime and all the screaming. He'd given Mimsy more in discarded Rolexes and pay-offs before he'd set her free by firing her while she was visiting industry people in LA, probably not without a secret severance package.

As the trip approached, I got antsy. I told myself I must get him to follow through.

Two days after Jooks flew to Italy with Corinne, his lawyer sent an email stating that he was summoned to an arraignment on the day following his return. The judge was going to tell him how much his bail was, and if Jooks didn't have the full sum, he'd go to jail. Then I would have to bus it out to Rikers every day, so I could pass him his tuna sandwich through an inch of bulletproof glass.

I called his burner phone to make sure he had gotten the news but waited a few days to ask for the money. "Jooks—I'm worried," I told him. "I was wondering if we could go through with what you mentioned before you return...I'd like to have a reserve so I can continue working for you should anything arise."

After some back and forth, Jooks called his banker from Italy.

JÖYCE

The day of the pick-up was soft and gray.

Jooks sent me to get $9,500 in cash from his banker all the time, but since it was for me now, my organs fluttered like everything would go wrong. I meditated into a space where $9,500 felt small. The slightest disturbance in energy could ripple over to Italy and conjure his change of heart.

The cab sailed down the island. I retrieved a bill-sized manilla envelope and slid it into the shoe compartment of my Lululemon workout bag.

An article online said a Lululemon employee murdered a co-worker who caught her stealing a pair of yoga pants for the mandatory uniform. Someone told me Lululemon was a cult based on the teaching of Ayn Rand. Their stock was doing well in the recession.

I kept the money in my bag for five days before I stashed it on a high shelf in my closet. I bought a lock for my bedroom door.

I wanted to build a better life for me

and Lemon. Jooks had promised to cover her expenses, but I knew he'd renege the second I left. I was the irresponsible single parent of a teacup Yorkie. My roommates were kind to her while I was at work, but she needed the stability of a retired couple or a house staffed with servants. Her medical fragility and maintenance threatened to bankrupt me.

Lemon was the only creature gentle and sweet enough to coax me out of my melancholia. We were parasitic twins, subsisting on the deep and toxic vein of Jooks' affections.

I welcomed Jooks and Corinne home. They handed me a vinyl tote bag embroidered with the word "Positano," and a cotton tea towel painted with a recipe for limoncello.

I went to the liquor store and bought a bottle of Danny DeVito limoncello. I wanted to feel what Corinne felt in Italy. Danny DeVito had a show called *It's Always Sunny in Philadelphia*, where I'm from. I brought the bottle to Alphabet

City and visited an old classmate, one of my last ties to the pre-Jooks world. She grew up in New York. I was in awe of her mesmerism. She'd internalized that downtown Edie Sedgwick vibe long before I even knew what that was.

Ina's roommate, some future Broadway dancer, slipped past an Indian curtain as I sipped the Limoncello—to show how great it was that I could drink socially and casually now. Ina was already teaching at NYU and had bought a fancy purse with the money. Ina was nothing like me—so I had no idea she was only a knock-off. She'd *All About Eve*'d me, all through Williamstown and the rest of Tisch, and I hadn't even noticed because I'd never seen the film. She was so good, to this day, I don't know if she was an undercover operative or just that skilled in subtle relational manipulation.

The artists around me regurgitated what they read in the newspapers, but I contended with fundamental truths. Religious truths. Only Jooks' primal rage, or my parents' homelessness, could scare me into societal participation. Everything in comparison was a petty exhaustion.

It was Ina's birthday, so I handed her some melted Häagen-Dazs ice cream bars as a gift.

CHAPTER 47

SPLENDA DADDY

Jooks was scheduled for his arraignment the next day. There were errands to run. Jooks' lawyer, Matthew Richardson, stopped by for morale. "Jooks, if you can get your assistant to come in at 8:00 a.m. tomorrow, that would be a big help. The jury will see how weak you are and that you really do have to be accompanied everywhere because of your health. Would you mind doing that for us, sweetheart?"

"Sure, I can do that," I said.

Corinne bowed over the photo album with the solemn grace of an organized crime wife. "I'll come in too, Jooks." She brushed a tear from her eyes and smoothed it over a picture of Jooks eating lobster at the airport.

"You come in at nine after I leave. I don't want you to cry and make me late."

That morning, Corinne and I had bought an $800 silver-leaf frame for a cellphone picture of them dining together in Positano. He'd enlarged it to a pixelated twenty-four by eighteen inches at the Rite Aid. His eyes and teeth were as yellow as the matte setting. Jooks loved the photo because of how happy he had felt in that magical moment.

He saw his lawyer to the door and came back asking to borrow $500,000 of Corinne's freshly gifted million for his bail. She complied without protest, eyes lowered, rhythmically swiping an Elmer's glue stick down the back of their pictures.

"Whatever you need, Jooks," she said.

"Go to the computer," he bade me. I made a tender cross to the desk chair. "Type 'I, Jooks, am borrowing $500,000 from Corinne, strictly as a loan, and will repay the amount.'"

I printed it for him to sign and date.

"Put that in my safe," he gestured to the wall closet where it nestled. I entered the combination, opened the door, and sealed the document within. "Alright, good. Now...l-let's watch some television."

After fifteen minutes, Jooks roused

me from the sunken place beside him. "Go and put that thing I wrote in the paper shredder," he whispered. Corinne kept tempo, sticking photos onto the adhesive pages, pretending not to listen from her swivel chair mere feet away.

I gave him a desperate look.

"Do it..." he jerked his thumb at the paper shredder between the couch and the desk. I took a pained stroll back to the safe. The paper shredder sighed the contract through rotating teeth, into a belly of strips.

Along with Christmas, exploitation of the poor, and prostitutes, now a thing Jooks shared with Dickens novels was trips to the courthouse.

Although drunk from the night before, I was awake at 6:30 a.m. in time for court. I was a woman now. I tempered my weightlessness with a sense of duty as I flat-ironed my hair and put on makeup, in case there were reporters.

An intact person would have left this job. I took a trust-fall into the void.

SPLENDA DADDY

Jooks sent me to Dunkin' Donuts for his small decaf coffee with cream, Splenda, and a cruller.

"Listen," he said when I returned, "if they send you home, I want you to go to Vern and g-g-get me $6,000."

"Jooks—is the bank even open this early? Your car to the courthouse will be here in thirty minutes."

"Not now—after I g-go."

"How will I get you the money?"

"P-p-put it in my safe."

"I'll need a note for that."

"There's n-no time."

"You want me to call your banker the second you get dropped off at court and tell him to give me $6,000?" I washed down a bite of cruller. "Jooks, how do you have time to send me for donuts but not write a note to your banker?"

"Don't you fucking tell me what to do."

"It's going to look like I'm trying to swindle $6,000 out of your banker while you're stuck at court."

"I don't care, just do it."

"Okay."

JÖYCE

Matthew Richardson rode beside the driver, a pure gentleman.

"Jooks, I need that note for your banker if you still want me to get $6,000 for you while you're at court," I interjected, so I'd have Matthew as a witness.

"There's n-no time!" he screamed.

"Then I can't go and get it for you."

"He gives you money for me all the time!" he shouted.

"Only with your permission. At least can you leave him a voicemail?"

"N-no. Just do it. If he says no, then forget it."

I had made up a bag of his Warfarin, Lipitor, Trazodone, and Klonopin with instructions.

Because of the religion I grew up in, which everyone claimed was a cult, I had a revulsion to psychiatric medications but an affinity for following instructions. I worried I was a Suppressive for administering the drugs, but the Church also insisted that one must never go off psychiatric drugs without the supervision of a qualified medical professional and that we were to obey the laws of the land. If only there was a way to make money that aligned with my spiritual goals.

In a small room with just two chairs, a table, and a lamp, we met the District Attorney. Jooks said she was getting her big break taking him to trial. She looked me over with a wince, like I had a wound that only she could see. My eyes welled up. It was the second time that year someone had pitied me. I expected her to accuse me of being a gold digger or sex slave, posing as his assistant. She wouldn't let Jooks take me with him.

"Here's his medication," I chirped. The cholesterol meds and blood thinner got through, but Trazodone and Klonopin had to stay back with me.

With Jooks occupied for the afternoon, his lawyer offered to drop me off at the apartment on his way downtown to the firm, where he'd prepare his statement that Jooks had a pacemaker for a heart and would die in prison.

"They're going to rape me in jail," he had whimpered, as Corinne and I meditated on his safety the night before. His jingle for the Orbit Soap campaign was drifting from the computer as she burnt a CD of his music to play in the new Mercedes Benz he'd bought her.

I thought: *what if Jooks decided to become a nice old man in a rocking chair with chickens and a garden?* Then, whenever he saw a pretty girl, he could write a song instead of committing crimes. Alas, he yearned wholly to be consumed body and soul by the flames of delusional obsession, so that his last remaining art form was an existence of profane defilement in the most violent expressionism.

Jooks' lawyer was an emblem of civilization in his tailored pinstripe suit, puffed hair, and office hung with romantic portraits of his wife in an off-shoulder pink gown, pretty as a prom queen gone missing.

"So how did you come to be a lawyer?" I asked, dainty beside him as the driver zoomed down Lexington Avenue.

"Well, I grew up in the Bronx where

cops would hit you in the shins with a nightstick just for walking down the sidewalk in threes. After law school, I did some years of pro bono work—because that was the only realistic way to pay off my debt. Then I became the lawyer of a famous rock band."

"Wow, that must have been wild!"

"Those were some great times, traveling around with them. But it became exhausting, and I wanted to have a family. Settling into white-collar criminal defense is a way to survive financially if you don't come from money. You know, I actually played Jooks' song at my daughter's wedding. He burned me a CD for the occasion."

If Jooks was guilty, he had a fake-it-till-you-make-it approach to innocence. He could think of nothing even falsely incriminating to disclose to his legal team.

I set about the day's first errand.

"Hey Vern, it's Jöyce. Listen, I know this sounds odd, and it feels odd, but Jooks told me to call you the moment he got dropped off at court and ask for $6,000 from his bank account."

"Ummm...."

"Yes, that seems like the right reaction. He told me to immediately ask you for $6,000 following his court drop-off but refused to give me a signed note, even though there was time to do it in the car ride over. Why would he do that?"

"Yeah...I don't really know..."

"Same. I asked for the note several times, and he refused—and just so you know I'm not trying to steal from you. Anyway, I trust your judgment. Should I come in and pick it up or is there some other way for Jooks to get money if he needs it? I'm just confused."

"That seems...odd. I'd really...rather not..."

"Okay, great, just wanted to make sure I was following Jooks' request. I'll relay that you declined. I hope he comes out of things okay today."

I went down to Hamburger Heaven and ordered Jooks' usual: tuna salad and a slice of tomato on toasted white bread with the crust cut off. I guess I was feeling sentimental. When I opened the wrapping, the crust was still on. The men who worked there knew I'd ordered it for myself behind Jooks' back while he rotted at the courthouse.

I caught up on the latest articles about the trial. Online comments said the girls should have known better than to audition in some creepy dude's apartment. Like they should have known their job interview, with somebody who won all these awards and paid to fly them across the country, was all leading up to a rapefest in his apartment.

Corinne arrived around noon.

"I couldn't sleep at all. I have bags under my eyes," she sniffled, opening a compact and dabbing concealer under her pristine lashes. I couldn't tell if she was faking or if my eyeballs were so deeply set into my skull that her definition of puffy was imperceptible.

"Did he tell you to throw away that contract he wrote saying he'd return the $500,000?"

"Yes, I knew you were watching. I had no idea what to do besides follow his orders."

"That was so stupid. I would have given him the money back if he'd asked. I don't know why he had to sneak around me," she said.

"I know. You obviously would have given it to him. It was like Jooks felt he had to con you."

"It's so much money. I wasn't even expecting it. Can we call him?" she asked, "I'm so worried. I was up all night crying."

"Matthew said they're preparing the case and in court all day..."

"I don't care, I'm so worried, Jöyce. Can we please call him?"

I acquiesced and rang up the phone.

"Matt? It's Jöyce...Corinne is really worried about Jooks. Any updates?"

"None yet, okay? I've got to prep some files, and then head over. I'll check back with you ladies if there are any changes," he strained.

"Okay, thanks Matt..." I put some concern into my voice. Not because I didn't have concern for Jooks as a basic human, but because it took effort to summon the gentler emotions towards someone who had given me low-grade occupational PTSD before YouTube taught me what PTSD even was.

"You think he did it?" Corinne said.

"It's impossible for me to know."

"When we were in Italy, he even looked at this girl who was, like, younger than me. Like, much younger than me, Jöyce. Like twelve."

"Are you serious? Why was he staring at her?"

"I was like 'Stop, Jooks, you're scaring her!'"

"Like, I've seen him stare at women over twenty-one that way. Wait, did she look twelve, like an actual kid? Like, there was no way he could have mistaken or been staring at her for some other reason?"

"Like, she looked twelve. I think Jooks might have done something..." said Corinne.

"You think?" I retracted to a crouch.

"I don't know if it was rape...but he

definitely did something...like there was this one time he grabbed me and, like, he was scary. I stopped him. I screamed at him. I totally went off on him, and then he was like 'Oh, I'm sorry, I'm sorry,' but..."

"...but if you were a girl who doesn't know that he responds best to being screamed at..." I continued.

"Exactly."

"Isn't it funny how when he gets angry, the only thing that snaps him out of it is to scream back?"

"I know," she said.

"You would think that screaming escalates the fight, but the more submissive you are the more ferocious he becomes."

"Exactly."

"The only reason I knew that is because the assistant he had from Hunter screamed back at him on her first day of training me. I would have never known."

"Do you think he did it?"

"He insists he has no idea who some of these girls are. One victim's testimony in the paper sounds exactly like him. Before he attacked her, he was like 'TAKE OFF YOUR STOCKINGS, THEY MAKE YOUR LEGS LOOK FAT.' Jooks' exact style of coercion: shame, confusion and intimidation, all mixed together."

"I can't believe he said that to someone."

"It's what the newspaper said. You'd think, given how obvious of a rapist he seems, he wouldn't actually do it. He's such an asshole, it's too easy to believe that he's guilty. Crime TV has trained me to expect a surprise ending. Of all the ways Jooks has failed humanity, being a repeat sex offender seems redundant."

"Oh," she said, "he's been so much nicer since the stroke."

Around 4:00 p.m., he knocked. The doorman gave no warning. Jooks wanted our unprepared reaction. Corinne raised her hands to her cheeks and gasped. She pulled him to her and laid her head on his chest, careful not to let their bodies touch below the neck.

JÖYCE

Jooks led us to the den. He had spent the day in a dingy hallway, summoned to and from the courtroom.

"What did they feed you?" I asked. Whenever anyone goes somewhere exciting, I always want to know what they ate.

"A piece of bologna on some bread." He waved his hand in disgust. I pictured poor old Jooks, his one-and-a-half octave hands grasping a flopping cold cut between two slices of bread.

I faded back into the conversation as Jooks recounted his big St. Joan moment. "...And I stood up. I said, 'Not guilty, Your Honor!'"

Corinne was like a displaced movie star. She rallied our good cheer with chronicles of Jooks' triumph at treating people like shit throughout Italy.

"We went out on a boat to this little island, and there was a boutique, so Jooks asked the sales lady about this sweater." Corinne fingered the edge of her vintage-style sheep wool cardigan. "She said it was on hold for an Italian princess. So Jooks was like, 'I WANT

IT!'" Corinne broke from her screechy imitation into giggles. "Jooks hated the woman who took us on a tour of the ruins." She dropped into a chortle. "So Jooks...shoved her."

She hit his arm. "You shoved her!"

"I did not shove her," Jooks said, clearly cheering up at the memory. "I just din' like 'er."

Marilyn Monroe said people will forget what you did but never forget how you made them feel, and Jooks made me feel like shit. I smiled anyway. Learning to smile while your mind is doing something completely different can be a valuable skill.

CHAPTER 48

BROTALITARIAN STATE

Jooks started taking Corinne on spending sprees so he would have less money to lose in the lawsuits. She stayed over every weekend but only visited for dinner on school nights.

She was wearing black quilted Chanel ankle booties and the black Chanel quilted cross body purse with leather and chain strap that I liked to search for on eBay and sometimes imagined owning. "The coat is Marc Jacobs," she said. "Ugh—but these sandals." She motioned her white-polish pedicured foot where the leather thong sandal bit into the skin between her big and second toe. "They keep hurting me when I wear them. I paid $200 for them at Bloomingdale's—with my own money."

I was sent to Gracefully Market on the Lower East Side to stock up on low-calorie foods for Corinne, who was getting her model figure back in honor of her new bank account.

BROTALITARIAN STATE

"I need Cornichon pickles, Kashi TLC whole grain crackers, Manchego cheese, Mighty Mango Naked Juices, blueberries, sliced deli turkey breast, Melba toast, grapes, watermelon cubes, Fage 0% plain yogurt, green tea, Sabra Supremely Spicy Hummus, two limes, and one whole jicama." Acai berry juice and Nopalina fiber supplement powder had accumulated on the credenza with the other signs of her inhabitance, bringing new life to Jooks' stagnant lair.

Jooks wanted two hotdogs from Katz's Deli. Iconic New York lunches surfaced in his memory, as from a shipwreck. "The hotdogs used to be twenty-five cents, and when I started at the Brill Building, some days I had enough money for the subway or enough money for two hot dogs from Katz's, and on those days, I chose to walk."

It was another lesson in marketing. I had no emotional attachment to food, being taught by my father from childhood that it was only fuel.

For myself, I bought three bottles of green potion, a European herbal digestive called Underberg, made from a closely guarded family recipe. *This, this is me,* I smiled, gazing at the little bottle wrapped in brown paper as I clutched it with my hand. *This is who I am.*

Jooks and Corinne's doomsday spending spree moved me to economic stimulus. That weekend, I got a black manicure and commemorated my independence by unwrapping an Underberg before going onstage to perform in a naked version of *Leaves of Grass*. It was forty-four percent alcohol by volume—the icy burn of European forest herbs and their secret magic.

We performed *Leaves of Grass* to packed houses. On opening night, an audience member snuck a video camera and zoomed in on someone's penis, so our director shoved him out the door. Another night, Marissa Tomei complimented me personally—thanks Marissa, I think your work is really great too.

I had the second bottle of Underberg

BROTALITARIAN STATE

at a theater on 72nd Street, watching *I Am Love*, an Italian movie starring Tilda Swinton. The movie was different from all the others I'd seen, which was not many. In the final scene, I couldn't tell if she killed herself or did a cannonball into an off-screen swimming pool to break the tension. I told myself that one day, when I was rich too, the movie would be about more than rich people in their nice-ass house.

I drank the last Underberg to celebrate my future and inevitable achievement.

Jooks bought Corinne a whole new top row of teeth and paid for laser hair removal on her bits. "The nurses were bitchy to me...like they thought I was his prostitute," she said.

I made an effort to look perplexed. Jooks only called them hookers when he was mad. She was not his prostitute. She was his girlfriend, and every hour, he gave her $1,500, because that's what you do when you love someone.

"They were like 'Oh, now you can have teeth to match your pretty face!'

but they said it, like, meanly. Then the dentist filed all my teeth down to little points and told me to go look in the mirror so that I understand how important it is to take care of your teeth. I saw myself and cried. I looked like a homeless person. It hurts so bad."

I imagined the indignation of the dental technicians that she, already young and beautiful, would receive free teeth to further advance herself in the world. The dentist had installed a pre-mold with no spaces in between, for her gums to accept while he finalized the real fake teeth.

"I swear, Jöyce—never do it. It isn't worth it."

"Why shouldn't she? You did it!" shouted Jooks.

"Her teeth, they're rotting out of her head," Jooks muttered in the cab. I worried that mine were too, and the longer I delayed addressing my spiritual ailments with The Ups and Downs of Life course to rid myself of suppression, the more they would decay.

(444)

BROTALITARIAN STATE

Jooks had just fired Corinne's gym trainer after the first session because of the way he touched her waist to help her balance on the machine.

"Corinne and I want to join a pool for the summer," he said. "Look up the best, most expensive swimming club in Manhattan."

Will recommended a place called the Soho House where he had a membership, but they didn't let Jooks join. "Tell them I'm an Academy Award Winner!" he ordered.

"I did."

"What the hell...I don't care about their fuckin' club!"

The rape trials weren't major news, but there were enough headlines to recognize his name. After car rides back and forth in negotiation, I got him two adult summer passes for the rooftop pool at the midtown Holiday Inn. The hotel costs hundreds of dollars a night, but the full sun and crowds of screaming kids seemed an alarming step down from his usual luxury.

JÖYCE

"Jooks wants me to see his psychiatrist, so he can give me some kind of medication," Corinne said in the cab ride to the gym. "He thinks I might be bipolar because we've been fighting a lot."

He'd switched to a more expensive gym farther east once Eclipse banned him.

"Oh...?" From what I saw, she had the symptoms of a girl my age dating an old freak, but I remained neutral. My childhood religion said psychiatric drugs were invented by the two percent of people truly capable of evil. But it also said what's true for you is true for you, and I didn't want to force my beliefs on her. I decided that considering the possibility of rapey old men trying to control you with medication through their personal doctor was not an act of religious intolerance.

"I'm not sure what to do, Jöyce..." The cab jostled her willowy torso.

"I would say definitely don't." I reached for precautions that would not offend her worldly sensibilities. "I think...if you're going to explore your options with an issue of that nature, don't do it with Jooks' doctor. Do it on your own."

I turned my head sharply to the window with nothing further to say. Discussing the human practicalities of things I fundamentally rejected, like society, was something I tolerated to survive the MEST Universe, which is the physical universe as we know it (comprised of Matter, Energy, Space, and Time).

I called the dentist to order more of the tube called Soothe. They had given Corinne three kinds of balm after the surgery, and she'd run out of one. I fantasized about a glamorous life of dosing up on topical gum painkillers in my own two-family home in Queens.

Corinne was very hungover and fifteen minutes late for a morning gym date with Jooks, who had already left the apartment and started without her.

"I don't feel well," she'd protested.

"That's the best time to work out!".

He lit my phone up like a poltergeist every five minutes while I waited at his apartment to shuttle her straight over.

"Is she there?" he yelled from the receiver.

"No, Jooks."

"Is she there?" he texted.

"No, Jooks," I texted back.

"Hi Jöyce—Jooks is on the elliptical. He asked me to call and see if Corinne is there," said his new trainer, who I could hear relish his own superior receptionist skills.

"You can go ahead and tell him no. Thanks."

"WHEN SHE GETS THERE, YOU TELL HER TO COME MEET ME IMMEDIATELY," Jooks boomed into the phone.

"I don't tell her what to do, Jooks."

"YES, YOU DO." He was always trying to incrementally initiate me into new, rapey skill sets, like pressuring girls my age to hang out with him.

"No, Jooks, I don't. And you can't be yelling at me right now. I'll let you know when she arrives and pass on your message. Bye."

[click]

Corinne was standing at the

bathroom mirror in her new black workout pants and shirt, with grey and electric blue Nikes. She ran a toothy comb through her long, black hair.

"Oh, my god Jöyce, I am so hungover," she moaned. "Does Jooks really keep asking if I'm there yet? I don't know why he can't let me rest."

She had been to the hospital a few days earlier because her mother had a recurring heart problem. "I drank so many Coronas last night. Can you just wait a minute before you tell Jooks I'm here? I'm so nauseous." She popped two Advil. I imagined her going out with a bunch of friends, knowing that her reason for celebration was because she had $1,000,000—well, once Jooks paid her back the half he borrowed for bail. I thought how wonderful it must feel and was happy because being near money made me feel like I could have it too someday.

Jooks called again. "Is she there?"

"Yes"

"WHY DIDN'T YOU TELL ME SHE GOT THERE?"

(449)

"She literally just stepped in the door, and I did not have time to pick my phone up between then and you calling me."

"Goddamnit! Lemme talk to her!" I handed my phone to Corinne.

"Jooks, I'm here. What? Let me get ready a minute!" I heard his voice buzz and snap back at her across the line.

"I will be there in ten minutes. Let me brush my hair and catch a cab—Jooks, I feel sick! I will be there! I have never stood you up! God! Now do not call here again or I won't come!"

Even if Corinne was only performing, she was doing a good job. All sexual and romantic relationships with men seemed like a performance to me. I told myself it was because I was broken and incapable of love. The loneliness would fuel my work, and people like artists who suffer terrible misfortune. Deep down, I knew it must be that my chronic tone level was so high on the Hubbard Chart of Human Evaluation that my sexual urges were sublimated into creative thought, while the materialist society around me was degraded into sexual aberration, and I might never meet my true equal.

In the cab, Corinne wept. "I'm happy... but I don't understand why I feel sad right now." I'd only ever heard anybody say that line in movies. I guessed the happy part came from having a $1,000,000 and the sad part came from having to fuck a hateful old man.

Everything filled me with dread. I had almost been extinct once already.

"Don't spend it," I said. The advice was my way of trying to help.

"I know. I won't. I'm not going to tell anyone I have it. I'll help my parents if I need to, but I won't tell them how much I have."

"You could live off the interest maybe. Twenty thousand a year, that's four percent of half a million, right?"

"I could if I worked other jobs."

"Are you an artist?" I asked. I always made sure to ask this question to everyone I met, because artists are the most revered beings on the planet.

"I want to be a teacher."

"I can imagine that."

JÖYCE

I paid the cab and peeled off to the gym café for my coffee and banana. Corinne headed upstairs for her conditioning.

For the rest of the day, I ran errands. I had to drop off paperwork for Corinne's marriage annulment and email Jooks' butler, Roberto, in Cabo.

Jooks had told Roberto to purchase a suit so he could fly up and go house shopping in New York, where he'd live and work for the soon-to-be-married couple. Then came news of another swine flu outbreak in Mexico.

"Ewwwwwww..." Jooks grimaced, "you'd better tell him never mind. Th-th-th-that's awkward...I'm glad I'm not the one who's gotta write that email."

"Jooks, he says the swine flu outbreak wasn't near the actual resort."

"I don't want to take any chances!" His gusto for infectious disease control was a far cry from Dr. Gordon's waiting room in December when he'd announced himself Manhattan's first recorded case.

"He said he already bought the suit."

BROTALITARIAN STATE

"Well, tell him to return it! Jerk."

Corinne went away to visit her family for a couple weeks. She called asking to transfer her $500,000 over to the Dominican Republic to make repairs on her grandmother's house. This made Jooks' banker hesitant. Corinne stepped back with composure but remained abroad.

As I left the gym with Jooks one morning, a man in his thirties intercepted us on the sidewalk.

"Jooks? Jooks, I'm not a reporter, I'm a friend of your daughter, Heather."

"Jooks, who's Heather?" I asked.

"No, no, no..." he waved his hand and continued walking, staring straight ahead.

"She's trying to get in touch with you," the man continued. "She's in New York for the next two weeks—she wanted me to give you this."

He handed Jooks a letter, which was immediately shoved into my hands.

The man trailed back into the gym.

I tiptoed beside Jooks, towards the

pizza parlor on First Avenue.

"Ah fuck, we've gotta catch a cab," he muttered. "I don't want them following me."

"Um—you don't want this?" I looked down at the letter.

"She's a jerk," he said.

"Why?" I asked.

"When she was nine, she told the school I was abusing her...so she could go live with her rich friends. I had to spend months trying to prove I didn't neglect her. She said there was no food in the cabinets. I always had food. She's a liar. In court, they each got to pick the parent they wanted. She went to live with her mother, and I took Will."

"How old was Will?"

"Will was six. I told him he was never to speak to them again if he wanted to stay with me."

We caught a cab to the pizza parlor, two blocks over around the corner. I had a classic New York slice, the best I'd ever tasted, and realized that making pizza is an art.

CHAPTER 49

STOCKHOLM SYNDROME

The stock market went down and down and down. Jooks sold his shares to collect before he broke even or lost. "But—but it's MY MONEY," he contested over the phone.

Jooks' broker said he had informed him of the fees.

I guess they weren't required to remind him, in spite of the stroke.

I'd bought Lululemon stocks on E-trade to emulate his high rolling life of prosperity. Too bad I emulated his selling habits, since Lululemon is bullish to this day. I didn't tell him he could play the Dow on E-trade right from his home computer with no broker fees. I imagined him screaming at me to sell when the price dipped, losing millions, and beating me to death.

Aashvi lived in the other apartment on Jooks' floor and worked for a banking firm that had taken a government bailout, then taken major criticism for sending its high-ranking executives on a lavish hunting trip right afterward. The American people just don't understand the stress of being a Wall Street baller. She was in her fifties and often showcased her perfect celebrity body with glamorous athleisure, of rhinestones and velours, satins and metallic threads, as fine as any of the reality television stars.

She said she was looking for an assistant. I said I was looking for a nicer boss.

"Oh, I couldn't do that to my neighbor," she said. "I don't want bad blood between us."

I referred my roommate's live-in girlfriend, Vine.

Vine said Aashvi's apartment was all white with lacquer floorboards like a Barbie mansion, with nothing in the fridge but a few bottles of champagne.

"Aashvi has me complete personal administrative and household tasks in exactly four hours, as detailed on a flow chart, while she's at work," said Vine,

STOCKHOLM SYNDROME

"and I, like, have to be gone before she gets back. Like she won't pay me after four hours, it's so weird."

Something rang a bell—the Scientology organizational technology I had studied and used in school would have called for the same thing. But I already knew not to admit this to outsiders.

One day in the elevator Aashvi said, "You know, if Jooks ever needs it, I'm willing to testify and say he's never tried anything with me."

"Thank you," I said. "I'll let him know that."

"Women of our age need to be, really, very strong."

"Yes."

Aashvi sent over an invitation to a birthday seance she was throwing for John Lennon.

"Jooks, do you want to go to this?" I said, thinking there'd be food platters.

"No," he sneered.

"Why not?"

"Because I don't wanna fuck'er!"

JÖYCE

I was deviantly prompt. Jooks wanted me there at 9:00 a.m. On the six train, I wore slip-on shoes of thick blue hand-sewn cloth printed with tiny brown blossoms that bound my heels and toes to rustic slabs of recycled rubber. The weather was mild enough for my new cotton frock. I was wearing the dress Jooks got me. The chest had a fabric panel embroidered with thick blue vines. That's why it had cost eighty-five dollars. Jooks had hovered it before my thorax at the gym retail store, "That looks n-nice. D-do you want it?"

"Oh, I do like it! But you don't have to get it for me."

"Okay," Jooks put the dress right back, attempting to enforce that playing coy gets you nothing. So I resolved with indignation that it must be mine. I complained to Mimsy, who had been re-employed for two whole weeks since getting fired, and magically, Jooks bought it for me the next time we went.

"I told Jooks how much you liked the dress, so he got it for you. Okay? Are you happy?" She rolled her eyes. So really, I

STOCKHOLM SYNDROME

was wearing the dress Mimsy got me.

The train was forty-percent populated. I felt something brush almost imperceptibly against the thin cotton at the apex of my ass curve. It had been years since I'd had the courage to confront someone over intentionally disrespecting my personal space. His touch was so faint, I clung to the pole, eyes forward with the assumption that this could only be an accidental violation. Seconds later, I felt the slight brush again, as before, and attempted to shrink. The touch was feathery enough to be imagined but creepy enough to exist. It was then I heard his low, ecstatic moaning.

Still too embarrassed to turn, I made a face of obvious disgust, hoping that someone, somewhere, would see. The train made a stop, and a man no taller than five feet in a baseball cap, oversized T-shirt, sagging pants, and large basketball shoes went bounding out the doors.

Two men walked right up to me.

"Was he doing to you what we think he was doing to you?" one said.

JÖYCE

"I couldn't believe it at first, but if you saw it too, I guess so," I replied.

"We're undercover cops" the other said. "We've been tracking that guy. He comes and does that on the train all the time and, yo, it's not right."

"Whoa," I said, nearly ready to swallow the whole ordeal. Two cops walking up to me, right after I was violated, and confirming that they saw it too changed everything.

"Ma'am, if you wouldn't mind, could we ask you to step off the train for a moment to fill out a report?"

"I have to get to work though," I stammered.

"It'll just take a second ma'am. We just really wanna catch this guy. It's not right for him to be doing that to women. We'll write you a note. We'll even stop the train for you so you don't have to wait for another one."

I was shocked that they could stop the train.

"Okay, I mean damn. I just want to get to work."

I needed to brush off the whole thing

like it didn't exist.

They said his name was Rafael Broncito, and they asked if I would be willing to tell the assistant D.A. what he'd done. I said sure, and they gave me a carbon slip of my report and appointment.

Having texted that I was late because of an incident on the train, I sauntered into the kitchen. "Oh boy—guess what?!" I said.

"What?" asked Jooks.

"A little shit on the train actually dared..." I paused "...to harass me." I laughed loudly. "So I'll have to go into court on the twenty-ninth," I said, rubbing it in.

"Wh-wh-wh-why do you have to go to court?"

"Because, they want me to confirm my story, and all of the female victims are coming in to testify. I mean, you wouldn't want a fucker like this to just, no pun intended, get off, would you?" I paused. "Anyway, that's why I'm late this morning. Sorry about that, Jooks!"

I handed him my note from the cops.

CHAPTER 50

SUMMONS TO LOVE

I had the desire and stack of bills to leave my job but no exit. I tried to motivate myself with a fear of going numb and getting stuck there for sixteen years like Pearl had done. But the more I allowed myself to imagine the unwanted possibilities, the more realistic they became.

I was a grain of sand trapped in a Nobu oyster at the bottom of his kitchen garbage dreaming of becoming a pearl. My mind was a detached symphonic computer. For sport, I could play dumb and helpless to see who tries to laugh at my expense. Unless I *am* dumb and helpless and only comforting myself with the illusion of control on the way to certain slaughter.

Either way, it still counts as a sport.

I waited for a truthful impulse to propel an organic exit as I had learned to do in scene-study class. Meantime, I strategized a raise. The internet said every sixth month of employment should be subject to a fifteen percent raise evaluation. I had been there over a year.

I couldn't go back to the Church until I was rich and famous, or I'd have to join staff and hit daily goals for how many copies of *Dianetics* I sold in Times Square.

Another summons came. This time, without an envelope. Alone on the elevator, I peeked. The plaintiff's name hit me with a cold flush: JANE DOE. I wondered if it was the one I knew.

Working here, I was learning legal terminology. The plaintiff makes the accusation. The defendant must defend themselves against it. Both plaintiff and defendant are innocent until proven guilty and given due process.

"JANE DOE...? I don't know who that is!" he uttered.

Coincidentally, the assistant director of a mainstage I did senior year asked me to be in his play. The mainstage had commissioned a Broadway and Pulitzer Prize co-winning playwright who developed a central character that matched my acting strengths so well, it was almost embarrassing when I read for it—until she mysteriously fell off the project. The professor directing it created a whole new show, positioning his favorite student to appeal to the industry with pole-dancing classes and a farcical newsroom strip tease, casting me as an old Iraqi woman. I had occasionally walked the two hours from Brooklyn to rehearsal because I didn't have train fare, and by tech week, I was living off discarded craft services from my roommates' film gigs.

In any case, I bumped into an actress I knew in the lobby of the rehearsal space. She said that she was working as a personal assistant too, but oddly, she seemed happy. When I mentioned my boss, she recognized his name and said I should get in touch with her close friend, JANE DOE. So it *was* the JANE DOE I knew—the girl from college whose mom said to go with the guy who keeps coming back.

Afterward, the play was canceled, almost like the whole purpose had been to lure me into that one chance encounter. I got a Facebook invitation to a record release party where JANE DOE was on the "going" list. It was fate.

Amongst the grand PBR windmills of the Bushwick Country Club, JANE DOE and I circled the beer-stained astroturf mini golf green as we had once trod the sprung floor of the Suzuki movement studio. Now I was beer-stained. I ran anonymously with struggling Brooklyn bands and was ousted from the crowd Japetto had leveraged against my reputation. I made myself available to speak but thought she should be the one to bring it up.

"I'm, uh, sure we're both trying to approach the same topic right now."

"Right," she said.

"Yeah. He's basically the worst person I've ever had first-hand prolonged exposure to," I muttered.

"Really?"

"I can't continue working for him now that I have this information. It's a wonder why I've stayed already."

"I can help you find another job,"

she said hastily.

"Oh, Jesus, no, you shouldn't have to do that," I said, perhaps too generously. There was Lemon, whose lifestyle and expenses were necessary for her dignity and stability. I couldn't maintain them without Jooks.

"We should get coffee and talk about it," she said.

"Yeah, definitely."

I left to see my boyfriend play bass with one of his bands.

JANE DOE was going to meet me after her audition in the Theater District, where I had a rehearsal for a one-act play written by an old classmate. She cast me as a stagehand who hides in the wings and threatens everybody with a gun at the end.

I went to the wrong Starbucks. Then, I found her at the right Starbucks, half a block over, sipping a chamomile tea.

I ordered coffee. I had taken to café au lait, which is half coffee and half milk.

"So what's he like?" she asked.

"Well..." I was tinged with paranoia, or, as I like to think of it, caution.

SUMMONS TO LOVE

I didn't want to be involved or blamed for Jooks' blights upon society. My boyfriend said I could become a character witness who could be called in without notice. I felt I owed JANE DOE answers for her suffering even though I had nothing to do with it. I tried to convey an honest portrait of Jooks without any upsetting reminders. "He's a total freakin' asshole," I went. "He's proposed about three different times to call girls and gym trainers in the year I've been working for him. You'd think from all those crime shows on TV, Jooks would cultivate a personality and charisma to misleadingly contrast with all the terrible shit he's being accused of. After working there a month, he became such a jerk that once the summonses started pouring in, I was like 'C'mon—that's too obvious.' You know like when you watch a movie and it's too predictable for one character to be suspected of something because they're already such a fucking asshole? Well, that was my reaction to Jooks being accused of rape."

"Really?" JANE DOE chuckled.

JÖYCE

"Yeah. I mean...he's just a dick. The accusations are consistent with everything I've seen about him. Like, he touched my knee, and I was like, 'Don't ever touch me,' so he laughed in my face and was like, 'You're funny,' and I was like, 'Why?' and he was like, 'Because you don't like it when I do THIS,' and pushed my shoulder. Right in front of his lawyers when we were in the cab—and I told him not to fucking touch me. He was like, 'Ohhhh I'm not doing anything that I don't do to my other employees!' and I was like 'I've never seen you gently brush your lawyer's shoulder or knee. I don't owe you an explanation. You are simply never to touch me.'"

"Wow..." she muttered.

"He's a total control freak."

"So you're...involved with his lawyers?" she asked.

"No, I just go to the office in a cab with him and stay in the lobby. I don't involve myself in anything but getting his meals and taking dictation for his emails and stuff. I make myself incompetent when he asks for dubious things."

"Interesting. Has he ever, like, hit on you?"

"Um—I'm really, really cold towards him. I shut him down at every turn and he's not a romancer, really—he's more like a predator. He watches and waits and feels people out for their loose bricks. Then he tries to loosen the brick, and before a girl knows it, she's been given a Chanel handbag and a couple dates to dinner and a Broadway show, and she's being harassed via text message over why she's not telling him where she is. In the trials...there are a lot of girls accusing him..."

"Yeah...I don't actually know those girls."

"I don't know how a lot of that legal stuff works."

"I actually don't know too much, either. Wait, so how did you find out about me?"

"Your friend mentioned it when I was bitching about Jooks. But I saw your name on a summons by mistake. He said it out loud, anyway."

"Did it say how much they're suing

for?" she asked.

"It said $2,000,000," I replied.

Her eyes widened a little.

"I'm surprised you don't know that."

"Yeah, it's weird—the lawyers do everything. I don't pick the amount or anything," she said.

"Wow...what was he like...um...that day when you met him?"

"Oh uh...just...what was described in the paper...pushing...shoving... shouting...."

I chastised myself internally for sensing something in her voice too vague and unemotional to be true. This wasn't one of our acting classes where we were striving for emotional availability. She could have been repressing the negative experience. Perhaps I was immediately doubting a victim as a coping reaction to avoid thinking I might become a victim myself. I didn't want to believe someone could be so powerless to protect themselves, because then it could happen to me.

There must be some factor that contributed to the situation, I thought, that I could isolate and avoid.

I felt guilty hiding my whole thoughts from JANE DOE, but I worried some of them would upset her. To be the same on the inside as the outside in all situations—to be so honest you don't need to hide anything—is the most noble human state. I heard L. Ron Hubbard say that in a lecture recording once, but I was not noble enough. So I could at least be considerate.

"He pulled some paper out of his nightstand and was waving it at me and shouting that it was proof he had a vasectomy."

She chuckled with faint memory.

"His vasectomy papers," I marveled. "He's always talking about that damn vasectomy—like it's the only thing stopping girls from wanting to sleep with him."

"He said, 'No' a lot."

"Yes!" I cried. "He loves to use the word 'No,' like to crush your hope."

"'N-n-n-n-no!'" She imitated him.

I went cold.

"Wait, how would you know about his stutter?" I asked. I wondered if his apartment was bugged and JANE DOE was listening.

"What? I mean, he didn't hide it very well. You mean, he doesn't normally stutter?"

How could she know about his stutter if the crimes had occurred before his stroke—unless she somehow came in contact with him afterward?

My thoughts spiraled. Had she fraternized with him a few more times? Was I being set up? Was the whole apartment being taped so she could get me involved in the trial? I couldn't tell if the man sitting a little too close to her left and scrawling on his notepad was a leery writer or some lawyer of hers.

"Wait a minute..." I continued, stabilizing myself in the immediate. "Jooks told me that his stutter happened because of his stroke. How would he have stuttered if the crimes took place prior to that?"

"What? No. Not unless he had a different stroke before I met him."

(472)

SUMMONS TO LOVE

"He's always made such a big deal that his stutter has only been since the stroke in April, and if he could fix it with his speech therapy, then women would be attracted to him again."

My heart flipped in my chest. It was inconceivable to me that Jooks would lie and that I had accepted something so easy to disprove as fact. Now, I would have to consider that any information I couldn't verify first-hand may contain a multitude of lies, just like Scientology had always warned.

"He had a stutter when I was there," said JANE DOE. Now she was startled by how startled I was.

"So then—what happened next, after you left?"

Today, I realize I was supposed to say, "Do you want to tell me what happened next?" but I would not have thought of it back then. I didn't know then what a rape even looked like—except that it would be dramatic and loud—in a dark alley somewhere—committed by a random mugger like in the movies and on TV. Then the cops would come, and

(473)

the criminal justice system would take care of it. I couldn't picture how it might work leaving a nice apartment afterward.

I thought that totalitarian religious indoctrination might be the only thing that gave my empath heart the necessary walls to protect myself from Jooks. But his emotional Tone Level was so low down, somewhere between "Body Death" and "Anger" on the Hubbard Chart of Human Evaluation, that I simply wasn't qualified enough in my Scientology training to confront the situation.

"Afterwards, his assistant called and told me I got the part," said JANE DOE.

"You mean Pearl?"

"Yeah, Pearl."

I thought about how it would feel to get called by an Oscar winner and told you got a part in his film with Scarlett Johansson.

"So did you get a rehearsal schedule or any kind of call from them after that?"

"No. Well...I'd better get going to my audition," she said. "This is all really good to know...we should get coffee again soon."

"I...I just have to leave him...this is too much and I feel horrible that I'm working for this man now. I...I'm leaving in six months when I save enough money... my parents lost their house...The trials should have been enough but...I know you and...well...there's...there's just one reason that I have to wait a little..."

"Why can't you leave him now?" she asked.

"I'll have to explain it later...it's nothing bad. It's just...surprising."

"Okay," she nodded, looking into my eyes and able to believe anything at this point. We said goodbye.

I would have to be sure that when I finally left Jooks, I would be ready to assume full financial responsibility for the dog. Jooks' embedding in my life was more toxic than the side effects of his extraction.

Ultimately, I didn't know what to make of Jooks' stutter. Either JANE DOE or Jooks was lying to me. One discrepancy in fact had thrown my entire model of reality out of alignment. Each pearl of data alters everything. No different than with one of Jooks' many Brooks Brothers sweaters. A bit of pilled cashmere, seemingly detached, skews the whole pattern when plucked. And things were not always as they appeared. A piece of lint Jooks picks from my shoulder might only be an excuse to touch me. I was too distracted by the fabric of the universe to recognize, in that moment, that society itself is wearable. I was left with my café au lait, remembering a news story my boyfriend told me about a man who had raped an eighty-year-old somewhere on the Upper East Side—who everyone decided was insane. Later, I read about a statutory rape trial against a teacher, where a judge said he was innocent because a picture of the middle-school plaintiff in makeup and a camisole made her "look beyond her years."

According to the Church, man is basically good. I am not an auditor who can assess the complexities of people and the corners they back themselves into.

SUMMONS TO LOVE

I stared through the picture window of bleary theater-district lights at street level. Mere blocks away, I had once chased MetRx protein bars with hot coffee before a fearsome and exhilarating dash out of the Hubbard Communications Office to the subway with a cluster of staff members bearing revelatory tomes that would lift our fellow man up from the mire. Now I was one more stagnant indulgence of a person. My parents had lost everything. I worked for a monster. I dated a musician who was an atheist. Everything they said would happen if you left the Church. I needed to return and gain the tools to change my condition in life, but I was too ashamed.

L. Ron Hubbard had once said something about the best Scientologists being the big thetans who had strayed many times to go on adventures. That's what I would be—wild and free, playing the game of life, unable to abandon the rest of humanity even though it was too aberrated to rise up from the mire and seize the tools to succeed in life. That's what made me not just a good actor but a great actor—so compassionate that I was almost wounded somehow. But I would go back one day, back to the Church, and bring with me the spoils of my fallen grace, of the true humanity that would make me so beloved among the masses.

CHAPTER 51:

A STREETCAR NAMED REPRESSION

I almost didn't make it far enough to study Scientology myself. Once in the eighth grade, things got so bad, I threatened to start seeing the school therapist. I had a friend who said her dad sometimes hit her. Finally, she and I decided to go together for an initial introduction. My dad told the Ethics Officer at the Church, and an alarm was sounded for the danger I was in.

At a Philadelphia graduate program for the fine arts he once attended, my dad's youngest brother Steve came back from a European painting scholarship because they found him riding the Eurorail for weeks on end in the same change of clothes, muttering incoherently. Uncle Steve was sent back to Maryland, where he wound up barricading himself in a house and claimed the SWAT team was coming for him. He's been in halfway homes and medicated into a daze ever since.

Occasionally, he was brought out for Thanksgiving or Christmas.

Uncle Steve has a freakishly high IQ, and just like Scientology said, was bound to attract suppressive old psychiatry for being an artist. My cousin said it was possible somebody gave him drugs in Europe that led to a psychotic break. Now that I've read a few history books, I'm thinking it was around the time they were doing the MKUltra experiments with LSD, so maybe Sidney Gottlieb slipped Uncle Steve something in the Eurorail coffee, trying to unlock his creative genius like Ken Kesey. My dad had always been scared for me, because I reminded him of Steve right from the beginning.

I was invited to meet with the Ethics Officer before deciding if I should go to therapy and brought along a list of every wrong thing my parents had ever done to me. Instead of addressing the list, the Ethics Officer had me write out every Overt and Withhold I could remember committing towards my parents and Word Clear a paragraph

STREETCAR NAMED REPRESSION

about *Responsibility* by L. Ron Hubbard.

Word Clearing is a Scientology Study Technology procedure wherein the student identifies all misunderstood and unknown words in their study material, and then thoroughly and fully learns their definition. In Study Technology, the Misunderstood Word is considered the greatest barrier to study.

It was then that I decided I was the only person with pure-enough intentions to effectively handle my situation. The only solution was to escape from my parents' house to college as smoothly as possible while internally severing all emotional expectation from them, limiting our interactions to that of co-workers or roommates.

The other girl with the abusive father spent the rest of eighth grade with a vitamin tube in her nose because of an eating disorder while I signed up for a bunch of extracurricular activities, so I had an excuse to avoid going home and could peacefully do my homework in the school library. If the only way for a victim to recover is to take complete responsibility for their circumstances in order to change them, how does it stop perpetrators who keep committing more abuses, knowing they'll be clean again once they confess? According to Scientology, except for the two percent of True Suppressives, most want to improve and avoid hurting others. In fact, claiming that man cannot change or improve is considered suppressive, and one of psychiatry's many crimes.

When I got to drama school, they said freshmen couldn't audition, but I had read all the best actors audition as freshmen anyway on the sly, so I showed up for a student film casting, auditioning for the role of a nun who was grappling with her sexual urges. That was when JANE DOE and I had first met. She was the only other actress to show up, and she got the part. I had the nun part down, but sexual urge was a level that I hadn't unlocked at that point, and I sensed something pass between her performance and the director that only seemed like an old shtick I had seen thousands of times, yet somehow held significance no matter how often it was repeated.

If the rigid form of religion's moral training wheels had robbed me of sex, Uncle Steve was still stuck living down in a halfway house somewhere, and I was playing a crazed stagehand with a gun up on 42nd Street.

CHAPTER 52

BIRTHDAY SUIT

I reminded Jooks I couldn't make it to work since I was needed down at the courthouse to share my story of subway sexual assault. There were big marble arches. I was sent to meet with the assistant D.A.—I didn't know if she was the assistant D.A. or if there were many assistant D.A.s, like VPs at Morgan Stanley. She was in her late twenties with wavy red hair.

"I appreciate you coming in," she said. She seemed less like a cop and more like a Writing the Essay Teacher from NYU.

"Oh, it's nice getting to come down here. My boss is kind of an asshole, so I'm glad to get away. He's in some sexual assault trials of his own."

"Really?" she replied softly.

"Oh, yes, well, I don't know if he's guilty or not, but it's just kind of a weird coincidence."

"It is," she agreed. She had the technique to navigate my combined pain and desperation for attention so I wouldn't feel outwitted or intellectually inferior.

"Well," I began. It was my time to shine. I shared my story and revelation that if the plainclothes policemen hadn't been watching, I may have gone on believing I invented the whole thing, and how pivotal it was to be validated at that vulnerable moment. I instructed her captive audience on my moral and behavioral insights, impressing my unique blend of highbrow concept with lowbrow execution and refusal to be a victim. "Really, more than anything, he was such an annoying little bitch and I was held up on the way to work," I bragged, defiantly reframing my assailant's crimes as nothing more than my momentary personal annoyance.

"Interesting." She gave a little smile. "Would you be able to come back and testify on October thirteenth?"

"Sure," I chuckled. "That's actually my birthday, so I'd be glad to have the day away from my boss."

CHAPTER 53:
THE FARE THEFT OF 2008

Defensive pluck is a legitimate alternative to letting powerlessness take you under, as long as you make sure that people don't take advantage of how much you are able to endure.

For some reason, for me, going to court has always involved strange synchronicity.

The summer before Jooks hired me, I was summoned for jury duty. Jobless and impoverished, the forty dollars per day had seemed promising. I hoped I got a big case. I was dismissed within an hour of showing up. The receptionist told me it would take four weeks for my check to arrive in the mail.

I went can-kicking back to the Court Street ACE subway to make my way home.

I was hot and hungry.

Discouraged by poverty and unable to hydrate for free, I drifted by osmosis through the first pore of the terminal. This happened to be an emergency exit left ajar.

FARE THEFT OF 2008

A wiry little woman sprung out of nowhere.

"Show me your ID," she snapped.

"What..."

I thought she was a clever, well-dressed grifter who used Pavlovian commands to con people. She wore civilian clothes, with no badge or explanation.

"Gimme your ID," she barked.

"What—why do you need my ID?"

She sighed in exasperation, like I should know. "How'd you get in here?" she interrogated.

"I just came in through there." I pointed to the emergency door propped open with a brick not two steps behind me. Then I thought maybe she'd been trapped in the subway for days and needed help figuring out how to leave.

"Hold on. Stay right here—Jason!" she shouted, storming off.

Two young guys dressed like guards came and stood beside me.

"Sorry," said one of them. "She's always like this."

I was ushered into a hidden office.

I wanted to ask if I could swipe my

Metrocard to prove I had a monthly unlimited and had only absentmindedly entered through the exit without motive. She was so nasty I feared the more I spoke the more she'd turn it against me. The desk attendant who filled out my sixty-dollar ticket for fare evasion said I would be able to contest the fine in court.

I swiped my Metrocard in the turnstile. Now, they would have it in the system as undeniable proof that I was not stealing. Surely then justice would come.

By the time I got a court date, I was working for Jooks and would lose more than the sixty-dollar fine if I took the whole day off work. A trial by mail made more economic sense.

I put together a meticulous account, writing that the lady didn't have a badge or uniform when she demanded my ID, had goaded me into confusion when I was only two steps through the open emergency exit, and that my Metrocard swipe was logged in the turnstile to prove I had no motive to steal the fare.

I received a letter back saying that while they could check those records—

and while I may not have had motive—I had still technically committed the crime by walking through the emergency exit, and there was no requirement to investigate whether I'd swiped my card. It was the cold metal instrument of the state snatching my fortune away through the willful exploitation of a technicality.

I won forty dollars reporting for jury duty and the MTA robbed me of sixty dollars on the way home. Spiritually, it made sense that this had happened to me. I needed to get right on my dynamics surrounding money.

I would return to court triumphant on my birthday. I strolled down Court Street to the ACE after the assistant D.A. let me go. Now poverty didn't nip at my heels, but my thoughts still hummed through the same old grooves, echoing whichever man is the loudest about achieving things and conquering life. "Looks like I'm gonna be down at the courthouse a while, Jooks," I texted. "Depending on how things go, I can join you this evening."

JÖYCE

Gauzy curtains swelled from an empty bistro where a lone waiter set the evening tables. The moments lost and stolen were the moments I was free.

If the time belonged to me to begin with, someone could take it away. It was the hour between lunch and dinner. I would treat myself to a single-player upper-income bracket casual supper for one.

"I think I'll have the baby octopus salad and a glass of something to drink," I told the tall young waiter with closely trimmed brown hair and an accent— Italian? Spanish? Eastern European?

"Prosecco?" he said, in soundbite.

"Yes thanks, that would be great," I trilled.

On my plate, I cut the morsels into tidy bits.

Table manners are such an art form. They make eating so fascinating. I was learning table manners from my boyfriend, using the fork and knife and placing them down on the plate between bites, looking up from one's food to listen and hold court, taking and giving focus to engage in conversation. My boyfriend told me this other thing about manners that stuck with me: he said that handshakes were first invented to show you weren't holding a weapon. I'd forgotten what he'd said about smiles. I only knew two kinds of smile: the kind where someone is trying to dominate you, and the kind where someone is trying to flatter you, and I hated both. The third kind of smile is the genuine spontaneous kind, which almost always looks ugly in photographs.

The waiter had the usual judgment masked with politeness, which I could never manage myself so I never got hired for waitressing jobs. Probably, he was making more money than I, but I had a manicure that day, did I not? Scrutiny told I was not accustomed to manicures, and that my imperfect hair was not a careful replica of bedhead or street style. I tried being as polite and untalkative as possible, listening and reacting warmly without offering information. This was what wealthy women did, was it not?

I was too fat to be from the Upper East

Side yet ordered the flourless chocolate cake. I ate it with delicate dents made by my spoon. The Prosecco was prompting my involuntary and prolonged smiles, lightweight that I am. Donning an air of sobriety, I paid my check and extracted myself from the billowing hologram of the bistro. I felt a sense of renewal, of the annoyingly stereotypical kind like on *Sex and the City*. I did not know the art of leisure, the beauty of entitlement. I knew struggle, work, self-deprivation, guilt, obligation, undeserving, co-dependence, subordination, servitude. There would always be assholes to take advantage of such qualities. I needed to experiment with abandoning these traits. I wanted to figure out how to be unexploitable, without being exploitative myself. To do that, I would have to treat myself to a good many luncheons of leisure. Jooks would have to be stricken from my sphere of influence.

Recognizing JANE DOE as one of his plaintiffs had peaked his toxicity. Then and there, I plotted my departure for six months in the future to the date.

CHAPTER 54:
DO RAPISTS DREAM OF ELECTRIC LOVE SONGS?

On the day I was to testify before court, I slept in. It was my birthday. They said he'd hover-crotched a lot of women on the subway. Nobody would need me there. I still went, in case they decided to put a warrant out on me for not showing up at all.

The boxy, dingy entrance had a security gate.

"You're too late," the guard said, like all women, disappointed in me. I was lazy and a coward. I didn't want to embarrass this small man in front of his family. I wanted my feelings of weakness to compress to the point of disappearance. I remembered his T-shirt, halfway down his shins. His pants were really only lengthy shorts. He was so small. Surely this must be taken into consideration.

I didn't want to participate in the justice system. True justice was in the void, where I liked it, and it was warm.

JÖYCE

I trudged from court with half a heart, past the restaurant where I'd lunched after the red-headed assistant D.A. interviewed me.

I fled the prescribed course of action and failed the specialness I'd been assigned. The police had stopped the train just for me and made important people sit through my improvised manifesto during the interview. Those had been rewards in themselves, enough for my ego to overtake the moment of intended payoff and plunge my shadow back into the lake, where I could gaze down at it forever.

I slunk back to work the following day. I was better suited for watching Jooks go batshit fucking insane than engaging in positive societal change.

"The watch got stolen." Jooks tossed his hands up.

"What?"

"The watch—Corinne's watch."

It was a rose gold Rolex encrusted with diamonds. I had never seen Jooks tolerate an unhurried transaction and began to wonder if he had fallen in love with the watchmaker. He deliberated back and forth, first over the engraving, then removing links to fit Corinne's wrist.

She had kept nagging, and he had kept stalling.

"Jooks," I said, "that watch cost a lot of money. I can't believe somebody just walked into your apartment and stole it. Why are you acting so calm?"

He shrugged.

"Oh—is it because you have insurance?"

He glanced to the side and nodded with a shrug.

"You do realize...this could mean that it wasn't actually Alina who stole the money from you, and now you've fired her for no reason?"

"NO...this is different. It's a twenty-five thousand dollar watch!"

"Which is why I'm wondering how you're so calm, but whatever. Should I call the insurance people? Or the police? Doesn't this scare you...?"

"First, we need to tell Corinne." He

handed me the phone. "Write: 'Bad news, honey—the watch got stolen from my apartment.'"

She could probably recover the price of the watch in a series of smaller gifts, but who was I to assume she didn't care enough to feel neglected? Maybe she sensed he was cueing the final scene of his girlfriend experience.

"Jooks. I'm not going to see you again until you get that watch back," she texted.

"Well, then, if that's how you feel, let's just call it quits," he replied. I did not see this coming. Celebrity unions are unpredictable. It almost felt staged.

An acting teacher once said the best performances were so engaging, they don't let your mind wander to awards season. But did the gold and black plastic imitation Oscar engraved with "World's Best Couple" that Corinne had placed between Jooks' Grammy and People's Choice on the piano mean nothing? It was a nuanced, layered girl-friend experience, steeped in magical realism and worthy of critical praise.

DO RAPISTS DREAM

"Please, Jooks. I still want to try and make this work," she texted hours later.

At home, I googled Jooks for new articles. In my one-day courthouse birthday absence, he filed a fraud lawsuit claiming Corinne had hidden her marriage to trick him into giving her fancy gifts. I guess he got bored with her and wanted to see if he could get any of his investment back. I hoped she wouldn't text me, personally.

The next day was very calm. I strode to the closet to help Jooks find his glasses.

"I'll check all your coat pockets."

"Nah, don't look there—"

I felt something cold and metal and extracted a diamond-encrusted Rolex.

"Uh...Jooks..." I said. "The watch that you got for Corinne that you said went missing."

"Yeah?" he said casually.

"You put the watch here in your pocket."

Now I had an example of how Jooks reacted to getting robbed for fake versus robbed for real.

"Yeah, what about it?"

"Uh...don't you think you should put this in your safe? I mean, what if you forget?"

I should have slipped it into my pocket, seeing how long he'd go before admitting he'd stolen it from himself.

The next day, his lawyers arrived and I was confined to the den.

"So, do you have the watch?" I heard Danielle say. I felt their reluctance and Jooks trying to control the whole situation by withholding information, as if his lie would become the truth by sheer will.

"It's right here," he said craftily. The closet door opened, and he rustled through fabric and umbrellas. "Oh, no... oh, no..."

"Jooks, the watch is in your safe," I called.

"Oh," he chuckled. His lawyers quartetted behind, their mouths in a silent O.

"Ahah!" he cried as the safe opened. He led them back to the living room, watch in hand, and shut me into my corridor. If I hadn't known that all of Western medicine is nothing but a moneymaking scam and that Scientology ensures total alertness and mental clarity, regardless of age, I would have suspected that Jooks' obvious failure to commit crimes at which he once excelled indicated dementia.

Danielle joined me in the den.

"Jooks seems to fall in love, propose immediately, buy a bunch of gifts, then try to gamble everything back with forms of harassment that cost even more. I couldn't tell what Corinne was playing at because I thought there was no way she could feel for him. My boyfriend told me that in the Dominican Republic, where Corinne is from, women date much older men and it's not taboo," I offered helpfully.

"Interesting," Danielle said.

He turned his call girls into girlfriends, and his girlfriends into call girls. He treated his business like personal relationships and his personal relationships like business.

His songwriting was so airtight though, you couldn't even tell it was written by a psycho.

"Did he get 'er yet?" he'd phone hourly, with all the giddiness of surprising a sweetheart on Valentine's Day. Jooks had to pay his lawyers to follow Corinne around until she let someone get close enough to serve her a summons.

Once Corinne's lawyer presented emails indicating that Jooks provided lawyers to help her annul her marriage a full six months earlier than he had indicated learning about it, Jooks lost his suit. For Jooks, it was part of the Girlfriend Experience. Corinne was doing her job perfectly.

"I have an idea," he said, gazing at the television.

"What's that, Jooks?"

"I wanna see if I can have her deported," he said.

"Um."

"Immigration Services...that's it... call them."

(500)

DO RAPISTS DREAM

"Um...Jooks...I can't do that...."

"Do it!"

"Jooks...I don't think she's even an illegal alien...I mean, you put the Mercedes in her name. Doesn't she have to have a driver's license for that to happen? She's enrolled in college...plus she was able to fly with you to Cabo... doesn't that require a passport?"

"Call them!"

"Hello? Immigration," answered a woman who sounded surprisingly casual.

"Yes..." I cleared my throat and altered the pitch of my voice. "I'd, uh, I'm uh wondering about...reporting someone..."

"Say she's an illegal immigrant!" said Jooks.

"...for being an immigrant. But, um, illegal," I went.

"Uh," she said, "we don't do that."

"Oh, okay."

"Okay, great thanks," she hung up.

"Thanks." I held my breath, hoping he wouldn't demand I track down a phone number for deportations. It was a balance, pantomiming agreement while proving ultimately ineffective. I infantilized myself. People are less likely to hurt an infant.

CHAPTER 55:
RUNAROUND SUE

With Corinne gone, Jooks' loneliness set in.

"You know," he said, "I think I need to find another girl like Harvest...who can introduce me to a girlfriend..."

"Welp, that's not going to be me," I said, flipping through an issue of *Highlights* magazine. We were in the waiting room Dr. Shore shared with the child psychiatrist, who popped into the lounge area to grab a box of Nilla wafers for her client.

"I didn't mean you!" he cried out. "My friends wouldn't like you!"

"Well, I wouldn't like your friends," I sneered over the top of *Goofus and Gallant*, not that I trusted either.

"Alright. That's enough," he said, husky with defeat.

My second Thanksgiving with Jooks rolled around. It was time for him to avoid paying the maid her bonus again.

"He no pay me extra on Thanksgiving. I work, but he won't pay me extra."

JÖYCE

"You worked on Thanksgiving Day?" I asked.

I'd begun informing him of my absence before bank holidays. This year, he'd spend Thanksgiving with his son Will at the River Café in Brooklyn.

"Oh, let me go ask him for you, Mar."

I went into the den. "Jooks, since Mar worked on Thanksgiving, do you think she should get paid time and a half?"

"Whaaaa?!" said Jooks, knitting his brows, tilting his head and gaping his mouth.

"I'm pretty sure it's standard labor practice. Possibly even the law."

"I'M NOT PAYIN 'ER EXTRA!"

I returned to the living room.

"Um, he said he didn't want to pay extra for a holiday. I would take that day off in the future so you can spend it with your family, but reschedule for a different day that week so you don't have to miss any hours—"

"What are you saying to h-her?!" Jooks asked, storming in.

"I was just saying that in the future, since you don't want to pay extra on holidays, she should reschedule, so that she can spend time with her family, but come in another day so you could still have your apartment cleaned."

"You're trying to make it so that she doesn't get to w-work!?" he said in disbelief, putting a protective hand on Mar's shoulder.

"No. That's just how you're trying to frame it," I said in monotone.

"Go in the kitchen!" he told Mar. She shrugged and went off.

"Listen, don't get involved," he pointed his big, knotty finger in my face.

"Jooks. You're perfectly entitled not to pay her extra on a holiday, but that means she should be perfectly free to go home—"

"Don't. Get. Involved," he said with a foreman's menace.

"Okay..." I said.

Jooks was saving to pay Masha $20,000 for a one week visit over Christmas. Masha had moved back to Russia after breaking up with her boyfriend. She was trying to buy an apartment there.

Before leaving the country altogether,

she told Jooks she might have to quit school for a semester and get a real job. Jooks offered to pay her tuition.

Even with a scholarship from Jooks, she'd returned to Russia.

He bought her Lufthansa airfare and booked the dinners, shows, and shopping trips.

Jooks made me accompany him to Roberto Cavalli, to buy her a warm winter coat. I yearned for Russia, all vast frozen landscapes, grand cathedrals with bulbed roofs and ominous church bells echoing through the dusk. To be a stern and beautiful woman, who never smiled unless it was genuine, and took no shit from vodka-crazed men or anyone.

The inside of Roberto Cavalli was a spotless white lacquer cube that I assumed was cleaned by a crew of styled and choreographed runway models for anyone who happened to peer in the glass after hours. The shelf beside the register had toy-dog mannequins in $600 puffer coats, but Jooks didn't offer to buy one for Lemon.

Jooks asked my opinion of the jackets,

then chose the trashiest in the store, teetering between wealthy Brazilian and boastful stripper. Ignoring a fur-lined shearling coat I thought would look nice in Russia, Jooks chose two identical belted-down jackets—one in glossy navy blue, one in snakeskin print—for $1,700 a piece, the warmest in the store. He hung them in his den closet for safekeeping.

Jooks booked a room at the Carlyle and reservations at Nobu for Will and his college girlfriend. William's grades and efficiency were supposedly up and so was the holiday cheer.

Jooks took me to an artist's studio on Eighth Avenue and 36th Street. He wanted to buy something for Masha's future apartment. He had met the artist's wife at acupuncture. She was young, pretty, also Russian, and looked just like Masha. She wasn't supermodel hot, a phrase I'd learned from my boyfriend, but more of a ballerina build, with curvy legs and a longish torso. She had an oval face and was a little shorter than me. To Jooks' mangled form, she must have seemed the fountain of youth.

The artist and his wife occupied a grand factory loft lined floor to ceiling with racks of paintings.

Jooks was obviously taken with the wife, who I chatted with on the reception couch while Jooks looked at art.

"Jooks'...um...girlfriend...is also Russian and looks a lot like you. I've never been to Russia but me and my boyfriend really want to go. What's it like there?"

"Eh...it's like garbage piled up two stories high in some places. I like being here better." I longed for the majestic heaps of garbage. The cold of Russia likely dulled their stench.

It dawned on me that we had come here so Jooks could compare himself to whoever married Masha's doppelgänger, demonstrate that his art was not good enough to purchase, but not without wasting a couple hours of their time. The artist was more than half Jooks' age, and almost double mine and his wife's.

I flipped through the paintings. One

RUNAROUND SUE

was a big canvas with a tiny school bus painted in the center. The next, a bigger canvas. In the center, an ice cream cone. It was just paintings of school buses and ice cream cones, over and over and over.

The artist must have been prosperous to have a large studio in midtown. There were articles about him on the wall.

It was in the high-rise where I'd once gone frequently to audition. I remembered the creak and fragrance of wooden rehearsal room floors, the early morning thrill of my first paid job with the Renaissance Faire for $2.33 an hour, the mealy succor of the protein bars purchased with my last pocket change, wolfed down on breaks. Those carefree days were dead and gone. We got home with bags of gifts for his prostitutes.

"I gotta see my fucking family for a holiday thing," he sighed. "Grab those." He pointed to the stack of free DVDs he received in the mail every year to vote for the Academy Awards.

"Um, Jooks, are you going to give these as gifts for your family?" Most

(509)

of the seals were broken and we'd watched them all.

"What? You fuckin buy 'em a present if you feel so strongly. Now, put this in an envelope with 'Joan' written on it."

He handed me a copy of *Milk* starring Sean Penn. "Meh, I'll keep this one." He set aside *The Mysterious Case Of Benjamin Button*. "This one sucks, put it in an envelope marked 'Ellen.'" He handed me *Rachel Getting Married*. "These two can be for Molly and Gail." He chose *WALL-E* and *Kung–Fu Panda*. "This can go to Mark." He gave me *Frost/Nixon*. He tossed out *Slumdog Millionaire*, *Doubt*, *In Bruges*, and *The Wrestler*. "Ugh, so many terrible movies this year. God, *Doubt*...so...boring! I couldn't watch more than five minutes! *The Wrestler*, what a loser! Why would Marissa Tomei do that shit? She was great in *My Cousin Vinny!*"

I went to close each manilla-letter sized envelope.

"Don't bother with that." He snatched the stack of envelopes and headed towards the door in his black

Burberry puffer and cane.

"Have a wonderful time with your family at the holiday party, Jooks," I tried to say with Christian warmth.

"See you," he sighed. The door slammed.

"C'MONNNNN!" I heard him bang on the elevator.

To Jooks, the most prominent filmmakers of younger generations were the latest crop of sophomores. He'd written hundreds of jingles and shaped the course of the American economy with the unshaped fantasy of public dreams, joined to our purchasing power by the beauty of his music and imagination. We bought those products, and the American Dream was born another day, in spite of all the odds and unseen casualties. It was a leap of faith to manufacture the product, to write the jingle, to buy the product, and to risk it all again without losing your investment or yourself. It is the occupation of generations after to complain of what those before us could not—hopefully never having to test our philosophies in war, if we can withstand peace. It's fun to be a generation of realism—when reality is one that we can face. A generation of nihilism, when our void is in the safety of a bubble, and every new ideal, a rebranded tyranny.

CHAPTER 56:
BRAH HUMBUG

I hope Will writes a book but doesn't bribe organized crime-affiliated fellow inmates to put a hit out on me in exchange for free legal help.

People just want to be loved and entertained—maybe fed, clothed, housed, and assured protection while watching their enemies suffer from afar—but mostly, loved and entertained.

Jooks aspired to this. I aspire to this as I write of him—of us.

It was approaching the end of 2009. Christmas Eve, Jooks noticed one of Masha's coats had gone missing from his closet. I assured him I would never want that trashy old stripper coat, which only made him madder, but he was certain Will took it for his girlfriend. If so, at least he chose the more subtle navy blue one.

I left on Christmas Eve as Jooks was departing for Nobu. Will's girlfriend looked TV pretty, Adderall thin, and so innocent.

(513)

JÖYCE

When I got home, Lemon was sickly. She had horrible diarrhea. We rushed to her Upper East Side veterinarian for chicken-flavored cold medicine that I was to administer from an oral syringe every six to eight hours. I thought I could leave her to recover overnight in my apartment, head to Philadelphia, then head back in the early morning to pick her up so she could meet my parents, but as I looked into her little black circle eyes, I realized I must vow to always protect her and that she was too frail to endure the journey.

I stayed with her through the night and took her on a bus to Philadelphia the next morning. I brought my parents exotic goods from Food Emporium: Norwegian chocolate dipped glazed spice cakes, which my father shoved into his mouth, tired of my mother's bland grocery budget, along with salamis, cheese, crackers, wine, olive oil. I brought a down-alternative comforter, a nonstick frying pan, a robe for my father, and the book of quotations my father wanted for Christmas a decade ago. It was the only gift he'd ever asked of us, and now he was unequipped to read. When I gave him the box of green tea and he couldn't remember that I'd grown up hearing him insist everyone drink it because of its health benefits, I saw he really had lost access to part of his mind. I had no answer for why my mother hadn't followed through with the right doctors' appointments. Our relatives had given her the money to pay for it. "He won't go!" she said. I choked on my helplessness. I couldn't think clearly around her, much less collaborate in anything but the most basic emergencies, and I needed to participate in other things besides emergencies.

I told my boyfriend proudly of the gifts, but he winced and said how Dickensian it sounded.

The day after Christmas, I returned to the progression of a vortex. Masha could barely contain her agitation as Jooks fixated on her every gesture. She was round-faced and had dyed her hair a dark reddish brown from the blond I'd once seen flash across the lobby. Her eyes were lined in thick unbroken black.

Jooks stepped out of the elevator with her. The old gentleman in a fedora and cane from the floor below followed Masha with his gaze.

"Pret-tyyy," he murmured.

I rolled my third eye, reminded of how adults grant approval to the children who behave as they wish and dismiss the ones who act up. I never fell for that trick, praise. What fucks did I give for an old man complimenting a whore's looks over mine? He only wanted to subordinate me because he knew I wasn't on the market.

I tossed my hair and chuckled smugly as I walked after Jooks and his long-lost Ukrainian granddaughter.

Of the four I had seen Jooks promote from call girl to girlfriend, Masha hid her resentment the least, and Jooks said he'd loved her longest. At her most polite, she was distant. Frequently and rightfully, she was cross.

The next day, she was sullen. I believe

BRAH HUMBUG

Jooks felt that Masha was becoming unmanageable and invited me to work as a way of embarrassing her.

Jooks sent me for their orders of liver and onions with rice from PG Bernstein.

"This tastes funny," Jooks pooh-pooh'ed from the kitchen.

"It tastes okay," she murmured.

Enveloped by pungent aromas of humble sweetmeats from Masha's homeland, I craved it like no other.

I trotted after them through the shops around 57th Street. Jooks took her into Cole Hahn for boots. She was sporting a large silk Louis Vuitton scarf around her neck and walked about the store, absorbing its opulence. Together, we silently willed away the painful humiliation of our chaperone and patron. The young sales girls grimaced in welcome. We could never tell where news of the trials had spread.

Jooks and Masha sat down at Viand, and I was sent to Louis Vuitton to pick up her new purse before returning home for the afternoon.

JÖYCE

Days later, it had all gone, of course, to shit.

I unlocked the apartment to Jooks pacing the living room.

"Look at this," Jooks murmured, holding his cellphone out. "Read the text messages."

Thus unfolded the morning's transcript:

"WHERE ARE YOU?"

"Just going for a walk."

"HORSESHIT. YOU'RE MEETING WITH THAT BOYFRIEND OF YOURS, AREN'T YOU?"

"I said I'm just going for a walk. Be back in fifteen minutes."

"OKAY, THEN HURRY BACK. YOU'D BETTER BE BACK THEN AND NOT A MINUTE LATER."

"You know what your problem is? You're a control freak. Fucking psycho."

I had never thought of his overwhelming monstrosity in such manageable terms. I understood why Masha secured his attachment. Of course, he'd metabolize the simple refusal to comply with his tyranny as

(518)

the oxytocin of love.

Time passed between text messages. The next read, "You better give me my passport or I will call the police."

"I DON'T HAVE IT. YOU MUSTA LOST IT."

"Bullshit."

"I'M TELLING YOU I DON'T HAVE YOUR PASSPORT."

Some more time passed.

"So, I'm leaving early. I can't take this."

"WHAT DO YOU MEAN? I FOUND YOUR PASSPORT, DIDN'T I?"

"Heading to the airport now."

"AFTER ALL I DID FOR YOU?"

"Please don't act like this is such a favor you're doing me. Twenty thousand dollars for one week is much lower than the proper hourly rate. You're the one getting favors."

"I WANT YOU TO RETURN ALL THE GIFTS."

"Okay."

"I read the text messages, Jooks," I said with sympathy, or at least discomfort. Masha hadn't made it through New

Year's. I don't know if she got the money. Maybe Jooks drove her away early on purpose.

"Also...there's this bag..." he said, holding out the Louis Vuitton box. "Take a look."

Inside was a beautiful checkered Louis Vuitton bag, but with bright, multicolored LV logos and sloppy flowers that looked hand painted in acrylics by a wealthy Japanese twelve year old from the UK.

"You like it?" he asked. I could tell he wanted me to ask for it. It was beautiful for its craftspersonship but distasteful for its imagery, destined to become an isolated emblem of fortune I could not keep up with, reeking of clinging servitude.

"It's nice, I'll go return it," I said, nicely.

I walked by a Hollister with a line of people waiting behind a velvet rope for a bouncer to let them shop at 2:00 p.m. Louis Vuitton was packed with assholes waiting to trade in as much paper cash as they could for whatever bauble or trinket they could afford to match their new Hollister T-shirt. It was the worst thing ever. I returned the overwhelming bag, hoping they would say they didn't do refunds, only store credit, but they weren't Prada, and they did do refunds.

My highly selective taste in trash was worth more than a fine-crafted Louis Vuitton emoji bag some Paris neon goth had printed out. I guess I choose the apocalypse over someone having more power than me.

New Year's Day, Will sat in the living room. I thought I heard him sniffle, eyes cast downward towards a pill bottle clung loosely in one hand. He was munching on Klonopin.

Jooks had warned me of Will's vulnerable state in a text: "LISTEN, WILL FOUND HIS GIRLFRIEND DOING HEROIN IN THE BATHTUB AT THE HOTEL LAST NIGHT AFTER DINNER. HE THREW HER LUGGAGE OUT ON THE SIDEWALK AND SENT HER BACK HOME TO CALIFORNIA IN A RAGE. HE PUNCHED A BELLHOP."

I felt bad for Will, bad for his girlfriend, and bad for the hotel employee who suffered the whims of people who indulged in the occasional bellhop punch.

I thought how he must have loved her, to want her health so badly that he refused to abet her addiction in exchange for the comfort of a relationship.

Thanks to Scientology, I had grown up free of psychotropics. I did not understand the culture and conspiracy of young adult drug use.

"Hi Will," I said, careful not to enturbulate him.

"Hey," he muttered.

I turned into the hallway towards the den. Jooks passed me quietly with his New York Times and orange juice.

"Ch-check my email," he said.

On the corroded salt flat of his spirit, familial strife gave Jooks a bit of warmth. I eyeballed him on the tone scale as vacillating between "owning bodies" and "being objects."

Finding no item of urgency in the morning emails, I crossed respectfully through the living room into the kitchen for a Diet Coke and slice of lemon. Their father and son murmurs curled softly as I passed.

"I know dad...I just lost it...she said she wasn't going to do it anymore. She said she was clean now. I really believed her. And she said terrible things about you."

"Ugh," Jooks moaned. "Do you think..." I heard him posit quietly as if to offer some comforting nugget of fatherly wisdom, "...that you would still be able to introduce me to any of her friends?"

"Dad!"

I sipped in the swivel chair for several minutes and let my mind wheeze in the day's narrow possibilities.

"L-listen," Jooks said, "we've gotta cancel Will's flight, and you gotta go to the hotel. He punched that bellhop, so here, give him this." He handed me a hundred-dollar bill.

"I'm sorry about what happened, Will," I said.

"It's okay."

Will dug a navy blue leather bracelet from his jean pocket and thrust it towards me.

"Here, do you want it? I was gonna

give it to my girlfriend. It cost $100," he said. It was a nice bracelet, and it had taste.

Here I was benefitting from Will's complete devastation.

For being so gracious, the bellhop was rewarded with a hundred-dollar tip.

The pharmacy denied Jooks an extra Klonopin refill, so he went himself to claim he'd dropped the whole bottle on the floor. Failing that, Dr. Shore supplied it direct.

Father and son collapsed into one another like stars.

"Ahh, shit! I don't want him here," Jooks moaned, booking the dinner reservations, but with an undeniable rose in his complexion.

There's no deep psychic stimulus like family, I thought.

CHAPTER 57

BRAND THEFT AUTO

"...and then, I want you to eat her out while I f-fuck you from behind," Jooks said.

"Um. Is this right?" I held out the text for him to see so I wouldn't have to repeat it.

"Good. Send it."

"Just sent."

Having exhausted all female companionship, Jooks went to Harvest. Harvest was Texan and had introduced him to the other girls. I pictured some seedy dude in an alley like the Scientology training films showed. She was a Columbia University student pursuing her master's or PhD in something having to do with biology, but I knew an elite school didn't matter in the grand scheme of your immortal spiritual potential.

"She's lying. She didn't go to Columbia," Jooks muttered, waving away the notion. "A-a-and get this—she's in love with a fifty-year-old woman somewhere in,

I don't know, Nevada. It's this whole stupid thing."

I found a long obsessive rant about the lover on her Facebook.

Asymmetrical haircut, bisexual, in love with an older woman, financially endorsed—she was a centerfold of the Columbia University brochure.

I tried to imagine being in love with an older woman but could only picture my third-grade teacher standing in the cubby hall in a turtleneck, denim shin-length skirt, and comfortable sneakers. I didn't get the attraction at all.

The morning had a drowsy silence. Harvest had flown in at dawn on the way to Nevada. Her slumbering presence deep within the apartment was heralded by a selection of the most whimsical deli pastries posed about the kitchen in varying states of unwrap and consumption. They were the pastries people admire for their gelatin layers and chocolate domes but never actually purchase. There were lady fingers and opera cake and tiramisu and macarons. There was a green glassy triangle of citrus cheesecake, rainbow almond cookies, and Ritter Sport, alongside some insulin shot cartridges. Harvest was diabetic.

"Have you met Harvest?" Will side-eyed.

"Yeah..."

"Nice haircut huh...," he smirked.

"Yep." I would invalidate neither Will nor the haircut, but listen to both sides fairly.

Jooks arranged for Will to stay at a hotel for a few days, in case denouncing Harvest's haircut wasn't enough to offset the sexual threat.

In her brief visit, Harvest made the notable and lasting adjustment of placing seven-dollar cinnamon-scented pinecones from Food Emporium in the large decorative hammered copper bowl on the credenza. I have never forgotten those pinecones.

"So—is the sugar good for you to have? Is that why you got all these cakes and stuff?" I asked. It was force of habit. Scientology is all about inquiring into different health problems that in most cases are the result of not applying Scientology. I thought anything positive could help. I also didn't understand how the different kinds of diabetes worked and wanted to talk about the cakes.

"Well, no, but I just have a tiny bit—like I'd just have a tiny square of chocolate."

"Huh."

"Hold on, my mom's calling me."

"She knows you're with Jooks?" I asked.

"No! I tell her I work as an assistant."

Maybe that's why people think assistants make so much money.

On the third morning, she stood swaying in the middle of Jooks' living room on a pair of platform espadrilles, in pressed white linen wide-leg chinos, and a striped boatneck three-quarter sleeve jersey fresh off a Ralph Lauren Bloomingdale's mannequin.

She uttered invectives like a Tennessee Williams heroine while Jooks quietly unpacked her suitcase of all returnables. Cast from his favor, it was safe to show her wit.

BRAND THEFT AUTO

I had never seen Jooks be discreetly expedient rather than pick a fight.

"O-okay." He gave her a dubious glance when the doorman phoned from the lobby to announce her sedan to the airport. "Your car's downstairs! Lesgo!"

"Hah," she chuckled in a relaxed wilt before the doorway, Klonopin bottle lodged in her little fist, eyes tending towards the heavens. "He's lost it completely."

Her eyes were wide open and clear. The Klonopin, or some force of energy, had cast away our shields for a moment, if also her physical bearings. The face right up to mine was innocent and clean, approaching in confidence.

"Yes well—consider yourself lucky to be going," I whispered excitedly, not knowing the reason for a willingness towards her that receded as quickly as it appeared.

What I didn't understand at the time was that this feeling of excitement is what people must have been talking about when they talk about attraction. We were oriented with each other in some way that I did not understand. It was so brief and natural—and I had rarely ever felt that way. Then, the portal closed. She shifted back into the Klonopin void, and I into my ready guard.

The Hubbard Chart of Human Evaluation did say that you could experience sexual feelings towards the same sex if you dropped down low enough on the emotional tone scale.

I slunk out the door after Harvest and Jooks, vaguely guilty over her drug-addled life.

"Hah," she laughed louder, intuiting some natural climax.

I could see she was quite hurt to be sent away, perhaps as a matter of professional pride.

There was a brisk knocking. The doormen offered to take the suitcase and Harvest had not the word nor the gesture to decline. I held my breath in the elevator, not wanting to be spotted in this tasteless exiling, or for anyone to think that I had invited Jooks into her life.

"Oh my god, look at her," Jooks

whispered as she sashayed through the lobby, doormen dutifully wheeling her suitcase. They maintained neutral faces, recording and judging everything that occurred. It was the doublethink of the high-class service industry. Luckily, no tenants were around.

"LaGuardia Airport, please!" she cried with cheer. If she didn't have a floor-length Isadora Duncan neck scarf trailing horizontally from the backseat window, she may as well have.

The doormen put her suitcase in the trunk.

"Jooks, does she have cab fare?" I asked.

"She's fine."

I worried. What if Harvest had no money and the cab driver kicked her out and she flew to meet her lover in Las Vegas, but they never showed up, and she became homeless?

We watched the cab speed away.

"Byeeeee!" Harvest stuck her head out the window and called back at us.

"Um. Is she going to be okay?" I asked.

It wasn't Harvest's pill-popping

monologues or nonchalance with deli pastries but the haircut that had pushed Jooks over the edge, and he didn't even know. The bisexuality he could pretend wasn't real, just like her Columbia education. He probably couldn't conceive of being in love with a fifty-year-old woman any more than I could. But the asymmetrical haircut had scrambled his brains. I'd been taught if you express too much with material things like clothes and whimsy, it will make your art bad—like foam at the top of a glass of soda that dissipates the carbonation. Forced into excruciating pressure, you can speak only through your art. For Jooks the anarchy of her haircut must have lodged somewhere in his subconscious, sending out synaptic misfires.

"I don't care," Jooks shuddered, sealing us back into the musty apartment, where all that remained of Harvest was the waft of cinnamon. "I'm glad she's gone."

It was good Jooks hadn't roped me into a prostitution ring, but things were lifeless around the house again. There was nothing to be done but barrel through it for my hourly wage.

We are all in the gutter, and Jooks was bored.

Harvest flew through incomprehensible youth while I shaved off each day like they were numbered, and Jooks had dismissed his last and final call girl.

It's hard to be a diamond in a pinecone world.

CHAPTER 58:
VINCENT VAN GOPHONE

"Guess what!" screamed Jooks. "Will rang up $20,000 on my credit card!"

"What?! On what?"

"On hookers!"

Except Will rang up $20,000 on their credit card. I knew because both times I'd accidentally lost it, the bank had sent one printed with Jooks' name, and another printed with Will's name that Jooks put in the paper shredder.

Jooks had me clean his file cabinet. I found letters signed by women stating that they consented to have sex with him, a photocopied picture of a woman in a hospital gown with bruises, and a letter from his accountant to his real-life true love from *Struck by Lightning*, promising to pay her daughter's tuition for life at any school. I also found an old interview that described the speech exercises he did every morning before acting on a film set, to deal with his lifelong stutter.

So that was why JANE DOE had

known about his stutter when she and I met for coffee.

"D-d-did you meet any g-good ones? Eh?" Jooks asked Will after a few minutes of screaming.

"Dad—there's this girl named Kiki—she's the number one Paris Hilton impersonator in the whole country..."

I wondered how you could stand being famous for pretending to be someone who was already famous, and how the world got to be trash.

"What about the girl—Dolores?"

"Sorry, dad...I just don't think she's interested..."

"Not interested?! I can pay 'er!"

Will gave him the slip with tact and compassion.

"I wanna show you what Will did for my birthday one year." Jooks brought me to the file drawers under the TV and pulled out an old section from the New York Times.

Before I could lift the page, Jooks began in the oral tradition. "During the seventies, I read an article about a scientist who was researching children's bone cancer. I was so moved, I told my secretary to call him up. She couldn't get in touch with him. I said, 'If you don't get in touch with him, you're fired.' Of course, I wasn't going to fire her, I was motivating her. So then, I got in touch with him and I said, 'I want to make a donation to your research.' I met with him and donated $1,000,000."

"Really, Jooks?"

"Really."

"Wow! That's amazing."

"I know. It was everything I'd saved from advertising. And I had no idea whether I'd ever have that much money again!"

"Jeez."

"And it was s-s-s-significantly more money back then. Today, $1,000,000 is... meh."

"Oh my gosh, Jooks. I can't believe it. What a crazy thing to do. In a good way."

"I had all these scientists in my living room smoking cigars. I did it anonymously."

"Oh, really? You didn't want people seeing your name and then hitting you up for money."

He shrugged.

"Wow, Jooks. Not a lot of people would do something like that."

"Read this," he rustled the paper at me.

In the one-page New York Times birthday advertisement, Will praised his father's anonymous charity, his venture into Hollywood, and being a super great dad. Jooks must have gotten tired of the anonymous part of the donation after a while and then leaked word of his generosity to Will so that he'd take out the ad.

Even as a teen, Will recognized that Jooks' love language was advertising.

I knew that trying to get pure fatherly attention from Jooks must have been like trying to breathe with a hole in the throat.

Will's $20,000 stripper bill brought them closer. Then, Will confessed he'd been talking with his estranged sister, mother, and grandparents, and Jooks threatened to disown him again.

"I just want my dad back—they can

help you with your legal problems! They have money!" I heard his voice rise from the living room. "I'll give my inheritance to your lawyer!" he pleaded.

Jooks had none of it, so Will agreed to disconnect. I assume he kept in secret contact.

"I wanna get Will an apartment," Jooks said as I browsed the website of Video Room. "D-d-do you know anybody?"

"Um. I mean the ones I know are in Bed-Stuy. It has the highest number of murders and robberies in Brooklyn."

"So?"

Will would not want to be involved in my crowd. I was not going to be Jooks' unofficial real-estate agent or get pestered to do things for Will's apartment simply because I lived nearby.

"Uh, yeah—I don't really know anyone with the apartment Will would want."

"Oh come oooooonnnnnn." Jooks glared at me for shutting him and his son out of my undesirable little life that

VINCENT VAN GOPHONE

Jooks would have laughed at anyway were it not for his hour of need.

"Oh boy!" Jooks navigated his meal full spirit. He had sent me to Nobu for take-out. They have a no-take-out policy, but he joked that he would fire me if I didn't lie and say he had just gotten out of the hospital.

"Guess who I saw today," he went on. "You'll never believe! I saw Baila at the gym."

"Oh, how nice," I smiled. For a moment I thought Jooks was excited to establish healthy boundaries with the gym trainer he had inappropriately proposed to.

"You know," he said, "why don't you call her up and ask if she's able to be my trainer."

"Um. Sure, Jooks."

There was no need for me to spoil his good mood when I could leave it to her judgment.

"Heyyyy, Baila..." I left a voicemail, and wondered if she got the same jolt of alarm from his BLOCKED number that

JÖYCE

I did. When I was still a kid, my mother would hiss at me to freeze and be quiet whenever the doorbell rang in case it was one of my father's debt collectors. She would yell at me never to pick up the phone for the same reason. So bells could have been more programmed into my nervous system than for other people.

"This is Jöyce..." I began the message. "Jooks said he bumped into you today... and was interested, in, ah, training with you again. Definitely call back and let him know! Talk to you...soon."

Jooks leaned back, smiled with forced contentment, and waited for her to call.

CHAPTER 59

DOC FUGUE

The blind shadows closed their crooked teeth over the small waiting room in the golden hour. Jooks and I were meeting Dr. Chaconne to determine whether Jooks was fit for trial. He was a nice man with Einstein hair, tufted and white. It was obvious but solid branding for a psychologist. He reminded me of the hippies-turned-professionals whose kids I'd gone to school with.

"Now, Jöyce, I want you to be here too. Because I wanted to ask you a few questions," said the doctor. "I'm going to also be recording this conversation, by the way, if that's alright with you both."

"Sure." I felt like I did in middle school before a test I knew I was going to ace. I had nothing to hide.

"Now, forgive me if this is a somewhat uncomfortable question, but I need to know everything is in order to correctly assess the situation. Did you at any point assist Jooks in—ah—in getting girls?"

"Oh! God no," I laughed, enjoying

Jooks' disgruntled silence. "No. No, not at all. That's not an uncomfortable question!"

"I see," said Dr. Chaconne, not quite able to hide his disappointment. I would not get in his flaming chariot to hell, which I had attempted to flag off the road multiple times.

"Have you seen any improvements in Jooks' symptoms since you began working for him?"

"Well, it's difficult to tell. Because I'm around him so continually, it's hard to track gradual changes. He says the acupressure helps his pain the most, and going to the gym regularly. He needs to practice his speech therapy every day, but we're not good about finding time. It was pretty amazing how much having sex with that one prostitute helped. I mean, I'm not okay with it. But it was like the very next day, the blood gushed back into his bad hand and he was able to play piano again. He's using his cane more and not just for show anymore."

Dr. Chaconne scheduled a visit to Jooks' apartment to speak only with me.

DOC FUGUE

"They want to determine that I'm not fit for trial," said Jooks.

"Oh, I see. You mean if you're not."

"We need to tell them I'm not!"

"Ohhh, I understand," reassuring him of nothing but my stupidity.

When Dr. Chaconne arrived, Jooks went out for an errand. He handed me a two-page form to fill out about Jooks' behavior since the stroke.

"Oh, I see there's a signature required. You didn't mention that."

"Oh, yes," he said of the oversight. "It's just to confirm you consider Jooks to be unfit for trial."

"Ohhhh, I see...well, I'm not actually sure that I do."

"Okay. Well, I want you to know that you can speak freely, which is why I wanted to meet with you alone. So that you're aware whatever you say is not going to jeopardize your job."

"Oh, I don't care about my job. I mean, I'm more concerned about putting my signature down, you know, when I'm not...sure."

"Do you think Jooks would be able to

undergo a trial in his current state?" he asked, aghast. "I mean, I don't know if I can picture it."

"Yes...I mean, he becomes... surprisingly lucid at moments of importance, or when presented with a situation in which gain or loss is involved. He seems very aware of how other people perceive him."

"For example..."

"For example...he walked to the front of the line at a theater, while laughing and commenting to me that no one would stop him because they think he's retarded, and what stupid jerks they are. Or how he brought his cane to every meeting with his lawyers but not anywhere else. Of course, now I worry he does need it. He looks so thin. Even for him."

"But I tried to test him in my office on that first day you both came, and he is one of the most depressed, uncooperative patients I have ever seen. We could not even get through the questions in a timely enough manner to finish the assessment."

DOC FUGUE

"Well, he's extremely savvy in determining which rules apply to him and which can be written off. He rarely socializes outside of his appointments. I think, because he feels you are on his team, he can use it as an opportunity for play. Or maybe he wants you to think he's not capable. I mean, that would be the obvious thing to do."

"I can honestly say that I can't picture him sitting in a courtroom without talking back to the judge or the plaintiff, or even one of the witnesses in the witness stand for god's sake."

"I don't know," I replied. "I've been surprised by his sense of gravity in relation to personal consequence. I mean...you should see him negotiating for first priority at the doctor's office. He's surprisingly calculating."

"How would you feel about putting someone on trial who isn't suited for it?"

"It wouldn't be me who puts him there. It depends on whether or not he's guilty."

"It's not a matter of whether or not he's guilty. It is strictly a matter of whether or not Jooks, in his current mental state, is able to go on trial!" He lost his patience.

"But what about those girls?" I said. "I mean, what about them?"

"I know," he sighed, "but do you think that Jooks, in his current state, would be able to participate in legal strategies with his lawyers for the better interest of his case?"

"Um," I asked, "what are some examples of a person being ruled unfit for trial?"

"A famous example is Jeffrey Dahmer, who claimed that the galaxy was opening up before the courtroom so that god could come down and speak directly to him."

"That's definitely not Jooks. Also, this form you want me to fill out is asking how his behavior compares before and after the stroke. You do know that I only met Jooks and started working for him after the stroke, right?"

"Oh. You didn't know him before the stroke?"

"No. His call girls did. One of them

said he became much nicer afterwards."

"Well, what I need are three people who knew him both before and after the stroke," he sighed.

"Oh, well. Then I don't qualify."

Had I qualified, I would have been sacrificed to public opinion either way—for denying justice to rape victims if I signed, or for trying to kill an old man if I didn't. For fifteen dollars an hour, plus jail bonuses.

CHAPTER 60

NOPE SPRINGS ETERNAL

Another lesson from drama school that helped me handle Jooks was practicing the rule of "Yes, and..." from improv comedy class. This rule consists of always accepting whatever new imaginary circumstance or idea your scene partners throw at you, adding your own, and then building the scene back and forth in this way. Example: your scene partner asks the girl in his psychiatrist's waiting room to give her phone number to his assistant, played by you. You then say, "Yes." When he leaves the room, you say, "...and the man who just asked you for your phone number is on trial for sexual assault."

The rule of "Yes, and..." has helped me shift a number of tricky circumstances, even when my scene partner was the universe itself.

"Hey, you wanna see my musical?"

Jooks had a Broadway musical. It ran for sixty-one performances.

"I taped it with a hidden camera.

You can never tell a soul," he grinned. "Because the union said I'd have to pay 'em. Why should I? I-i-i-it's my musical! I already paid 'em to perform."

"Yeah. Unions," I agreed. I wasn't in the union, but I wanted to be. The theater I did probably wasn't even legal.

His musical was about a composer with Tourette's syndrome who falls in love. There's a child ballerina who died and went to heaven. She sings a beautiful song that made me cry. There was a glam-rock angel master of ceremonies, a scene where the stage was covered with ten-foot tall lemons, and another where the entire upstage wall was made of file cabinets. If he wrote the character of the dead child ballerina inspired by the living daughter he'd abandoned, that would be fucked up. Channeling his speech impediment into a protagonist who suffered from Tourette's was another possibility that I considered, one that would have been surprisingly socially adept.

I was conditioned to never lie. At acting school, a teacher once said that being truthful made you sexy. There were always quotes about the truth, and how being truthful as artists and actors was the whole point. If I developed a habit of trying to lie, I feared I'd lose my emotional connection. Maybe I didn't know how to lie properly.

Illusion and confession and art are different media for the truth. Like the oxygen you breathe versus the oxygen in your blood versus the oxygen in the water. The molecule needs to travel to different parts of the organism through different vehicles, but straight oxygen would just kill you.

We arrived ten minutes early for Dr. Shore. He was taking Jooks' appointments at a new location with a smaller waiting room and no adjacent offices.

The pretty girl who also saw Doctor Shore was there. I was always thankful that we left as she arrived. Whenever Jooks noticed her, he would stop, turn, and drag his old watery eyes up the length of her body. She was about my age, just past pediatrician coverage.

NOPE SPRINGS ETERNAL

I avoided interactions with attractive females when Jooks was there because it made me the bearer of bad news on both sides.

On this specific Friday, she was over an hour early. She had the peaceful glow and abundant golden curls of a Renaissance painting. Jooks sat in the chair facing her. I shrunk into the wall.

"He-he-he-hello!" The size of the waiting room allowed no more than twenty-four inches of space between their knees.

"Hi, how are you?" she spoke with tenderness.

"Wh-wh-what's your name?"

"It's Chelsea."

"Jooks."

"Nice to meet you!"

"A-a-a-are you here to see Dr. Shore?"

"Yes," Chelsea smiled. "I'm about an hour early."

"A-a-a-are you an actress?"

"Yes," she said, pleased to have given the impression.

"I see," he said. "I'm a director."

"Oh!"

JÖYCE

"I won the Academy Award..."

"Oh!"

"...and the Grammy Award, and on and on. I had a stroke. Which is why I t-t-t-talk like this."

"Oh, I see. I'm so sorry," her voice warbled. Her eyes filled with tears at the sight of this once giant man, now feeble, drowning in a Burberry puffer coat. Like most people at this stage of introduction.

"Don't worry," he chuckled. "I just wanted you to know the reason that I t-talk like this."

"I can understand you perfectly! I barely noticed."

"Ah. Thank you," he said.

"What did you win your Oscar for?" She beamed again, in the simple joy of kindness.

"Tell her," he instructed me.

"He wrote the song 'You Fill Up My Void,'" I said, trying not to kill the good spirits.

"I wrote the biggest song of the seventies, and now—I can't even t-t-talk."

"Oh, gosh. I can understand your frustration," she said.

"It's hard, but every day I'm getting back to normal. I'm working on a script right now. D-d-d-do you have a boyfriend?"

"You mean *Struck by Lightning*, Jooks?" I interrupted. I hadn't heard about any project except the auditions where he allegedly raped everyone.

"No, not that one," he waved me away, returning all his focus to her. "It's a new script. There's a part in it that might be perfect for you!"

"Really! Well, can I give you my contact information?"—Dr. Shore summoned him in.

"Give your number to my assistant," he said, drifting into the office. I marveled at his ability to feign good nature in the first interaction. The door closed. I turned towards Chelsea, who sat pondering her good fortune.

"Well! I guess I should give you my info?"

"Well—you see," I began, "if I was in your position, I would be excited too, and I don't want to ruin it for you, but..." I lowered my voice, "he is actually on trial. For numerous charges of sexual assault. And rape. He did have a stroke—right after the alleged crimes. He totally did win all of the awards he said. I've only been working for him since the stroke. As far as I've seen, he's not working on any new projects. I do all his typing and dictation. I'm with him twelve seven. I'm pretty sure he just made the project up on the fly so he could talk to you. If you want to give him your number, that's totally up to you, because I can see how you might worry that maybe I'm an actress too, and I don't want competition...or something like that...but he'd probably just end up trying to date you, or text message stalk you, or something creepy. I mean, post-stroke he seems too feeble to, like, commit rape, but...I would say this is definitely not going to be anything that helps your acting career.

"Oh," I continued, "and the way he allegedly raped and assaulted, like, a dozenish girls (I think that's the tally so far, at least according to the newspapers) was by soliciting them in the Craigslist acting gigs section to come audition for his screenplay. I mean it was a real screenplay, and I think he did want to make a movie but...he's also super fucked up, and like...rape and assault might be part of his movie-making process. Assuming he did it. Which is still not proven. But yeah, you can look up his trials in the news and...I really don't want to be complicit in giving this man your number."

We chatted about acting school.

"Why do you see a psychiatrist?" I asked, concerned.

"It feels good, I guess." She shrugged. Her dad must have been the kind of man who could send her to $500-an-hour sessions. I rattled off advice about showcases and "the business," envying her and thinking that maybe she could make it since she had money and time and looks and youth.

We brainstormed over how I would break it to Jooks that there would be no phone number and considered just giving him a fake one, the old one-digit-off. After an hour of cautious whispering, Jooks breezed out, the picture of stability, and we departed without fanfare. He scraped alongside, sustaining his performance of restraint until we were halfway down the block. Then, with all the nuance of Judy Dench, he casually remembered:

"Oh, did you get her number?"

"Oh...she actually didn't give it to me. It was weird." I cinched my brow.

"What?! Wh-wh-wh-why not?" he asked.

"I don't know I...didn't want to push the issue, you know?" I shrugged.

"Wha?! Not give her number?! Boy, that's..."

"Yeah. I don't know. It's such a weird reaction."

He scraped along, lost in thought.

"When you meet a big director who wants to talk to you...someone who tells you they won a Grammy Award...an Academy Award...You stop everything and you go meet with them. Not give you her number?! It's senseless!"

"Well..." I could lie because it was the greatest good for the greatest number, "she did tell me a story about how one time she gave her number to an important Hollywood dude, and he kept saying he wanted to cast her, but in the end just ended up being really creepy. Even though you wouldn't be anything like that. She must have had a bad experience before."

"Huh. Okay. But still. Not give her number?!"

"It's frustrating to see someone miss out on an opportunity like that," I agreed.

We got into the cab. Central Park scenery scrolled along as he stared glumly out the window in the ringing silence.

"What did you say to her?" he said.

"We just talked about acting and stuff," I said. "I told her your awards. And I told her that story about how you managed to get your first movie into theaters," I chuckled fondly. "Maybe you freaked her out by asking if she had a boyfriend like the minute you started talking to her." This was not inaccurate, turning his attention back on something he had done that he could blame.

"Oh. Really?"

"It did seem unrelated to an audition. Why did you ask her if she had a boyfriend?"

"But that's just because the lead actress in each movie I did was always my girlfriend."

"Wait. So you mean, you always cast whoever happens to be your girlfriend as the lead in your movies, because you date talented women who you believe in? Or do you mean, whichever girl gets cast in your movie becomes your girlfriend?"

"Th-the second one," he said.

"Ohhh, okay..." I gave the old nod and smile, just until I could turn my head to share a bug-eyed grimace with the fields of Central Park. I had two faces now. One for Jooks and one for private enjoyment of what sanity remained.

"Boy," he muttered to himself. "She's finished. She is no good!"

"Yeah," I murmured. "It's just so weird.

I mean, what could she possibly lose by giving you her number, or even coming in to read? She'd only gain, if anything. By the way, what's the new play you're working on? That's so exciting you're starting a new project."

"Oh, it's huge...so big." He stretched his wingspan.

He spoke no more of Chelsea and her waiting room career suicide. I fetched a sulking Jooks the Wednesday-night spaghetti Bolognese from Elio's.

Come evening, I uncurled from the couch and prepared my exit speech. Jooks was settled before *Grey's Anatomy* with a Diet Coke, his plate already polished off.

"Soon," he began, in tones of layered calculation, "I'm going to need someone who can stay during the night and help me write this play."

"Okay. You mean to take dictation."

"Yeah...that's part of it. But I need somebody who can stay nights. If it's not you, tell me now, because I need somebody who can give that kind of time."

JÖYCE

"Okay," I said, since he was threatening to replace me with someone more available and possibly more willing to help him rape people. "I can stay and take dictation for you." I could still delay him while earning my wage. There could be no harm in taking down a writer's words.

"We'll start posting on Craigslist to audition girls for some of the songs."

Nope.

"Umm, are you sure that's wise...right now..."

"What?!"

"Okay..." It seemed likely that if I couldn't say no to Jooks, I could signal his lawyers to shut it down.

"I need to cast two girls...and two guys," he added, for non-bias. "You see," his voice retracted, his eyes seemed to flicker into the oldest reptilian layer of the human brain, so that I felt even a twitch would provoke his deathly suspicion.

Every cell of my body felt monitored.

"I know what you want," he charmed.

It was to leave now and go home.

"What do I want?"

(560)

"I know...what you want," he repeated with a tone of mercy. Everything but his face went into soft focus. His gaze honed into mine. I could almost feel his brain waves pulse.

"What's, uh...what's that, Jooks?" I stammered. I was transported to exactly how his last rape spree must have started. Alleged rape spree, I reminded myself.

"You want to act," he said. There may as well have been spinning cartoon hypnotic spirals in his eye sockets. He was literally steepling his fingertips.

"Right," I agreed easily, curious what else he had to say.

"I want you to be in the show," he continued in his quiet voice, "but you have to help me with it." I imagined Pearl in my spot, being asked to do the same for *Struck by Lightning*. I wondered if he'd baited her with the promise of a role, if she'd done it from pity, or even faith in his artistic vision.

"Okay," I said blankly.

"I've been watching this..." He gestured to *Grey's Anatomy* playing on mute. "I've been thinking...fooling around on the piano. This could be big, really big."

I looked hard at Katherine Heigl in medical scrubs, holding a clipboard.

"Wow," I murmured, my eyes straining as they stayed locked with his.

"And so," he soothed, "we'll have auditions for a number of different girls...and boys too!" I remained stone-faced, my thoughts tucked deep away where he couldn't read them. A warlock caught up in the game of being human, he peered down from the edge of his fate, unable to see the coming cycle of destruction identical to the ones before.

"I'd be happy to help out, Jooks," I smiled gently.

"Yeah? S-sound good?"

"Sounds good."

"Okay. Goodnight." He nodded gravely at our pact.

I left the apartment. In the elevator, I let the blood surge to my face, surrendered to a panicked breath, my heart battering in alarum.

Perhaps Jooks wanted me to be tried

one day for facilitating rape, just like Pearl was being tried now. Maybe after his stroke, Jooks was more transparent, no longer the commander of his once-robust faculties of deception. The cloak had been lifted, but the patterns of his tactics, his motives, his indulgences, and boundless entitlement at the scarred and knotted core of his personality, could not be destroyed. Statistically, this opportunity was rare—the workings of such a personality, partially dissected by way of brain trauma. As much as I hated to see anyone in his weakened state, I would have feared him at peak health.

I exited the lobby. The doormen smiled at me as they had probably smiled at other girls who'd fled the lobby in ghostly terror. That's why they'd been assigned a lawyer. Why were there no doorwomen in the building?

I briefly entertained contacting the assistant D.A. who'd called me in about the train harasser. Maybe she could send someone undercover to get hired as Jooks' second assistant. He was too much for me alone.

CHAPTER 61

FAUX COUNTRY FOR OLD MEN

"I want more!"—Jooks rose from the chair—"It cured me! You don't understand. Please...doctor...please...oh please."

"No. I can't do it," said the doctor.

"Why not?!"

"You had the injection three weeks ago. At most, at most, you can have a cortisone injection three, maybe five times. Over the course of your lifetime. Anything else is unsafe. It's unethical of me to do what you're asking."

"But why?! Unethical? Doctor, I was cured! You don't understand—I felt alive again! My pain was almost gone! Maybe it's not safe for some people, but for me—for me, it's the cure!!"

"No. That's how a lot of people feel when they take it—but it wears off. And there are side effects. I'm sorry. I can't give it to you. Hold on, I'll be right back." He stood up from his chair, slid between Jooks and the front of his desk, and ducked into the atrium of the hospital.

FAUX COUNTRY FOR OLD MEN

Jooks had darted in unannounced while the doctor was alone in his office.

Three weeks earlier, he got a referral for the injection. Within the space of our cab ride home, vitality and relief surged into the decimated right side of his body, letting him believe, for the first time since the stroke, that full recovery was within reach. Then it wore off.

"Jooks, have a seat. You're freaking him out. He's probably telling security about us. He's more likely to listen if you're reasonable," I said with uncharacteristic command. He situated himself in the chair facing the desk as the doctor returned.

"Sorry about that. You were saying," said the doctor.

"L-l-listen, I want to try it again. It's my body, not yours. I don't care what happens. I'll take full responsibility. I'll sign anything. Now, I want monthly injections..."

"That's impossible, no, I'm sorry."

"O-or every six weeks. Please, doctor!"

"No. No, I can't. Do you understand? I can't. Even if I thought it was a good idea."

"Well then why did y-y-y-you give it to me?" Jooks was near tears.

"It's supposed to help with physical therapy. Cortisone gets your body into a temporary state where it can heal faster."

"Why would you do that to me? Why would you want me to feel that way if it's only temporary? Why?" He gazed into the doctor's eyes.

The next day, we took a cab to the Sam Ash music store in midtown. Jooks admired the instrument-lined walls and high ceilings with a sense of the sacred and familiar. For once, he didn't say to find the manager and announce his accolades. For once, I felt the urge to do so.

"E-e-excuse me. Where are your k-keyboards?" he spoke to a young musician working at the counter. It was his holiest moment. My defenses came down enough to like him. "I might want to buy a weighted keyboard. So it's easier on my fingers than the piano."

He bowed over an expensive

(566)

keyboard with a little smile. He didn't look around for attention, for he knew he was in his own home and improvised a chord progression. He listened for the quality and feel of the instrument. The store employees left him alone.

"Ah, would your grandfather like some assistance?" asked a young man.

"Oh—I'm just his assistant. He actually, um, he's a musician. He had a stroke over a year ago, and he has a baby grand piano at home. But I think he wants something that he can compose on a little more easily, because his fingers are weak. Don't tell him I told you all that...but...just so you have an idea..."

Minutes later, I saw him and Jooks chatting and strumming guitars in a glass cubical chamber suspended at balcony level. Forty-five minutes later, we left. I was disappointed he didn't buy anything for himself. I realized he never spent time around other musicians anymore, only doctors, lawyers, sex workers, and salespeople.

JÖYCE

"Nnnn...short shirts...T-shirt/she's cheer captain and...nnnn...bleachers," he tapped along to "You Belong With Me."

"Boy, Taylor Swift—she's great! The Grammys were incredible! Taylor Swift! Oh Boy! And Lady Gaga—you shoulda seen'er do this thing where she was flying from the ceiling? Who's that one girl—Be—"

"Beyoncé?"

"I don't like her." He made a face. I gave my best sympathetic grimace. Her glistening sonar vocals and skill as a singer sometimes raised vulnerability to a level of transcendence not often seen in pop music or on this earth. And that may have alienated him, depending on which songs he'd listened to. I also considered that he could just be racist. "Racist" rhymes with "rapist" and is only one letter off. I was tempted to make him listen to "Crazy In Love," but then I would have had to laugh and dance, and maybe even, god forbid, groove alongside him. I lost that opportunity for Beyoncé because I was weak. Not every girl gets to be lucky.

(568)

FAUX COUNTRY FOR OLD MEN

Jooks had sent me to purchase every single Taylor Swift album at Best Buy during his psychiatrist appointment. He'd started seeing his psychiatrist four days a week.

"Look at that!" he slanted a CD case in the light. "It's a hologram!"

"That's so cool," I smiled in the cab. "How long have you been seeing a psychiatrist?"

"Well, after my father passed away, I was left a modest amount of money—ten thousand or something—and I used it to see a psychiatrist."

"Huh."

"I was very different than I am now—very different. I had very low confidence. The doctor gave me an IQ test. He said I had the eleventh-highest score in the country. So he said, 'Jooks, it doesn't make any sense for you to have low confidence, because wherever you go, you will be the smartest man in the room.' Ever since that moment, I knew I was."

"Isn't being the smartest person in the room supposed to be a bad thing?" I asked.

"But I actually was!"

"Unless one of the ten people ahead of you in the country happens to be in the room too."

"Oh, but that's not likely to happen."

"Wow. That's incredible," I said. Before psychiatrists, friendships must have been more of a sacrifice, and public meltdowns much bolder.

"He's the reason I ended up being brave enough to go and pursue my dreams out in Hollywood," said Jooks.

"Wow. You mean after getting into Juilliard, making shitloads of money in advertising, and winning twenty-seven Clios, you were actually afraid to go out to Hollywood?"

"Yep." He shook his head and laughed. "They don't give a fuck about me. I would have phone appointments with him when I was out there. But then, something happened."

"Oh no, what?"

"Well, I met an actress, and I left my wife and kids to be with her. When I told my psychiatrist what I'd done," he chuckled, "he got very angry. He said, 'You didn't talk to me about this or consult me at all or tell me what you were thinking about doing. You made a decision that had a big effect on your life and other people's lives and I can't work with you anymore.'"

"Wow. How long was the relationship with the actress?"

"Two months."

It seemed dramatic to dump Jooks just like that and leave him floundering out there in Hollywood. Scientology says psychiatrists are the ultimate haters. Maybe he could have helped Jooks deal with his sexuality and intimacy and mental problems in a way that would have prevented all those rapes, except the news said Jooks was raping even before. Maybe the psychiatrist had been waiting for a big excuse to cut him loose before some inevitable monster surfaced for which he would be blamed.

Maybe the psychiatrist only told Jooks he was the eleventh smartest person in the country, knowing the narcissism would give him enough sex-fueled ego and rogue desperation to get his movie made. I wished someone cared that much about me.

CHAPTER 62:
A CLOCKWORK I'M NOT REALLY A WAITRESS

"Why can't you work?"

"I'm filming a short film that a friend of mine wrote," I offered modestly, so Jooks would worry it was something important.

"What's the budget?" he asked.

"Oh, hardly anything."

"Oh, no," he waved his hand. "I didn't think otherwise."

"I'm not sure. I don't really deal with those details," I smiled. I'd be reimbursed for my Long Island Railroad ticket. My friend, the director, would front the cash for our only prop, a bottle of Vitamin Water.

"Wh-wh-what is it about?" Jooks asked.

"It's about a female celebrity in her early twenties—who I'll be playing. This weekend, we're shooting a fake interview about her charity, Change Children Change, in a sound studio. Then we're filming at a mansion in

Long Island. She's supposed to be very rich and very crazy."

I looked down at the manicure I'd gotten to look the part. The color was called I'm Not Really a Waitress. I thought: *Because I'm an Actress.*

"Is sh-she married?"

"Well, she's twenty two—no, she's not married."

"I don't understand. How could she be rich if she isn't married?"

"She's a movie star who's been earning since she was, like, a teenager."

"Still..." he said, hurt and confused all at once.

"You met a lot of women like that in the entertainment industry, didn't you?" I returned.

The trouble with me is that I just love men. My dad was one. And so I overindulge them sometimes.

"Well, have a good weekend...I don't know...I just don't know."

"What don't you know?" I asked, turning back from my exit.

"I'm afraid to be alone."

"Afraid?" I asked.

"Because of what I might do to myself."

"Jooks—I can't hear about that," I said as if it upset me too much. I didn't allow for the possibility of Jooks' suicide to cross my mind as a real option. He had plenty of professionals to consult. If he was willing to invoke suicide to get me to work more, he'd be willing to invoke suicide to get me to start pimping him women to sleep with.

As usual with Jooks, oblivion was the best cure.

"Boy, if this legal stuff gets bad enough...my doctor taught me where to put the knife to kill myself."

"Your doctor showed you that?"

"Well, yeah!"

"That's horrible, Jooks. They're a bad doctor. They shouldn't show you that."

"My doctors are the best doctors. Listen, honey, I'm not stickin' around for jail. You think I can survive in jail like this? With a cane?"

"Maybe jail isn't so bad, Jooks...it could be like camp or something. Maybe they have jail for old people. I've always thought going to jail would be a great opportunity to focus on writing."

"Camp? God, you're a fuckin' idiot. I dunno...I dunno." He led us into the kitchen and handed me a Wüsthoff steak knife from the wooden block on the counter. "I want you to get this knife sharpened at Gracious Home."

"Why?"

"Never mind why."

"You never use these knives. They're perfectly sharp already."

"Sweetie, I asked you to do it, so please, just do it."

"Okay. I can do that for you tomorrow."

I smiled as if there were no meaning behind it, in hopes that my innocence would confuse him out of any ruminating thoughts. He was trying to pull me into some kind of web.

"In fact," he said, "here, do it first thing in the morning. Put it in your bag."

"Jooks, what if I arrive late?"

"I don't care. Here, take it. Do it first thing."

"O-okay," I said.

I'M NOT REALLY A WAITRESS

I wrapped the blade in a paper towel, in case he was trying to get my fingerprints on it for some unknown reason, and slid it into the secret shoe compartment of my Lululemon bag.

CHAPTER 63:
THE ESCAPIST

"Check my email."

"You got an email from an old friend."

"Read it out loud."

"'Hi Jooks. Glad that we heard from you. We've opened our business here—it's a restaurant that serves only hotdogs.'"

"Wha?!"

"You haven't heard of stuff like that?" I said. "It's kind of a thing now. There's a place in the East Village that does only rice pudding. It's called Rice to Riches."

"Only rice p-pudding?"

"All different flavors. There's a place called Criff Dogs that does only hotdogs. There's lots of places doing that in Brooklyn, where you only do one thing, but do it extremely well."

"Like a hotdog stand?"

"Oh yeah, I forgot about those. No, like a restaurant."

"Really? Huh."

"'The business is actually doing pretty well,'" I read aloud. "'How are

(578)

you? Are you currently working on any new musicals or movies?'"

"Write back: 'Dear Pete, I am doing great out here in New York. I got an idea for a reality TV show that'll knock your socks off—it's about a guy who opens a restaurant that serves only hotdogs. Let me know what you think. Jooks.'"

"Okay. I wrote it. Want to look at it?"

"Good. Send it."

"You have another email here from a university asking for the rights to perform *Metropolis*."

"What'd they say?"

"'Dear Mr. Jooks, our University Theater League has performed your musical three times over the past decade while I have been head of the department. I am a great admirer of your work and dearly hope to have the opportunity to continue my work with the students as benefitting from your talents. Your request of $25,000 for the rights to perform is well above our budget, and we only have $10,000 at our disposal. We have had to manage our budget very strictly in recent years, and the arts department is certainly affected by the budgeting decisions that have gone into effect. Is it possible to persuade you to take our available funds even though they do not meet your requirements?'"

"Write back: 'sorry, not interested.' Don't capitalize it."

"Okay."

Later that day, Jooks came home from a meeting with his lawyer.

"G-g-go and look up private jets on the internet," he said.

"Um. Why?"

"Go do it."

"Where do you want to go?"

"Don't worry about it."

"I feel like I have to know the destination in order to look up private jet services."

"Colorado."

"Oh. You're trying to hide out?"

"Maybe. Just go do it."

"Jooks?" I called into the living room.

"What?"

"Every time I click on the link to a private jet company, a form pops up asking me to enter your address, name, and social security number."

"What?"

"Yeah. Every website for private jets requires it before allowing you to proceed."

"So just go ahead and enter your information, h-h-honey," he coaxed gently.

"...No..."

"Ah, well."

A phone call rang from his lawyers.

The next morning, Will sat in the living room. He'd been staying overnight on the fold-out in the den. Jooks walked across the living room to the kitchen.

ZZZT!

"You're late! They called me down to court and put on this goddamn ankle bracelet! Will h-h-had to go with me." He stuck an accusatory finger at a black plastic cartridge locked around his tube sock and protruding beneath the hem of his chino pants.

ZZZT! The cartridge gave another harsh jolt.

"Goddamnit!" Jooks blurted. Will broke into muffled laughter. "It's not funny!" Jooks said, trying to suppress a smile.

"I'm sorry. It is funny," said Will.

"Aww, screw you!" Jooks waved his hand at his son and chuckled. He turned to me and became serious again. "I gotta charge this thing every six hours. When the battery's low, it vibrates like that every two minutes."

"You've got to charge your own tracking device?"

"Yeah! If you're late, I could run outta the battery!" His voice rose. "Then they'll come a-a-and take me off to jail!" he screamed. Will hung his head and bit his lips shut in hysteria.

ZZZT!

"Jooks, how do you charge it? Can we charge it now?" I asked.

"Here, lemme show you." He scuffed to the den and returned with a cheap AC adapter. He sat down on the couch, so I could plug him into the wall.

ZZZT!

"I gotta pay seven dollars a day to

rent this thing."

"You have to pay for your own tracking device?"

"If you can't pay, you go to jail and they keep track of you that way for free!"

"If you can't afford to rent this thing for seven dollars a day, you go rot in jail, when they haven't even finished the trial? That's so unfair. How is jail cheaper than seven dollars a day?"

"Well, be glad I can afford it and don't worry about other people!"

I said nothing.

"You were late, dammit! Why were you late?"

"Sorry, Jooks."

"I need you here! Or find me someone else who can be!" he screamed. "Do you know someone else who can work here?"

I didn't.

"Please be on time, honey. Please. Please. I need you here." His voice sunk to a whisper. "I don't want Will here all the time."

Jooks was paying $210 per month for his own tracking device, around half my rent at the time and the maximum allowance for food stamps in New York City. The little black cartridge could have passed for a medical device, but in some circles, it was a status symbol.

CHAPTER 64:
CANE & TABLE

"You won't make it in this world if you do it that way. TELL them you want a reservation! Don't ASK them if you can have it! None of this 'Ooo, can I please have a reservation?'" he sneered.

"Jooks, I phrase my appointment requests as questions because I know the answer will be yes—hello, I'm calling to make a reservation for Jooks, party of two, at his usual table."

"Ahhh...what date were you looking for?" asked the hostess.

"This Saturday at 7:00 p.m."

"I'm sorry, we're actually all booked then."

"Oh really? Huh. Jooks, they're all booked then."

"TELL THEM I WANT IT!" he shouted next to my ear.

"Yes, but they always make room for you so I'm thinking this time they're really—"

"TELL THEM!!!!"

"Sorry—uh, I was just speaking with

Jooks. You see, he's a regular and he was really hoping—"

"DON'T SAY I WAS HOPING TELL THEM TO BOOK IT!!!"

"—I understand. Let me check with the manager. One moment," said the hostess.

"Jooks, she's checking with the manager, she's probably just new and doesn't know you."

He sighed and rolled his eyes.

"Hi there, I'm the manager. I'm so sorry, but we're actually completely full that day and do not have room. We're using all of our extra tables and chairs, so I can't legally take another reservation."

"Would it be possible to put the reservation on your waiting list and call if there's an opening?" I asked.

"Certainly," he said.

"Thank you so much." I hung up.

"WHAT?! Waiting list?"

"They're physically full."

"You call them back."

"It's because of some event they have to do. They're going to call if an opening comes up."

"Call them back and see if they have another day!" He scuffed out of the room.

"Hello?"

"Oh, hi, this is Jooks' assistant, I just called a moment ago. Could I be able to speak to the manager?"

"Hello, this is the manager."

"Hi, sorry to trouble you. Jooks wanted me to see if I could book another date. He's on the waiting list for Saturday, February 6, but maybe he'd be able to get a definite reservation for later in the week."

"What date were you thinking?"

"The following Saturday."

"Umm...no, we're booked that day."

"Oh, okay, what about the Wednesday after that?"

"We're actually booked that day as welllll..."

"What about ummmm...hold on I have to make sure it works with his calendar... Thursday, February 25?"

"I'm actually booked then as well."

"Um. Is there a reservation you do have available within the next six weeks?"

"Uhhh, I would have to get back to

you on that. I couldn't give you a date right now, unfortunately."

If civilization consisted of designating one space for fine dining and a separate one for rape and murder as accepted acts of warfare, Jooks had disqualified himself from his favorite restaurants: Daniel and The Four Seasons. He didn't bother after that, letting it go out with a whimper rather than a bang.

I was going out with a whimper. It was as if I could do nothing about my total lack of regard for his time or his anger for that lack of regard. One morning I arrived three hours late.

"YOU WERE LATE, YOU GODDAMN... FUCKIN..." He came rushing at me with his cane raised as though to strike.

I summoned the posture of a lion tamer and glared him in the eye.

"You'd better fucking put that down," I said.

I wonder if Jooks would have been the kind of master to box his servants' ears if this were a Dickens novel.

CHAPTER 65

MADMAN BUTTERFLY

I was called for jury duty and had scheduled work off. I slept in and made a half-assed attempt to get to the courthouse in Queens before calling and testifying from the outdoor subway platform that I was making a great effort but feared I'd miss the appointment. They said I could fax in a note and request another date. I was at the Jamaica train stop when the lady on the phone sighed and relieved me from my assignment that day. It was around 2:00 p.m. I felt light, like all my troubles lay within the walls of Jooks' apartment—and that I'd been kept from the magic of the outside world.

I'd been to the Jamaica Queens station every weekend of my seventh semester of college, for *Julius Caesar* rehearsals in Long Island. I asked to audition for Antony instead of one of the wives and got the part. Protecting a great big spirit like *Julius Caesar* in a world of haters so resonated with me. It was as if the "Friends...Romans...countrymen..." speech was born from within. I didn't know much about *Julius Caesar*, except that he was successful, and I wanted to surround myself with success. The taste of Special K cereal bars and microwaveable Dinty Moore beef stew from the nearby Duane Reade is stored fondly in my memory. At my final review, my soap opera acting teacher admitted the faculty had thought I had a drug problem all semester without even bothering to ask me, because of how exhausted I seemed. It was from traveling to Long Island all weekend to perform in *Julius Caesar*.

Now I could explore the area. There was a Mattress Warehouse, a Dunkin' Donuts, Popeye's, McDonald's, gas stations, an antique store with shiny things made of synthetic materials, a local health-food store with a man in a daishiki selling containers of shea butter and scents in cylindrical glass bottles, wooden masks, drums, wall hangings, carvings of elephants and giraffes. There were bodegas, a struggling coffee shop—a haven for artists and thinkers with grimy cracked linoleum and stale pastries behind oily plexiglass. There were stores filled with expensive sneakers and cheap clothing with names like Beauty and In Love Clothing, where you could feel beautiful or in love. I ordered a beef patty from a Jamaican restaurant, and the cashier rolled her eyes at me like the Upper East Siders did. The tranquility was only disturbed by feeling that everyone wanted to sell me something. I guessed this is what it was like to be rich—to travel not because I was going to work, but because I was going to explore. The sidewalk was damp from a light rain, with a wet-pavement smell and the tires going shhhhhhhhh on the wide road. It all feels right at home because I made it feel that way in my memory.

I saw that I must and would leave Jooks at any minute. I was young and free. Jooks was old and trapped. One day I'd think, *I had all the opportunity in the world—why was I so frightened of other people's reaction to me?* I didn't think I'd look back and see that I had narrowly escaped a trap. It was better not to know that it was there. In order to escape, I had to believe in the shape of the positive space and ignore the negative space closing in around me.

I lost my will to arrive on time to work. Jooks no longer flew into a rage. Now he begged, "Please, honey—why? Why are you late?" But I couldn't respond. I had too many overts and withholds and wasn't trained enough in Scientology to deal with somebody so low on the tone scale. I just couldn't make this go right.

In the waiting room of some lawyer or another, he was chewing me out for my tardiness.

Thoughts hummed in my mind: *You haven't given me a raise, ever. It is customary to give a raise every six months. I have adopted what were once the duties of three separate assistants. I have acquired indispensable skills and information specific to your lifestyle. My value now exceeds my pay rate, and it has for some time. If you want me to supply you with*

a certain level of performance, I will need
appropriate incentive.

I unstuck the back of my throat and squeaked, "Uh, well, usually people give a raise..."

"That's nonsense," said Jooks.

When he complained that I was late the next day, I realized the motivation I lacked was monetary.

"I should have a raise," I said.

"How much?" he sighed.

"It's usually twelve percent every six months according to my old Starbucks training manual. Going up to twenty dollars an hour from fifteen seems fair since I've been here over a year."

"Fine," he said. "But if you're even one minute late, no more raise."

"Okay, Jooks." That fucker. I was totally worth it even if I was late. I was working for an hourly wage, after all, not a salary. But I figured I'd take the challenge.

I would sprint from my house to the G train to the L train to the 6 train to Jooks' apartment. Once, I was three minutes late because the subway stalled, which almost lost me the raise. After two weeks, I slid into my old patterns, but by then, we were both too used to my new promotion.

Being on time every day improved relations. Maybe my lateness was the reason everything had gone wrong.

My dad was always early but when my mom dropped me off at school I was late every day since the age of three. Walking into class late every day and being alone waiting for my mother in the playground at the end of the day had helped to shape my outsider identity. I was taught to live on the cathartic cycle of stolen and scarce time. I found daily renewal in the Aristotelean plot structure of guilt, pity, and shame, despite the disapproval from peers and authorities, and my ultimate permission to redeem myself through apology and hyper-creative acts that were less fearful, having been outcast already. I was trained to live in fear of being late, rather than in anticipation of being early.

Time is our most valuable resource. I don't mean figuratively or sentimentally, but in a way that is economically very real. Unlimited time is how vampires become so rich. This, and they kill people.

My boyfriend said that Jeffrey Dahmer worked briefly as a low-level clerk at his father's business before he became famous for murder and was never once late. That comforted me.

Then in acting school, they trained me to be early and to know that nothing at all would be given to me unless I was always early. Once I figured out how to be early, people started trying to make me late and telling me that being early demonstrates a lack of compassion. I guess I have to find new cycles of societal abuse to get addicted to in order to extort enough pity for people to let me keep being an artist.

The date I vowed to quit, May 31, came and went. I did what cowards do and began to phase myself out. My generation invented ghosting. We ghosted our lovers, our parents, our schools, our employers, and by god, our own country. Jooks was vengeful and proud. There could be no grand exit.

Like all promises, I knew he'd withdraw his patronage of Lemon, who I still referred to as Mila in front of him, so he would not accuse me of corrupting her. When he said he was only leaving her $5,000 in his will, I created a five-page contract, projecting her lifetime expenses of $35,000 for a dog of her breed expected to live fifteen to eighteen years, securing his signature to pay for all of it. It is also stated that I was the permanent and sole caretaker for the remainder of her life so that he couldn't use custody to manipulate me.

I knew damn well Jooks could do whatever he wanted, but I wanted to make him sweat a little, like an embittered ex-wife. I certainly didn't want him to feel like he could use the dog as emotional or financial leverage over me. I'd need as much help as I could get supporting Lemon and didn't want her forced to work at a job like this, one day.

"You'll support her for life, Jooks," I reminded him. "It does NOT depend on whether or not I continue working for you!"

"OH, YES IT DOES," he growled.

"No, it doesn't. Do you think I'll be here in eighteen years? If I left tomorrow, you'd still be accountable for the dog. You knew that when you signed. Or were you just trying to get what you wanted at the time?"

"If you're late one more time," he said, "you'll be fired, AND I won't pay you."

"Whatever money you owe me for hours I've worked will always be paid to me, no matter what," I replied calmly.

I missed three days of work in a row. Jooks asked if I could work just every other day. I said, "Sure, I guess so." After two weeks, I failed to show up again, not out of strategy, but intolerance.

"You're fired," Jooks texted.

"Okay. I'll need to pick up my last check."

He didn't respond. I emailed his lawyers who had his money in escrow.

Dear Matthew, due to changes in my schedule I will not be able to accommodate Jooks and need to pick up my final check. I am sure you understand how forgetful he can be with this sort of thing. I would be happy to come by the office once you sort it out and confirm that the amount I stated is correct.

I was getting my goddamned $300.

Jooks asked me to meet him in his lawyers' office.

"I couldn't ask you to come in because I needed to get away from Will. I stayed at a hotel for three days. He wanted money but I wouldn't give it to him. He got upset and broke the window. So I kicked him out." Jooks shook his head.

"Do you no longer want to work for Jooks? If she doesn't, Jooks, you need to accept that," said Matthew.

"You don't understand! I want her working for me every day!" Jooks said.

"Well, I mean, I sort of want some time to pursue my artistic goals..." I muttered.

"That seems reasonable," Matt nodded.

Jooks sat looking down at his hands.

"Jooks, we can help you find somebody

else to replace her. Or, Jöyce, would one day a week be doable for you?"

"Um, yeah," I said.

The lawyers cut me my check, and I followed Jooks to the apartment.

"Look!" he pointed to the large picture window in the den. "Will broke the window." I expected howling wind through broken glass, but someone had only yanked the blinds up at a seventy-five-degree angle on one end, so it looked like a paper fan.

A week later, I signed into Jooks' email account from my apartment for the first time ever. He wanted to know about his Broadway tickets, and I wasn't working that day.

There was an email from Will. He described that he was living with friends on the Lower East Side and that he worked in a bakery from 6:00 a.m.– 4:00 p.m. and barely had enough money to buy things like a toothbrush, but that this could be one of the best things to ever happen to him, since it was forcing him to be more independent. He said he really missed Jooks and wanted to see him. The next day at work, the email was gone.

I came Mondays from 9:00 a.m.–3:00 p.m., completing a bundle of tasks in a mad scurry as he watched on with no one to torture.

"Y-y-y-you have s-somewhere to be?" he asked, as I dashed out at exactly three.

"Yep, got an audition."

I had no audition. That was none of his damn business.

My boyfriend and I walked across the Brooklyn Bridge to Zuccotti on one of the first Occupy Wall Street marches, with Lemon in her tote.

One day a week with Jooks still drained my life force. My spirit was too depleted. He might convince me to work full-time again. I could get trapped there by another parental emergency. I needed to close the portal.

One spring day, I deposited my paycheck and kept walking with the hope that each step would land somewhere, a little further away from him.

CHAPTER 66

LOOK HOMEWARD SATAN

Jooks didn't bother to fire me this time. The worst part was having no finality. No big fuck-you exit that many dream of yet few achieve. I never quit. I just stopped going.

I thought I'd never be able to get another job because of the shell shock. I thought of him day and night, fearing I might bump into him or get roped into the court case, or even framed for dognapping, waiting for his phone call to find me at a weak moment when I could be convinced to start showing up for work again.

I had no choice but to make it as an actress—in the six months before my money ran out.

In my first week of freedom, I was called in to audition for a true-crime television series. When I stepped off the elevator onto the ground floor, Jooks was hailing a cab on the sidewalk with his back facing me through the glass double doors. He wore his Burberry puffer, leaning on his cane and the April breeze. I curtsied back into the elevator before it could close and let it take me back to the casting office. It hadn't even registered that the building was identical to and right across the street from Matthew Richardson's office. It was odd for him to hail a cab on the opposite side. I returned to the lobby. Jooks was nowhere to be seen. I flitted out a side exit through a Kinko's copy center and onto the street.

Late in August, I got a voicemail from BLOCKED. It was his voice drowned out by the wind. I hoped he'd only called by accident.

Eventually, Lemon's Park Avenue veterinarian notified me that Jooks had requested a chargeback on her bills from after I'd left, including one check-up, the purchase of heart-worm prevention, plus a week of boarding for when I stayed at Fire Island with my boyfriend and his mom in a rental house that didn't allow dogs. If the credit card company did the chargeback, I would owe the vet money.

Already desperate for work again, I stayed up all night to compile a four-page statement. I attached a copy of his signed agreement with his acknowledgment of her projected lifetime expenses, noting his voluntary addition of Lemon to the will. I cited her $4,500 retail price, her twelve-inch stature, her medical fragility, the luxury bedding, the tiny sweaters, the faux alligator harness, the $100 grooming sessions, all of which he had insisted on.

None of my charges were reversed, but Jooks canceled the card on file at the vet. Lemon and I were on our own. I wasn't going to bother suing him. I was grateful to have covered my ass enough to keep him from framing me. At least we didn't have to depend on him for anything now.

Autumn came. My money was gone. Cue the soundtrack from *Requiem for a Dream*. My return to the workforce was a commission-only job selling water purification coolers at a company called

Watermatic, run by a fifty-year-old Wall Street crash survivor named Franco who was married to a twenty-two-year-old ex-Victoria's Secret model. He had cult-like charisma. Despite no hourly wage, people really did make money at the company, I heard, so I knew it was just a matter of time before my deals would start rolling in. The highest earner there was this girl my age getting her master's in music composition, but when Franco had her take me out to watch her work door to door, I saw she got into cold-sell meetings by doing this horrendous flirty thing with her face.

When we weren't out pounding the pavement with a list of leads, we'd be cold calling people from a nice office, northwest of Union Square, and encouraged to enter all of our personal contacts into what the managers called "The Pipeline." The good thing about working for free at Watermatic was that it forced me to buy some brand-new office clothes from Banana Republic right before I auditioned for *The Caucasian Chalk Circle*, directed by my favorite acting teacher, so I appeared professional and confident and ended up getting invited to callbacks.

This one dude at Watermatic got hired with his girlfriend and made a big show of treating her with favoritism, prioritizing them building a future "as a couple." My supervisor lent him a book by a broker he'd worked with back in the eighties called *The Wolf of Wall Street*. I resented him not lending me the book, so I went to the library and read it anyway.

It was about a man who worked his way up from nothing, trading millions on Wall Street, then stole stuff and committed crimes and went to jail. In jail, he wrote a book about what he learned, and now, he tours the country on speaking engagements and had his book made into a film by Martin Scorsese.

Once, Franco pulled me into his office for an inspirational pep talk. "You know, I see you here in your nice necklace and heels—but you have to be honest about who you are. Like, my wife was a Victoria's Secret model, and I said,

JÖYCE

'If you wanna marry me, I can't have other guys jerking off to you in some catalog. You have to choose between me and modeling.' She chose to marry me." I guessed he meant that spending my last $100 on a fitted blazer and some corporate chic costume jewelry at J. Crew wasn't being honest about the fact I was poor.

I didn't make a single sale or dime, but I showed up at the office every morning with just enough money to buy a delicious chocolate croissant from the kosher vending machine. Eventually, I did need to start eating again, so I applied for another job on Craigslist that paid a normal hourly wage.

I interviewed for coat check at a Michelin-starred restaurant near Washington Square Park but impressed Delfino, the manager, so much with stories about my dad's homemade yogurt and alfalfa sprouts that he asked me to train as a hostess instead. I was reluctant to get re-routed into the more commitment-heavy position when coat check was supposed to be ideal for an actor because it took place only at night and got good cash tips, but I was relieved the interview went well, and more than anything, I needed a job and didn't want to disappoint Delfino. Things were looking up in general, and my boyfriend asked if I wanted to go to Costa Rica with him and his family for the holidays.

The lead hostess, Emma, was intentionally confusing. She'd been there longer than anyone and said she wanted to leave soon to become a computer programmer. She was dating the assistant to the restaurant owners, who were from an oligarch bloodline that had once opened fire on a camp of protesting coal miners with machine guns but were now shifting into the slow-food movement and replacing workers with robots. He would bring her a venti Starbucks Frappuccino that further accentuated her willowy frame whenever he visited, and she would thank him in a creepy baby voice. Another hostess, who was dating the sous-chef twelve years her senior because it pissed off her dad, was only working there while she went to Med School. Her mom would casually eat at the restaurant for hundreds of dollars per meal. She said Emma was crazy and pointed out that she hummed to herself in a high-pitched soprano at random moments, which I did notice during the trainings.

Every day, Emma would explain the OpenTable Reservation software to me like she was marking the lyrics of a non-rhyming Mary Poppins song, not because it taught me anything, but for her own amusement, and she wouldn't let me take the manual home to study. Come October, after four weeks of reporting to Emma, Delfino told me I seemed like a very scared person who needed therapy, and that it was strange of me to still be writing everything down at this stage of the training, but the whole reason I had become afraid was because of Emma, being intentionally confusing, and then pretending she had been clear. He said that nevertheless, they couldn't afford to keep training me. It had already been a month, and he dismissed me right before I was supposed to buy a passport to go to Costa Rica. I couldn't risk spending almost $200 until I could secure another job.

I asked Delfino if I could do coat-check, since that was the job I had originally applied for anyway. He said the coat-check positions were no longer open, but he would put me on the alternate list, so they could call me to fill in.

When I had auditioned for *The Caucasian Chalk Circle,* I was optimistic in my new office clothes. At callbacks, I was downtrodden. Suddenly I had to scramble for a new job when I had planned to research the play, and I was unable to get my fancy clothes back from the dry cleaner anyway because I could not pay them. I was now too persecuted to compete with the rich girls for the lead role of the servant. The director said the show did have an investor but didn't say who. She said we could bring in a song and a monologue for the group callback. I secretly planned to sing "Four Generals" for the bravado and well-suited vocal range, and, as if by psychic powers, before I could get up, the director said that very song was cut from the play because she didn't like it. So I didn't sing.

In early December, I read that Will had committed murder at the Soho House. His girlfriend had been found strangled in their bathtub. I was really surprised by that because I had never seen Will even raise his voice and had dismissed the whole punching a bellhop thing as a one-off display of tormented romance. New York Magazine did a father and son feature called "The Curious Case of Broseph and William Jooks." It said Will reunited with his sister during the trial and claimed to be innocent, but Jooks had nothing to do with him anymore. The article noted the siblings shared the habit of ordering a selection of dishes at restaurants, taking a few bites of each, and discarding the rest.

A *Jekyll and Hyde* theme restaurant called to offer me a job just before the holidays. I'd applied because you automatically got to join Actors' Equity if they hired you. I dreamed of joining Actors' Equity, so I could sign up for Equity auditions without having to wait all day at the Actors' Equity Center for only a chance of getting in. They told me they could only hire me if I stayed and worked on Christmas and New Year's Eve, so I had to turn down the job because my boyfriend told me his parents already bought my ticket to go to Costa Rica. I was doing the one thing I'd vowed never to do since the fourth grade: compromise my career for a man.

I applied for a Craigslist gig that paid more money than I'd ever seen, $800 for a few hours' work passing out cigars at a theme party, only the theme was *Eyes Wide Shut*, the Tom Cruise movie about a naked sex cult, so we could only wear lingerie and Venetian masks while we worked. I went to the photographer's apartment by Union Square for my interview. The living room led into the bedroom, which led onto a small terrace, so I thought he must be *making bank* (a phrase I'd learned from my boyfriend).

"Why are there cans of Rockstar

energy drink on your bed?" I asked.

"I'm photographing them for a promotion."

"Do you think there's weird drugs in those energy drinks?" I thought maybe psychiatrists were using them to dose the population.

I wondered if he was into other drugs as well.

"No...just some caffeine and maybe a little vitamins," he said wearily.

"I brought my underwear," I said. "Like the Craigslist post said. For the picture."

He sounded gay so I wasn't worried.

"You can choose a mask and change in the bathroom there," he said.

I chose a black half-mask with deep green feathers and crammed myself into the little white hex-tiled bathroom. I changed out of my coat and the layers beneath. Then, I presented myself.

"You have a nice butt," he said, zooming in on my butt with the camera.

"Oh, thanks," I said. "That's what my boyfriend says. I mean I can't tell, I don't really have anything I can compare it to.

My boobs aren't very big though."

"Can I touch it?" he asked, moving his hand gradually through space.

"No," I flinched away. "Wait, you're not gay?"

"No," he said.

"Oh. You sounded gay."

He was like this new genre of New York boys who sounded gay but weren't, and it scrambled my brain. My boyfriend kind of sounded gay when I first met him.

"And can I ask, let's say at the party, a guest tries to touch you. What would be your first reaction?"

"Oh. I guess I could just start screaming."

"Great. Thank you so much." He smiled, and I believed him. "I'll be sure to follow up with the details of the party."

"Thanks!"

I waited for the job, hoping he'd call me. I was an actress and could stand there and act like I wanted to be at their stupid-ass party for $800. I told myself he'd tried to touch my butt as a test, to make sure I knew how to protect myself.

JÖYCE

The ad said there would be no touching, so I figured I could just work at the party, and if someone touched me, I could scream and it would be okay. He didn't call, though.

Just in time, I found a job working at a spice and tea stand in the Union Square Holiday Market for $900 cash at the end of the week. I worked twelve hours a day and took a hot bath each night to thaw my bones. Sheer terror drove me to speak at length on every bowl of tea, spices, and herbs, as if by divination, to all who passed. The owners of the company were French. One was the entrepreneur. The other said he came from a family who'd traded spices and teas for three generations. The trader's girlfriend, cousin, and I would huddle for warmth and get Waffles and Dinges and cider with our spare dollars. I'd eat candied ginger from the bowl like it was potato chips. On the last night, we broke down the stand and they popped a bottle of champagne in the freezing winter. Working out there in the cold instead of at the sex party was more life-affirming, I thought at the time.

They said I could take whatever spice and tea I wanted for free, so I packed myself baggies of fragrant and exotic goods. They handed me my envelope of cash, short a few twenties, and I was like "Why did you short me?" and they were like, "Because we gave you that free stuff," and I was like, "But I can't pay for things with Turmeric," and I made sure I got the cash they said they'd give me. It was snowing outside in big white cornflakes—the dandruff of god. I was riding high on the adrenaline of an eighty-five-hour work week and the smoked paprika fumes of success.

The owners took us to Blue Water Grill. We got to order whatever we wanted, so I had the salmon. We were the only ones there. The trader's girlfriend, who was from Miami, ordered a Sprite and then sent it back because she said it was watered down. When the waiter tried to explain that the soda fountain was malfunctioning, she scoffed and wouldn't look at him. I wondered, if she was used to such fine dining, why was she ordering a Sprite, but figured it must be her abundance mentality since she was dating the boss.

I went home and set my envelope of $900 cash out in a fan, over the folding seashell-printed snack table I'd used to replace my writing desk, and positioned small bags of Za'atar, Sichuan Pepper, Masala Chai, and Lavender Rose Petal tea, then took a picture and sent it to my boyfriend, like *Scarface* after a big score.

Sunday morning, a blizzard began and didn't stop. I went to The Container Store for packaging to make a spice and tea gift set for my boyfriend's parents. I shouldn't have spent the money, but I had to buy a gift since they were paying so much to bring me on vacation. At night, I took the subway to Woodside, Queens, with Lemon strapped to my bosom under my coat. Then I got out and walked for an hour in the snow when the trains shut down on the bridge. I was dropping her off at my boyfriend's friend's place to dog sit. It was the drummer friend who insulted me whenever we all hung out, but he loved Lemon and didn't mind the few hundred bucks.

I went to the passport office at 7:00 a.m. Monday for a same-day passport, which would cost much more, but a government employee said the office was closed. "It's a snow day today. Everything is closed."

Numb with defeat, I wondered what I'd do next. I hadn't been able to get a passport appointment until I'd had the money to buy a passport, but I hadn't been able to have the money to buy a passport until I got paid for the job that ended yesterday. And now, the snow ruined it all. I went home and sat in my bed and cried.

Then, I called my boyfriend. "Hey— the passport office was closed because of the snow. I was going to get an expedited passport today so I could fly out this afternoon. I—can't meet you in Cincinnati until I get my passport," I said meekly, over the phone. He was having cheery holiday breakfast with his family.

"Oh, no."

"I don't know what your parents are going to do about the flight. I feel so bad, but I wanted to tell them as soon as possible."

"They can change it."

"Okay. The soonest I can get a passport appointment is in Philadelphia tomorrow."

"Jöyce...why didn't you do this earlier?" he mourned.

"I didn't get paid until two days ago," I pleaded. "The restaurant got rid of me right before I was supposed to buy my passport back in October."

"I know but...okay."

"I made a gift box of exotic spices to bring to your parents."

"Don't bring it on the plane," he sighed. "Customs will confiscate that."

I took a bus to Philadelphia and waited in the passport office the next day. A boy who looked exactly like my seven-year crush from middle school sat across from me with a dreamy smirk. I wondered if I looked haggard and downtrodden with the black canvas parachute duffle I'd just purchased from I. Goldberg Army Navy surplus. He'd come from Russia with his parents as a young boy and rode the inner-city school bus out to the suburbs like me. While he infiltrated the inner circles of popularity, wealth, and the Ivy League, I went deeper and unlocked my potential with Scientology, sublimating my silent love for him into my art.

I got my passport and headed back to New York.

It snowed again on the day of my flight. I would catch up with my boyfriend's family in Costa Rica after spending the night in San José.

It was my first time flying and staying in a hotel alone. I bought an eight-dollar steak dinner with room service. I woke up three hours later and got breakfast in the casino, which was still pumping club jams at 4:00 a.m. A man approached me with a big smile as I had my eggs, hash browns, orange juice, and coffee at the sticky bar, under darkness and blinking lights.

"Hi!" he said with an accent. He

looked so happy.

I smiled back and waved.

"He thinks you're a prostitute," said the bartender.

"Oh," I said. I had thought he was only a friendly man who wanted my breakfast to be filled with welcome.

I took a cab and then a plane and then a smaller plane to a tiny island, where—oily and weary, and still dressed for New York winter—I met my boyfriend and his family under the warm sun by the sea. It was New Year's Eve.

That night, we went all around the island. I drank about twelve drinks at three different clubs. It must have been the altitude, because I usually never drank more than two or three drinks at one time. My Spanish-speaking abilities emerged in ways I'd never imagined. A street cart was selling giant steaks the size of my head for eight dollars, just like at the hotel, and I carried on a full fifteen minutes of negotiation trying to get the price down, impressing everyone with my global business acumen, but the vendor refused, so I paid market rate. There was a club where we went to dance, and the DJ kept blowing this big loud emergency horn to punctuate the music. A few months later, I started hearing that horn in every new trap song.

My boyfriend and I had sex in the hotel at 5:00 a.m., and I felt myself become impregnated. Of course, it would happen the second I missed a birth-control pill, with money being so tight. I was so guilty and so late to the trip and such a costly inconvenience. I had never refused to fulfill my boyfriend's request for sex, and I could not do so now, on New Year's Eve, on top of everything else, except, in addition to not having my thirty-dollar monthly pack of birth control, I would have to buy a thirty-dollar single dose of Plan B.

Two hours later, we woke up for the fishing trip. We took Dramamine and ate a breakfast of tropical fruit, coffee, and toast with poached eggs, but the moment the boat left the dock, I got sick. I have never wanted to die before, but the feeling of unrelenting nausea on a moving boat was enough to at least consider that it would feel better not to be alive at all. I made sure to vomit over the side of the boat. Eventually, we turned back. I was deposited on land, and the fishing trip went on without me. I spent the day swaddled in towels under an umbrella by the pool with my boyfriend's mom, who already knew about her own motion sickness.

I secretly hoped all that vomiting was just as effective as taking the Plan B pill. What a burden I was already—and I'd only known his parents for less than twenty-four hours.

"Geez, Jöyce," my boyfriend later said, "you could've told me you stopped taking birth control. I don't know if we're gonna be able to find plan B out here. I haven't seen any pharmacies. We can try to go to the general store."

We went, but there was no plan B where we were in Costa Rica.

I could definitely feel something going on with my body. The baby couldn't be normal because I'd had alcohol. Surely the birth control residue in my system would alter the chemistry somehow. It was my fault and my problem to handle. I could feel my stomach churn and twist and hoped it was a lack of probiotics.

By the time we were at the airport, ready to fly back to the U.S., it was too late to buy a Plan B pill anyway. My boyfriend suggested I purchase some bulk cartons of Marlboro Reds at the duty-free store to sell outside of bars. As his parents departed, his father handed me a hundred dollar bill for a Christmas gift, but now that it was too late to take a Plan B pill, I was going to need birth control that cost more than $100. I spent it on groceries and a dress that was on sale for ten dollars at Urban Outfitters.

When we got back to New York, it was time to start rehearsals for *The Caucasian Chalk Circle* by Bertolt Brecht at Theater for the New City.

The blizzard continued through the whole winter of 2011. I scraped for work and read *Anna Karenina* between sips of ice-cold Absolut Kurant from the duty-free store on the roof when I'd clear a path in the two feet of snow for Lemon. It was too cold to do anything but read, starve, and pray for work. I wasn't confident enough in my nightlife sales skills to peddle cigarettes outside of bars, so occasionally, I'd indulge in one when I drank a vodka in the snow while Lemon took a piss.

In *Anna Karenina*, which my boyfriend and I were reading together, everyone drinks vodka like it's nothing, so I had a shot before the first read-through of *The Caucasian Chalk Circle*. I spoke minimally, with no sudden movements so no one would know, and decided never to do it again.

Delfino offered me coat-check jobs only for the exact times when I had rehearsal, as if someone knew my schedule and was trying to get me to skip out in financial desperation, and then get fired from the show. I gave the cigarettes to my boyfriend after they sat unsold in my freezer for a month and patched together an income fishing

LOOK HOMEWARD SATAN

Craigslist for odd jobs.

I lived for five days on a carefully rationed box of Pop-Tarts and a six-pack of Snickers bars, the highest calorie count I could find at Kmart for my last ten dollars, before trudging through the snow to the government aid office on DeKalb Avenue and signing up for food stamps. One morning, I had a day-long flyering job, but the change I dug up that had fallen out of people's pockets in the couch and washer/dryer unit wasn't enough for train fare. I'd be paid in cash at the end of the day but the reel editor whose business we were promoting said that anyone who was late would lose the job. I went to the subway and risked jumping the stile. The train arrived just as I got there and a guy saw the squirrelly look in my eyes. "Want a fare?" he asked cheerfully and heaved open the emergency door with a flourish. I could have wept for my good fortune and his kindness and used my change for a cup of hot blueberry coffee from Dunkin' Donuts. It tasted like the nectar of freedom.

JÖYCE

The lead character in *The Caucasian Chalk Circle* was smuggling a baby, just like me, but the actress playing her had $400 highlights. One night, I was playing the rich cousin who wouldn't let her have a place to stay and started coughing from some dust in the theater, so I played it off like my character was coughing due to some infirmity her poor uninvited guest brought into the house, and an ex-classmate I never trusted because of her profuse flattery said how brilliant I was. On the day we finally struck the set, I was showing and had just gotten my first food-stamp distribution. I brought some snacks to share with the cast. One of my castmates told me I looked good with a broom.

By that March, I was behind on four months of rent. I would hand my roommates the rent check on time, thinking the money would somehow follow, but it never did. I wished my mom hadn't yelled at my dad so much for bouncing checks when I was a kid, otherwise I might have never known it was an option. Thalia had a dog Lemon's size and contacted me on Facebook to see if I wanted to be roommates with her and her coworker Robert from Lomography in Bushwick. Not having rent was making my whole situation at Myrtle Avenue toxic, and I thought a little distance could help me focus on paying the landlord back. I worked non-stop shifts at four jobs through the spring to pay it off while paying my new rent and expenses. I worked in health-food stores demonstrating paleo cookies, a Chelsea pizza shop heating slices and ringing up orders, a Staten Island Costco selling leather goods at a pop-up table, which I didn't get paid for since I got fired halfway through for not being able to make the commute, a low paying catering company, and by demonstrating cheese samples at Zabar's. I promoted the Justin Bieber Someday perfume at the Brooklyn Macy's on Fulton Street, which left the cartilage of my nose tingling for several months after. I had pledged to send my old landlord, who I'd never met because the building was a large Hasidic-owned real estate LLC, about $700 a week. Each week, I'd put the envelope in the mail and call the receptionist to tell her. I did it right on time for a few weeks until that rent was paid in full.

I wished I could make that much money just for myself, and not when I was desperate to pay a debt.

One Sunday in May 2011, I was putting up posters for a private yoga instructor, making twenty dollars an hour, when it started to rain. I decided to go home on the nearby 6 train at 86th and Lexington, but it shut down at 59th Street, so I had to get out and walk to the 63rd Street F train, right on the corner of Jooks' apartment building. I assumed Jooks still resided there, though my googling had shown he was being sued by the owner who let him stay on condition that he pay maintenance and a lump sum of $2,000,000 at the end of 2011.

It was the third time I'd passed this corner since I'd quit, almost two years ago. I feared I'd see him crossing the street, catching a cab, or heading to the deli. Maybe he would beg me to come back or call the police or not acknowledge me at all. It was lunchtime, and I shuddered thinking of him gazing out at me from Hamburger Heaven over a tuna sandwich.

I swooped into the steamy subway with a quick glance at his window, daring to catch his silhouette peering down from the sixteenth floor.

The next morning, I awoke curled up beside Lemon, still in my catering uniform from a job the previous evening, not thanks to any referral from Mimsy, but to my own Craiglistery. I fell asleep with the laptop glowing and bedroom lights on, so the day could never end.

It was the first I'd slept in some time. My bed filled more than half the room, but the room was paid for. There were two new text messages on my phone.

"The old man. Oh, Siezer of Tritons, did you see?" Hazel texted.

"See what, Scotchbright?"

"You must look it up, quickly," she wrote back.

JÖYCE

"Oh, dear. Did you read the news about Jooks today?" Ryan texted.

"What? No. I'll check."

I rapped out his name on the keyboard. A catalog of headlines loaded onto the screen. Within the very hour after I had walked by his apartment for the third time in a year on the previous day, Jooks had been found dead in his apartment.

Only then did I feel like the job was gone for good. Privately, I shed tears for the old man and his misery.

The articles said he left a long and rambling suicide note with no mention of family, only of his innocence and a woman who physically abused and stole from him.

The circumstances of his death underwent little scrutiny. His body had been found by a *friend* meeting him for a lunch date, yet I knew both were out of character. The news later said it was the husband of a gym trainer he had recently started working with who was meeting him for lunch. He'd left them everything in his will.

(630)

LOOK HOMEWARD SATAN

He was discovered with a plastic dry-cleaning bag tied around his head, attached to a helium tank. I was glad I left when I did, because it would have been me who he'd have set up to find him.

Within hours of the news, someone anonymously uploaded a video on YouTube, "The Suicide of Oscar-Winning Composer Broseph Jooks." It showed a man from behind, singing along to a recording of his hit pop song while placing a dry cleaning bag that was hooked up to a helium tank over his head, swaying back and forth to the music as he slowly suffocated.

Someone else anonymously uploaded his cover of "Nobody Waved Goodbye."

Three days later, Pearl pled guilty to criminal facilitation.

The following week, I thought I saw him sitting on a bench on 68th Street, gazing at me in bewildered silence. It couldn't have been him, because he was dead, but it looked enough like him for me to stop and stare for a minute. Tall, skinny, ashen, dressed below his pedigree. He looked right at me for a split second. It was like seeing Jooks from another dimension. Maybe when a celebrity malfunctions, I reasoned, the government wipes their identity and sends them out to live on the street.

Being around him that long had showed me a side of humanity I didn't expect but am glad to know about. The moral tight-ass tendencies I got teased for may have been the only reason Jooks couldn't get me to do shit for him besides run his errands and schedule his appointments, no matter how isolated or full of despair I became. I wouldn't do it when my immortal spiritual potential was at stake. I'd rather be brainwashed by the rigid dystopia of a totalitarian church, I thought, than a fucking rapist.

YOU CAN GO HOME AGAIN IF PEOPLE AREN'T A DICK ABOUT IT

A customer eyed my belly as I slid his slice of pizza into the brick oven and said, "Bless you."

"What do you mean?" I said coldly.

Even my boyfriend hadn't noticed I was pregnant while we were having sex. How dare this man assume. I had finally paid off the rent I owed my old landlord. I did not need to be pregnant. Even my old castmates from *The Wizard of Oz: Lord I'm Coming Home* didn't seem to notice. They wandered in, exchanged casual greetings and ordered some pizza like nothing was happening. It felt kind of good to be disgraced before somebody I knew.

The poor baby was doomed and probably had several engrams already from my not having the willpower to tell my boyfriend that Scientology said having sex would damage the unborn fetus.

With my finances restored, and enough frozen pizza filed away to secure the near future, I went to a doctor who confirmed what was happening. At Planned Parenthood, someone said I could consider adoption and I got mad. It was very late in the term, but the Thetan only enters the body at birth. They said I might have to go to Albuquerque, New Mexico.

Planned Parenthood sent me to Bellevue. As I waited in the emergency room with a jar of my urine, a man with no apparent reason to be there appeared next to me on the bench, told me he thought I was beautiful and asked for my number.

"No. Leave me alone," I said. Maybe he'd been hired by the Church. If only I'd learned to say no before that moment.

A caseworker who was also a doula said there was a grant I could apply for at a clinic down in Maryland, but I might need a person to go with me. Since no one could know, that person would have to be my boyfriend. Not because I was ashamed, but because what people will do with controversial information about you is beyond your control. It usually places you at the mercy of their personal shortcomings, rather than your own.

"I have concluded that I am with child," I said, staring out over Bushwick from the roof of the cement cube Lemon and I now called home.

"Jesus, Jöyce—" I'd been trying to inhale as much of his second-hand smoke as possible for the past few months in the hope that it would help the baby pass naturally out of my system.

"I've made all the arrangements to follow through with a termination."

"Oh..." he said, the color returning to his face.

"I'm only bringing you into this since I may need you to come with me for part of the three-day trip..."

"I have a show..."

"I might be able to go alone...I know you have a gig that night." My voice rose. "I got one of the grants they have for this, and they'll let me know if I got the other one once I'm down there."

"I mean—we're gonna have to ask for help," he went on. "We're going to have to ask our friends...my parents..."

"We can't. We can't. No," I said. "I'll go down there. They said I'll find out when I arrive, whether or not I receive the other part of the money I need."

"Well, how much do you have"

"Only $300. I have to leave in the morning. On an Amtrak. It's probably enough for the tickets."

"And you're gonna need how much every day for food?"

"Uhh...ten..."

"Twenty dollars a day for food."

Better to give the baby a chance of being born next lifetime without any engrams, I reasoned, taking a cab to the hotel from the Amtrak station in Maryland.

I told the concierge at the front desk, "I booked a room."

"Yes, I have your key."

"Thank you."

"May I ask as to the purpose of your visit?" He glanced down at my stomach.

"Oh, I'm visiting a friend."

"I see."

The clinic was right down the

street. I assumed he did this for regular entertainment.

I was early for my appointment, so I headed to a Turkish grocery store at a strip mall down the highway. They sold Turkish delight, the candy my entire generation grew up craving because, in *The Lion, the Witch, and the Wardrobe* movie, the White Witch asks Edmund what he most wants to eat in the world, and he says Turkish delight. I'd been waiting all this time to finally have it.

The cab drove through picketers waving blown-up photographs of bloodied fetuses. I stepped onto a sprawl of green lawn and small brick office buildings. A friendly man traipsed over the grass and said that he happened to be on his lunch break and pointed me to the clinic. He seemed like he'd done this for other women who'd driven past the protestors.

They said I couldn't go through with the procedure unless someone escorted me home. I would have to stay one more night and call my boyfriend to meet me the next day. They sent me back to the hotel room with six pills I was supposed to take every two hours, to poison the child inside me.

It was July, and the abortion clinic was my first vacation since Costa Rica.

I took photographs of myself on my MacBook and sent them to Hazel. I had a brand new look. I had found a Craigslist ad for a free haircut, but when I asked for a short bob, he said, "No. Just bowl cuts and pixie cuts." Far be it from me to hamper another artist's creativity. The salon, called "Crops for Girls," was generous enough to have me for free, so I told him, "Whatever you want." I looked like a second-grade boy, but I had a bowl cut before they started appearing at fashion week. To ease the shock, I found another ad for free platinum blond coloring at Arrojo Studio. I sat in a four-hour session with the stylist and went back every few months to touch up the roots.

I was a welfare mom getting an abortion with a laughably trendy haircut, but it was other people, using me as their lab rat, that had put me in that situation to begin with.

In the hotel room, I got a text from my boyfriend's mom. "Are you sure you don't want to keep the baby? I will help you." But I knew she was only asking me at the last minute, so she could say she'd tried.

"Thank you—I have made up my mind. I'm just glad I didn't have to impose on anyone," I wrote back, making sure to be clear I'd gotten the grants all on my own, except for the Amtrak tickets they'd bought my boyfriend. What if I became completely under the ownership of their family but my boyfriend left me for someone else? My parents had nothing, and I could get mangled by the pregnancy and tossed out onto the street.

Since the concierge had been such a bitch to me, I stole a cheap terrycloth towel and the unused coffee and creamer packets from my room on the way out.

"At the last minute, your mom texted asking whether I was sure I didn't want the baby," I told my boyfriend on the cab ride back to the Amtrak station."

She said that she would help me."

"She wants grandchildren."

I took full responsibility for the situation—by not disrupting my boyfriend's life or hurting the baby's immortal spiritual potential.

We were going to be late for my show so we ran. I wasn't supposed to run according to doctor's orders, but maybe I was helping my body heal faster, like in the wild.

I had stayed in control for the entire process, except I asked, "What was the gender of the baby?" on the operating table.

"It's...better not to know..."

"Poor little guy," I said, wanting to feel for a second what it was like to squander myself on sentiment.

"I was cracking jokes the whole time," I told my boyfriend. They had given me some potent meds, which probably disqualified me from ever going clear in Scientology.

"Oh man, so you were like the Larry David of the recovery room kinda thing," said my boyfriend. I thought about the horrified expression on the face of the woman who had been there with her husband to terminate her baby, due to a life-endangering medical complication.

"I guess."

After that, I didn't fall for my roommate's prying eyes and concerned "Is everything okay?" when I got back from my trip. I wasn't going to tell her anything. Women's idle sympathy never fooled me. I had to appear functional. We had just started our life together as roommates.

I had to spend three days recovering and doing nothing. My breasts became swollen with milk, and it was painful to shower. Once, a Scientology spy who nearly tricked me into having sex with him told me I had the most beautiful breasts he'd ever seen and that men were obsessed with prostitutes who had "little perfect teacup breasts." I didn't believe him, but now that I had bigger boobs I wanted the small ones back. In order to stop lactating, I had been instructed by the doctor to wear cabbage leaves in the lining of my bra. I was emotionally numb, and it was necessary to be so, to ensure that I would survive and not accidentally become someone's property or homeless. I'd walked away from my jobs when I left for Maryland. I'd fallen behind all of my self-scheduled shifts and couldn't tell them why I was going out of town so abruptly.

Periodically, I had to cleanse myself of society's trappings so I could start fresh. Nothing outside Scientology was sustainable for long.

My mom had an extra $1,000 lying around, and my body needed rest and nourishing food. I told her I had to recover from a physical ailment but didn't say what. So I lay in bed for three days eating fruits and prepared sandwiches and non-dairy ice cream and watching movies too vapid to make me cry, not that I knew what to cry about.

The first mistake made me feel like I wasn't worth preventing a second. I felt so bad depriving my boyfriend of sex and grossing him out with my post-pregnancy body that I let him have sex with me before the birth control pill could kick in after the month of healing.

(642)

EPILOGUE

Sex was uncomfortable. I caught another pregnancy. I saw a doctor early enough to use a pill this time, so it was secret and less traumatic. Afterward, I went to Shake Shack.

After a year in Bushwick, my boyfriend invited me to move in with him. His parents were buying him a brownstone.

I got a call from my parents, but I let it go to voicemail like always.

"Please, Jöyce, call me, call me," said my father's recorded voice, a warbling, cavernous realm between ecstasy and weeping, as it had become since the start of his decline.

"Jöyce, please call," said my mother's voice in a message the next day, soft and irritated as usual. "Your father wants to talk to you. Here, Jay wants the phone—" and then my father's voice, "Please call me, Jöycie. Please call."

I would call soon, but I was working. They were always leaving voicemails, but my dad sounded especially urgent.

"Please call us, Jöyce," my mother's voice left a message on the third day.

JÖYCE

The next day came, and I finally called.

"Jöyce, Jay passed away," my mother said.

"What happened?" I asked.

I would cry later after the call.

"He fell. In the bathtub, and he didn't want to get out. He hit his head, and I heard a crack. He wouldn't let me call an ambulance."

"Why didn't you tell me what was happening?"

"He didn't want you to call the hospital."

"Where is he now?"

"The police came. They carried him from the bathtub, took him to the living room, and laid his body out. On a yoga mat."

"What did they say?"

"They said, 'It looks like he's gone. I'm sorry, Mrs. Miller. It looks like he's gone."

"Did you murder him?"

"No, I didn't murder him." She started weeping.

"But you didn't call the police or the hospital."

EPILOGUE

"He didn't want me to. He wouldn't let me."

Knowing that he could rest at ease now that I'd been married off, my dad had died over the course of three days in an empty bathtub, refusing to call an ambulance.

I went to work the next day at a new catering company with better pay.

I thought I'd never let another man make me feel as trapped as Jooks had. When Adam at the Church of Scientology had me read the Org Bulletin, stating that they'd canceled the Fair Game Policy, where the Church is allowed to harass, trick, lie to, sabotage, and spy on anybody who attacks the Church, I believed him— so at first, I thought the professional hackers, honeytraps, and surveillance operatives were all hired by Jooks' and Mimsy's families or legal teams.

I guessed for all his jingle writing, Jooks' family suddenly wasn't into capitalism if it meant I got to write a book and make money too. My thinking is, if you don't want to be a bitch in my

JÖYCE

art, don't be a bitch in my life. This is not a story of redemption. It's not like I did anything wrong.

EPILOGUE 2:
THE PEPSI GENERATION

You had a lot to live, and Pepsi had a lot to give. Now, on some level, Jooks, you are dead, and Pepsi can do nothing but take and take.

Despite coming from such a religious background, I can't call myself Jooks' moral superior. I dated two separate guys who were both named Richard Jordan right before I started working for Jooks, and one of them conned me out of my virginity. If they were hired by the Church or the government to spy on me, then I guess that means I've been with sex workers as well. I can't fault Jooks for spending his final years almost exclusively with hired staff and financially dependent family members. At this point, I don't know if I even have anyone left who isn't being compensated to follow me around and smear me.

Lemon passed away right after my boyfriend and I moved in together and never got to enjoy the life she deserved in the brownstone. One day, a few months after we moved in, my boyfriend kissed me goodbye for the recording studio, and she ran off with a bit of apple that fell to the floor from the cutting board. We used apple to give her trachea pills all the time, so I didn't think anything of it. Then I found her seizing and choking under the couch. I tried to save her while I called car company after car company like I had so many times for Jooks, but it was right after Hurricane Sandy, and it took twenty minutes to get a cab. I breathed air into her nose while we waited, and on the ride over, as her little lips turned blue and she faded in and out of consciousness. At the animal emergency hospital, Lemon was still alive. A few minutes later, a nurse walked over to my chair and told me they couldn't save her.

My boyfriend and I wept together in the bed for hours.

"Why didn't you call me? Why didn't you knock on a neighbor's or a tenant's door?"

"I was trying to give her mouth-to-mouth. I thought you didn't want to be interrupted."

"You should have told me while you were at the hospital. I could have come and said goodbye to her. I wouldn't have cared about recording. The band would have understood."

Lemon was cremated and buried in Kentucky, on one of my boyfriend's parents' estates, where her grave remains memorialized to this day. A few months later, my father got a memorial too after my mother finally got us to take his ashes down to West Virginia, where my cousin arranged a service in a small Baptist Church. Mother's still nagging me about a burial and headstone. I guess I've always been way too chill with graves.

Foreclosure, Bankruptcy, Heartbreak, Tyranny, Jooks' Suicide, Will's Murder Sentence, Pearl's Criminal Facilitation, Totalitarianism, Espionage, Abortion, Dad's Surrender to Quiet Desperation, and Lemon's Possible Assassination, staged as a suicide by the FBI for her indirect ties to the Occupy Wall Street Movement, make 3.25 Great Misfortunes per year in my four-year, post-college life.

Like rape culture and the patriarchy, I continue to reinvent myself. My plan is to be skinny, get treated like shit, and then write about it. Calling it "The Patriarchy," is smart branding because then you're attributing the genderless behaviors of power gone amok to a specific gender. Like how people call all tissue Kleenex, even though tissues, paper towels, napkins, and toilet paper all pretty much do the same thing.

You might accuse me of being a hater whose bad vibes caused Jooks to die faster—especially if you're a man who aspires to genius, fame, and fortune. As a man who also aspires to genius, fame, and fortune—well, not a man—but as a person reading these final sentences to Jooks' ghost, I can guarantee you that he hasn't indicated any disapproval.

Artist, father, rape suspect. No one could put him in a box.

Jooks had true intellect. No matter

how rich and corrupt, he still had a curiosity about ideas for their own sake, which seems to offend the status quo more than being a rapist does. It's too bad he cultivated the wrong trait.

Sometimes people want to destroy someone for being sexier, smarter, or richer than they are, more than they want to destroy a rapist, or someone doing evil things. Compared to other criminals, Jooks wasn't the hottest or most talented by any means.

Maybe the qualities that make you a rapist and an asshole also make you more successful. Maybe, in a different system, Jooks wouldn't have raped anyone or succeeded in advertising. For a few years after the recession, there were a lot of articles published about how people with sociopathic traits were more likely to become leaders in business, and how our society needs to stop incentivizing narcissists and sociopaths.

I used to think attracting narcissists was my main problem too—until I realized the real problem is that I'm surrounded by spies. Jooks' family may have even got a honeytrap to trick me into writing about the Church of Scientology so that I would blame all the spying on them. That way, Jooks' estate won't have to pay anyone to assassinate my character, and Mimsy can get one of his call girls or victims or kids to co-write a book that won't make her look like such a dipshit, using this hacked manuscript as stolen source material.

I'm sure that not asking me to sign a non-disclosure was Jooks' way of commissioning this biography. It's not like I have to answer to him anymore. I got a job at the corporate offices of a soda company as a Brand Ambassador, no less—at least for the day. I can't say which one, because they made me sign a non-disclosure. I know how to respect the rules. Not that I'd damage the brand. The latest advertising is all about individually customized consumer relationships. Today, I work at an interactive virtual-reality station where employees can walk right up and design their own labels on blank beautiful silver soda cans.

EPILOGUE 2

Things aren't so corporate now—it's about community, and that really showed when we braved the storm together. We Brand Ambassadors held our ground while the employees darted out from under the office building ledge, one by one, to snatch a free T-shirt from our hands and then retreat, back out of the rain. I had to move to where it was dry since I was getting sick. At every train station and business and municipal building, the air conditioning was cranked up to November temperatures in the middle of summer.

"We don't need to be in the rain," I told the other brand ambassador, but she stood her ground, a hero passing out T-shirt after T-shirt like they were FEMA emergency packs. She was a New York native visiting from New Orleans. It was inspiring to see her rise above adversity instead of go where it was dry and just pass out T-shirts there.

In capitalism, the revolution of yesterday is the experiential marketing of tomorrow.

JÖYCE

After the event, we pushed a shopping cart full of the leftover blanks into the basement. I stood with five other girls by a utility sink, emptying can after can. Each one was filled with water we were warned was unfit for consumption. I maneuvered the pad of my finger under the tab without chipping my manicure at all, resenting that Mimsy had lied years ago when she asked me to open her Diet Ginger Ale so she wouldn't ruin her nails. Then I remembered that now durable gel manicures were the fashion, and hers had only been lacquer. Besides, maybe she just wasn't as good at opening cans, and I needed to be more considerate. I remembered how happy I should be that Mimsy is getting film and TV jobs now. As a reward for my goodwill, the universe chose me from the row of can expressers to leave early. On the way out, I passed a photograph from the 1969 commercial featuring Jooks' first big jingle, with the name "Broseph Jooks" on a plaque right underneath the frame.

I didn't expect to see a memento of

the man who helped get me where I am today.

No longer do I curse his name as if he were alive. In the Great Void, he is screaming for the lunch that never came when his spirit summoned me in the hour of his death. I have an endorsement from the finest jingle writer of all time, because he never asked me to stop. But don't take my word for it. Buy the book and find out for yourself.

Joyce Miller has written Almost Rapist: A True Crime Memoir (Enthusiast Press, 2025). Chapbooks: Bluebird (Bottlecap Press, 2023), John (Bottlecap Press, 2024). Poetry: Pyramid Scheme (Bookleaf Press, 2023). Anthology: Stage It and Stream It: Plays for Virtual Theater (Rowman & Littlefield 2020, Bloomsbury 2024), Keep Scrolling Till You Feel Something: 21 Years of Humor from McSweeney's Internet Tendency (McSweeney's, 2019). Online Satire: McSweeney's Internet Tendency. Mentions: "McSweeney's Top Ten Most Read Articles of the Year," AfterEllen, Autostraddle. Awards: The Handmaid's Dianetics (Best Satire, United Solo Festival). Born and raised in Philadelphia, she lives in New York.

www.ingramcontent.com/pod-product-compliance
Lightning Source LLC
Chambersburg PA
CBHW021208130626
46554CB00004B/1126